Stewart Binns began his professional life as an academic before becoming a teacher and a soldier. Later in life, he trained at the BBC and began a successful career in television, during which he won many awards, especially for his 'in-colour' documentary series, including a BAFTA for 'Britain at War'. Stewart has since published several fiction and non-fiction books. *Japan's War* is his fourteenth book and seventh work of non-fiction.

Also by Stewart Binns

NON-FICTION

The Greatest: Who is Britain's Top Sports Star?

The Second World War in Colour

Britain at War in Colour

America at War in Colour

British Empire in Colour

Barbarossa: And the Bloodiest War in History

FICTION

Conquest – The Making of England I

Crusade – The Making of England II

Anarchy – The Making of England III

Lionheart – The Making of England IV

1914 The Shadow of War – Great War I

1915 The Darkness and the Thunder – Great War II

Betrayal

JAPAN'S WAR

HIROHITO'S HOLY WAR AGAINST THE WEST

聖戦

Seisen

STEWART BINNS

First published in 2025 by Wildfire
An imprint of Headline Publishing Group Limited

This paperback edition published in 2026

1

Cataloguing in Publication Data is available from the British Library.

Paperback ISBN 978 1 4722 9522 4

Maps © Tim Peters

Designed and typeset by EM&EN
Printed and bound in Great Britain by Clays Ltd, Elcograf S.p.A.

Headline Publishing Group Limited
An Hachette UK Company
Carmelite House
50 Victoria Embankment
London EC4Y 0DZ

The authorised representative in the EEA is Hachette Ireland,
8 Castlecourt Centre, Dublin 15, D15 XTP3, Ireland (email: info@hbgi.ie)

www.headline.co.uk
www.hachette.co.uk

*This book is dedicated to all those who suffered
across the vast expanse of Asia and the Pacific
in one of the most brutal wars in history.*

The horrors of the Second World War in Europe – especially the monstrous crime of the Holocaust – are rightly regarded as belonging to one of the darkest chapters in recent human history. However, there is no doubt that the events unfolding in Asia at the same time also gave rise to acts of unspeakable barbarity.

Like the conflict in Europe, it is important that the horrors of the Asia-Pacific War are not forgotten. Nor should we hide from future generations what humanity is capable of when we are at our worst.

The stories and first-hand accounts contained in this book challenge us to confront uncomfortable truths, to re-examine what we think we know, and to remember what can happen if we succumb to the maelstroms of hatred that warring nations often create.

Japan will rise and fight for her rights like one man, even if this should reduce the whole country to a heap of smoking ruins.

Count Kōsai Uchida,
Prime Minister of Japan 1921–23

For twenty-six centuries we Japanese had been ruled by an emperor. We worshipped him as a god. We believed he was descended from gods. To us, the Imperial Family was sacred, the heart of the Japanese people.

Hiroko Nakamoto,
a seven-year-old schoolgirl who watched her father go off
to fight at the beginning of the Asia-Pacific War

CONTENTS

LIST OF IMAGES

1. A Yokohama Samurai Warrior, Edo Period (pre Meiji Restoration), circa 1865. (Felice Beato, public domain)
2. 1st Sino-Japanese War 1894–1895, Imperial Japanese Army opening fire with their Japanese-made Type 22 repeating carbines. (Public domain)
3. The 1904–1905 Russo-Japanese War. 500lb shells to be used in the Japanese attack on Port Arthur, January 1905. The massive weapons were central to Japan's success. (Topfoto)
4. The Japanese Invasion of Manchuria 1931: Imperial Japanese Army Cavalry entering Mukden (Shenyang), September 1931. (Public domain)
5. The Nanking Massacre 1937: Following the capture of Nanking on 13 December, a Japanese officer prepares to execute a Chinese prisoner of war. (Getty)
6. Pearl Harbor 1941: USS *Cassin* (right), a Mahan-class destroyer, was in dry dock in Pearl Harbor on 7 December 1941 when her neighbour, USS *Downes* (left), was hit by a 500lb bomb dropped by the Imperial Japanese Navy. *Downes'* fuel tanks were ruptured, causing huge fires on both *Downes* and *Cassin*. Both ships were lost and decommissioned. (Public domain)
7. The Fall of Singapore 1942: With fixed bayonets, soldiers of the Imperial Japanese Army guard men of Britain's Suffolk Regiment, some of the 120,000 British, Australian, Indian and Chinese forces who surrendered at the fall of Singapore on 15 February. (Getty)
8. The Battle of Midway 1942: Japanese prisoners of war aboard USS *Ballard* after being rescued from a lifeboat fourteen days after the Battle of Midway. They were from the Engineering

Corps of the Imperial Japanese Navy aircraft carrier *Huryū*, which was scuttled the day after she was attacked from the air and set on fire on 5 June. Thirty-nine men had been aboard the lifeboat. Thirty-four survived to be picked up by *Ballard*. (Public domain)

9. Kamikaze 1945: The USS *Missouri* about to be hit by an A6M Zero Kamikaze off Okinawa on 11 April. The plane hit *Missouri* below her main deck, causing minor damage and no casualties. It is likely that the Zero's bomb load did not detonate. The name of the pilot who died on impact is not known. (Public domain)

10. Okinawa 1945: Some of the survivors (military and civilian) of the Battle of Okinawa, one of the bloodiest of the Asia-Pacific War, which lasted from 1 April to 22 June. (Alamy)

11. The Firebombing of Tokyo 1945: The charred remains of Japanese civilians after the firebombing on 10 March. As many as 100,000 people died. One million were made homeless. (Alamy)

12. Hiroshima 1945: Taken on 5 October, two of the victims of the atomic bomb detonated above Hiroshima on 6 August. They are in a damaged bank building in the centre of Hiroshima. Well over 100,000 people died in the blast, but thousands more died from injuries, disease and radiation sickness. (Getty)

13. Surrender 1945: General Yoshijirō Umezu signs the Instrument of Surrender on behalf of Japan aboard USS *Missouri* moored in Tokyo Bay on 2 September. (Alamy)

14. Hirohito 1947: His rehabilitation complete, Hirohito is given a rapturous welcome as he visits Hiroshima. (Alamy)

MAPS

Japan

CHINA
RUSSIA
Sapporo
Hokkaido
Sea of Japan
NORTH
KOREA
Akita
Honshu
JAPAN
Sendai
SOUTH
KOREA
TOKYO
Kyoto
Nagoya
Yokohama
Kobe
Hiroshima
Osaka
Kitakyushu
Fukuoka
Shikoku
Kyushu
East China
Sea
North
Pacific
Ocean

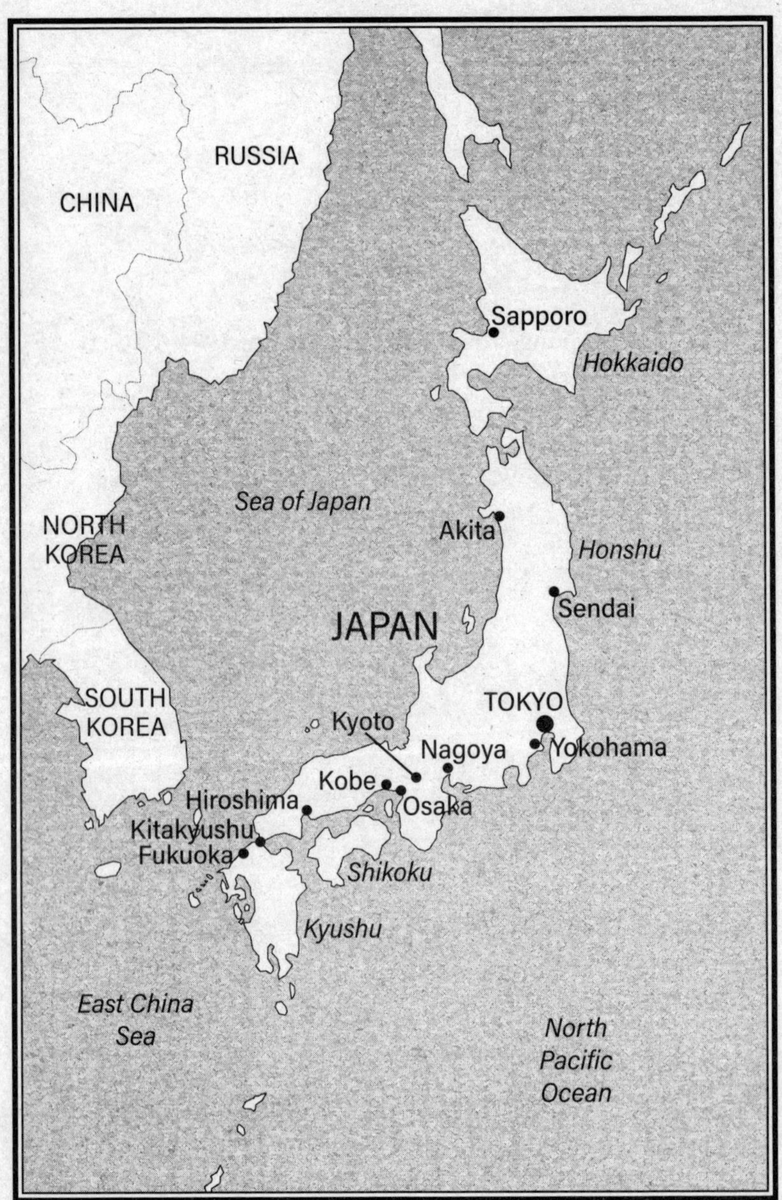

The Beginning:
The Russo-Japanese War 1904–1905

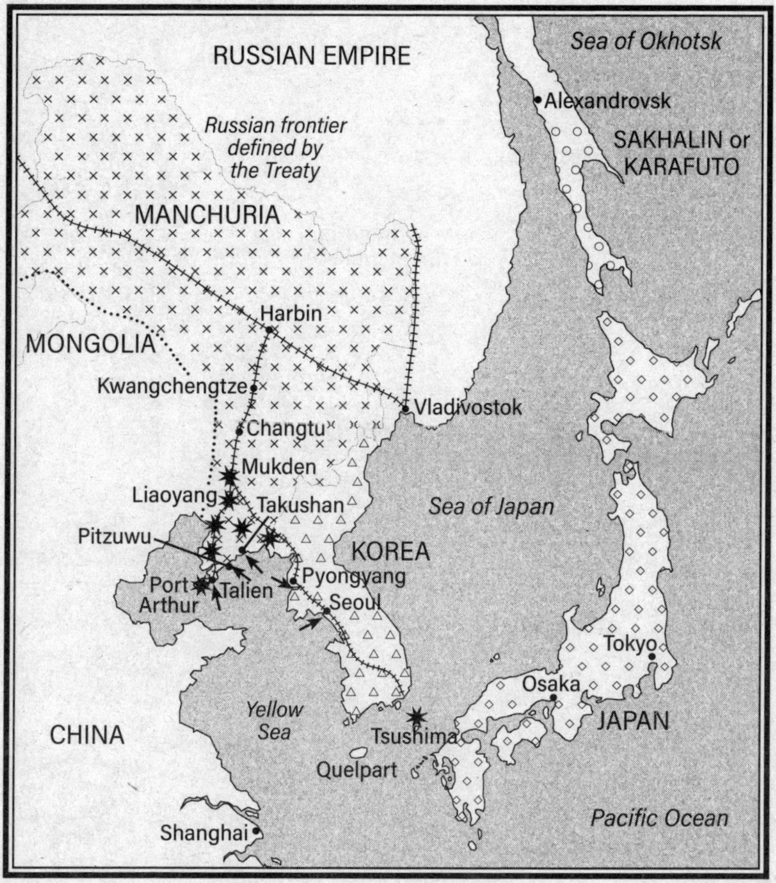

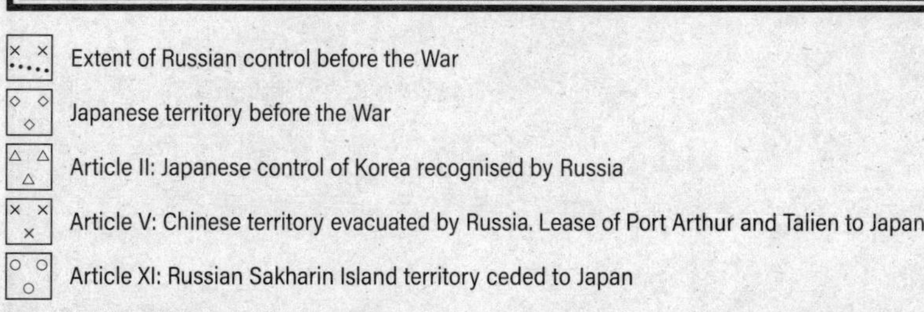

Inexorable Growth 1931–1940

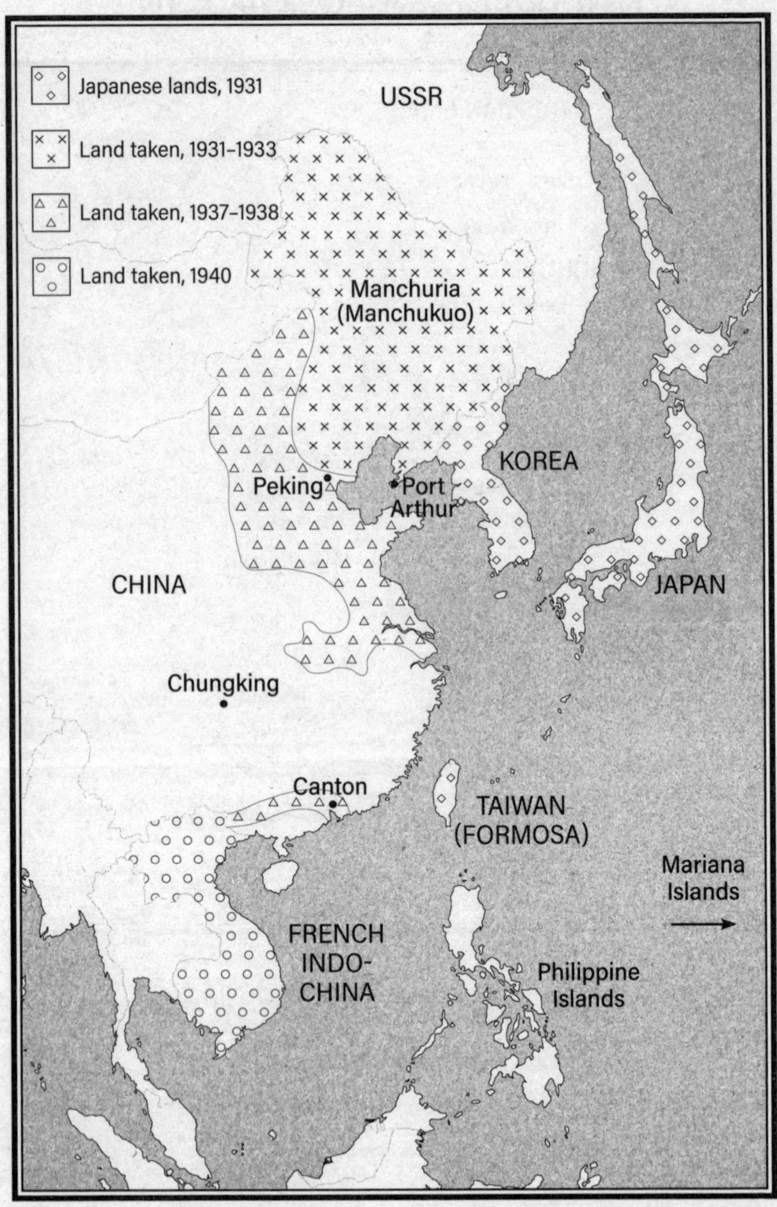

Japan's Holy War:
The Rise and Fall 1941–1945

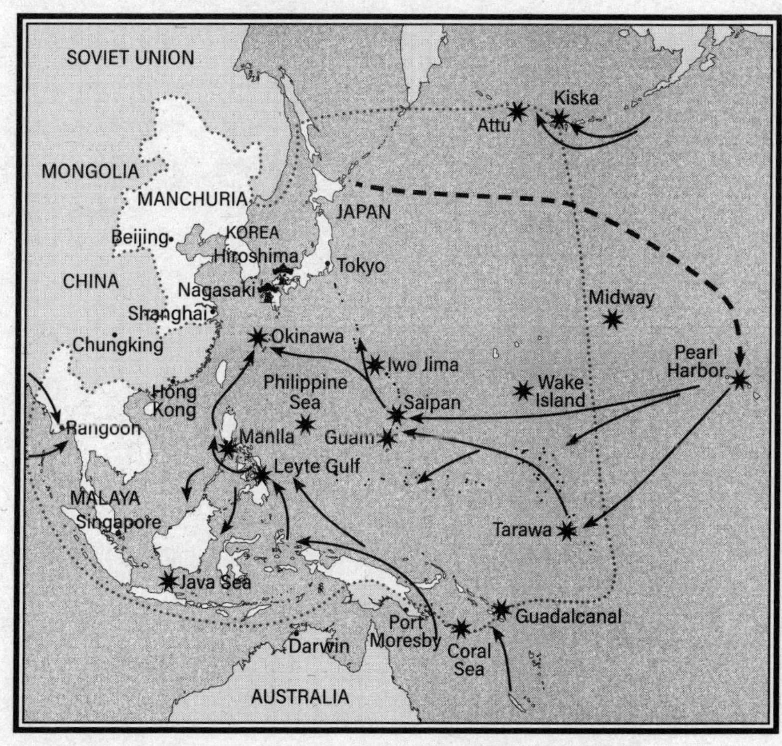

Japan and Japanese controlled areas, May 1942

Farthest Japanese advance

Allied countries

Japanese fleet, December 1941

Allied offensives

Major battle

Atomic bombing site
Hiroshima: 6 August 1945
Nagasaki: 9 August 1945

Pearl Harbor: 7 December 1941
Wake Island: December 1941
Java Sea: February–March 1942
Coral Sea: May 1942
Midway: June 1942
Guadalcanal: August 1942 to November 1943
Attu: May–June 1943
Kiska: August 1943
Tarawa: November 1943
Philippine Sea: June 1944
Saipan: June–July 1944
Guam: July–August 1944
Leyte Gulf: October 1944
Iwo Jima: February–March 1945
Manila: March 1945
Okinawa: April–June 1945

AUTHOR'S NOTE

I have made three documentaries about Japan. The first, in 2000, was a detailed account of its participation at the Olympic Games, a co-production with Japan's national broadcaster, NHK. The last, in 2011, for Discovery Asia, was a history of the country from 1904 to the end of the Second World War. Both productions were completed with no issues or problems, but the second documentary, in 2003, proved to be a profoundly insightful experience.

At the turn of this century, thanks to the remarkable talents of the renowned film researcher Adrian Wood, we had some success with what became known as the 'In-Colour' genre of documentaries. Adrian had become aware that, thanks to advances made in the 1930s by Agfa Colour in Germany and Kodachrome in the US (both widely embraced by amateur cine enthusiasts), there was far more original colour film in existence and from far earlier than most people realised. This previously unused cache of 'lost' film – much of it sitting on the dusty shelves of the world's archives, or languishing in the attics of homes around the world – provided us with a very fortuitous opportunity to rescue many of the significant moments of the twentieth century from what had previously been perceived as a black and white world.

Adrian's treasure trove allowed us to make a series of films that recaptured the drama and tragedy of the Second World War, including Britain's story, *Britain at War in Colour*, the stories of America and Germany, and also of Australia and New Zealand. However, there remained a gem that both Adrian and I wanted to reveal: Japan's story. By this time, we had a strong relationship with Japan's national broadcaster, and we pushed for a co-production with NHK and Channel 4. The film would be edited in Tokyo: most of the colour footage prior to 1945 was found in NHK's own archive vaults. It was also where the letters and diaries for the Japanese witnesses to the war would be researched. In an exciting development, the excellent Japanese researchers we hired began to discover home movie material from all over the country.

The early days of the co-production proved to be promising. However, language issues, technical conflicts, and significant differences between Western-style documentary making and NHK's approach, meant there was little contact between the Japanese and British editing teams. Our ambition had been a laudable one, but it became inevitable over the ensuing months that our aspiration of the same film being seen by both Japanese and British audiences was a pipe dream. Eventually, we went our separate ways and two versions of the documentary were made: one for UK distribution and one for Japanese transmission.

During my years as a documentary-maker, I went to Japan many times. From the late eighties until recently, I paid at least thirty visits to the country, spent long periods of time in Tokyo and travelled the length and breadth of the country. I never mastered its language, but I could exchange pleasantries and order food and drink; the food and drink were vital for me, the pleasantries crucial for the Japanese.

In this text, macrons are used for long vowels except for place names well known to the Western reader (for example, Tokyo rather than Tokyō) or words that have passed into common usage in the English language (for example, shogun rather than shōgun).

Japanese names are presented in the Western style: given name first, surname second.

Since the majority of Chinese names in the text refer to the war years, Chinese names and words have been used in the Western style. So, Nanking rather than Nanjing.

PREFACE
THE 'ENIGMA' THAT IS JAPAN

Much has been said and written about the 'enigmatic' nature of the Japanese. Not all of what has been written – and certainly most of what is said about the Japanese – bears much scrutiny. The defining traits of any nation are legion: from physical to behavioural; from cultural to metaphysical; and from the idiosyncratic to the profound. It is tempting to indulge in caricatures and stereotypes when the name of a people is mentioned – automatically painting pictures and using words derived from familiar descriptions of past and present events. Even when a country is hugely diverse and complex, we all too readily ascribe to all of its population characteristics that we suggest they all share. So it is with the Japanese.

Tāro Asō, Japan's right-wing prime minister from 2008 to 2009, wrote about his people, '*One nation, one civilisation, one language, one culture, and one race. There is no other nation that has such characteristics.*' His words were regarded as controversial at the time, both at home and abroad. Even a rudimentary knowledge of the nation and its people would suggest that Asō's view was, at best, a little simplistic.

Although today 98 per cent of Japan's population identifies as Yamato – an old clan name that has come to identify 'original' native Japanese – this is, in fact, misleading. Genetic and other research shows that Yamato people are a mixture of two groups of migratory settlers from mainland Asia: the Kofun and Yayoi. In addition, Japan is home to the Ryukyuan Japanese, whose origins range from the southern island of Kyushu all the way to Taiwan and who share a distinct language and dialects. Moreover, the Ainu people of the northern-most islands of the country, including Hokkaido, also have their own languages.

Distinct vestiges of Japan's ancient caste system still survive. 'Burakumin' is a polite name used to describe people who are descended from an outcaste class, the work of which was regarded as *eta*, 'defiled', like butchering animals, preparing the dead for burial, executing condemned criminals or tanning hides. Their status is remarkably similar to that of the Dalits in the Hindu caste tradition of India. Although official discrimination against the Burakumin no longer exists, there is still a social stigma attached to being a resident of certain areas traditionally associated with the Burakumin, as well as lingering discrimination in marriage and employment. Cases of continuing social discrimination occur mainly in western Japan, particularly where many people, especially the older generation, stereotype Burakumin residents whatever their ancestry, and associate them with impoverishment, unemployment and crime. No official figures exist, but it is thought that there are about 6,000 segregated Burakumin communities, containing between 1 million and 3 million people.

Religious affiliation, too, is a complex picture in Japan. The Japanese concept of religion differs significantly from most other societies. Spiritual beliefs are diverse, and worship is highly varied. Religious rites and ceremonies are more associated with well-being and worldly benefits, while doctrine is less important. Japanese religion is rarely preached, but rather seen as a moral code. Religion is usually a private, family affair with no religious symbols or practices in schools.

Where figures are formally recorded, they suggest that 70 per cent of the respondents follow Shintoism, 67 per cent are Buddhists, 1 per cent are Christian and that 6 per cent follow other religions. As you will readily calculate, the numbers add up to 144 per cent. This is because large numbers of people identify with both Shintoism and Buddhism. And of the majority who follow Shintoism, only 3 per cent will identify as Shinto in formal surveys, because the term suggests membership of organised Shinto sects. The 62 per cent who identify as *mushūkyō* ('without religion') do not necessarily reject faith but would prefer not to be labelled with a particular set of beliefs or practices.

There is a Japanese term, *Nihonjinron* ('discussions about the Japanese'), which has produced a significant body of literature that focuses on issues of Japanese national and cultural identity. *Nihonjinron* became popular after the Second World War, when the perceived behaviour of the Japanese, both in truth and in myth, became the subject of much debate. A vast range of material – some worthy, but some markedly less so – tried to analyse the peculiarities of Japanese culture and mentality, usually by comparison with those of Europe and North America. Given the many strongly held views about the Japanese during the war, this is perhaps not surprising. Even after eighty years, simplistic and usually negative attitudes about Japan are still deeply entrenched, especially in countries that were at war with Japan between 1937 and 1945.

Just after the Second World War, eminent American anthropologist Ruth Benedict made her excellent contribution to Japanese studies with her book *The Chrysanthemum and the Sword*. Pointedly, on the opening page, she wrote:

> When a serious observer is writing about peoples other than the Japanese and says they are unprecedentedly polite, he is not likely to add, 'but also insolent and overbearing'. When he says people of some nations are incomparably rigid in their behaviour, he does not add, 'but they also adapt themselves readily to extreme innovations'. When he says a people are submissive he does not explain too that they are not easily amenable to control from above. When he says they are loyal and generous, he does not declare, 'but also treacherous and spiteful'. When he says they are genuinely brave, he does not expatiate on their timidity. When he says they act out of concern for others' opinions, he does not then go on to tell that they have a truly terrifying conscience. When he describes robot-like discipline in their army, he does not continue by describing the way the soldiers in that army take the bit in their own teeth even to the point of insubordination. When he describes a people who devote themselves with passion to western learning, he does not also enlarge on their fervid conservatism.

When he writes a book on a nation with a popular cult of aestheticism which gives high honour to actors and to artists and lavishes art upon the cultivation of chrysanthemums, that book does not ordinarily have to be supplemented by another which is devoted to the cult of the sword and the top prestige of the warrior.

Not surprisingly, the Japanese are perfectly capable of making succinct observations of those who would comment about Japanese foibles. Yoshisaburō Okakura, a leading teacher of English in Japan, was addressing a Western audience in America in 1913, when he asked:

Did the idea ever occur to you that your own ways might appear to us no less curious and strange than ours do to you? Do you know how amusing it sometimes is to us to see you at your daily performances? Your mode of expressing friendship by a grasp of hands; your manner of imparting affection by an application of lips; your fondness of hopping about on tip-toe in a dancing-hall, with your arm round the waist of a person of different sex; your readiness to wear indoors the same pair of shoes in which you have shuffled about the street – all this and many other oddities cannot fail to attract our attention.

He then added, much more scornfully:

You seem to us strongly convinced of your superiority. You believe in one God, and all are hopeless heathens who do not do the same. You belong to the Caucasian race, and all are hopelessly inferior who do not belong to it, so much so that an American authority on Japan kindly proposed to vindicate in his new book the possibility of our being a great nation by pointing to the probable existence of a drop of your blood in our veins through our early intermarriage with the hairy Ainu, the Caucasian aborigines of our islands!

German-Japanese writer Komakichi Nohara offered another perspective on the Japanese in 1935, just before Japan's Holy War began in earnest. It doesn't tell of aggression or conquest, but of character.

> The coats of varnish that are laid on the foundation by laborious work throughout the years, the more valuable becomes the lacquer work as a finished product. So it is with people [. . .] It is said of the Russians: 'Scratch a Russian and you find a Tartar.' One might say of the Japanese: 'Scratch a Japanese of the varnish and you find a pirate.' It should not be forgotten that in Japan varnish is a valuable product [. . .] There is nothing spurious about it; it is not a daub to disguise defects. It is at least as valuable as the substance it adorns.

Put simply, it is Komakichi's contention that the 'lacquer' of painstaking self-restraint is the virtue that helps the nation to control its menacing impulses. It is Japan's character that says more about the nation than its actions.

This book is committed to hearing Japan's voice, so let us return to Yoshisaburō Okakura. In his address to Western audiences, Okakura describes the importance and symbolism of 'sakura' – the cherry blossoms of spring – for the Japanese.

> It is to this day one of our highest ideals to live clean, undefiled lives, which seem to us as serene and beautiful as a cherry-tree in full bloom. The sakura with its gay blossoms, seem to us to set up every spring an exquisite example for us to follow in our worldly existence. To live like the sakura and then die, when die we should, like the sakura, has been ever the ideal of a true son of the Land of Yamato [Japan]. Our love of Nature, and our love of the child, the symbol of undefiled humanity, are these not also expressions of the same mental craving for the pure and the beautiful?

Okakura firmly rejects the prevailing Western view of the Japanese as a bloodthirsty nation that poses a risk to global development and stability. Instead, he points to his nation's reverence for the beauty and fragility of the cherry blossom.

It is my strong belief that she [Japan] will remain the peaceful and faithful admirer of the sakura ideal, and never be consciously the cause of social disturbance in her intercourse with any of her sister-nations [. . .]

Okakura's conviction about the true nature of the Japanese people is compelling. However, he ends with a proviso, which, given that it was said just twenty-eight years before Pearl Harbor, is starkly portentous:

[. . .] unless the wantonness or greed of other nations force us in self-defence to an attitude which we should find it very hateful to assume.

INTRODUCTION
THE PRICE OF WAR

The statistics are stark.

An estimated total of between 70 and 85 million people perished in the Second World War – about 3 per cent of the people on Earth in 1940. Deaths attributed to the war are estimated at between 50 and 56 million, with an additional 25 million deaths from war-related disease and famine. In addition, it is thought that at least 5 million prisoners of war died in what was often murderous captivity. More than half of the total number of casualties is accounted for by the losses in China and the Soviet Union – at least 15 to 20 million, and 20 to 27 million respectively. The economic and social costs of the conflict are impossible to calculate; it took decades for the world to recover from the full impact of the destruction and chaos caused by the war.

As for Japan, 800,000 Japanese civilians and over 2 million Japanese soldiers died during the war. According to a report compiled by the Relief Bureau of the Japanese Ministry of Health and Welfare in March 1964, combined Japanese Army and Navy deaths during the war (1937–1945) numbered approximately 2,121,000 men, mostly against American forces (1.1+ million) in places like the Solomons, Japan, Taiwan, the Central Pacific and the Philippines, or against various Chinese factions (500,000+) during the war on the Chinese mainland, Manchuria and the Burma campaign.

The Imperial Japanese Navy lost over 341 warships, including 11 battleships, 25 aircraft carriers, 39 cruisers, 135 destroyers and 131 submarines, almost entirely in action against the United States Navy. The navy and army together lost 45,125 aircraft.

The US Strategic Bombing Survey found that the damage to Japan's urban centres was enormous. In total, some 40 per cent of the built-up areas of sixty-six Japanese cities was destroyed, and approximately 30 per cent of the entire urban population of Japan lost their homes and most of their possessions. In addition, Hiroshima and Nagasaki suffered the new horror of an atomic detonation and its subsequent radiation.

•

The consensus among historians about Japan's purpose in attacking Pearl Harbor on the morning of 7 December (8 December Japanese time) 1941, is that it defied logic because it began a war that it was impossible for Japan to win. Given the price of war, that assertion begs several questions, the most telling of which is: What drove Japan's leaders, and the millions of its people who followed them so devotedly, to embark on a war that led to inevitable defeat, and one with such a catastrophic conclusion?

The simple answer lies in the one-word subtitle to this book, *Seisen*, which loosely translates into English as 'crusade'. The Asia-Pacific War was Emperor Hirohito's Holy War. A more subtle answer lies in a combination of factors that will be addressed in this book – some cultural and emotional, some political and strategic, and some pragmatic and logical.

The sudden shock that was the Japanese attack on Pearl Harbor in December 1941 was the culmination of a complex set of circumstances that began with Japan's expansion on to the Asian mainland almost fifty years earlier. It was also a direct consequence of the enormous watershed that was the Meiji Restoration, a generation before that. Like the history of all nations, Japan's modern history has been shaped by its past. In order to better understand the dynamics that underpinned Japan's ambitions, actions and attitudes during its Holy War, I aim to describe its complex history, demographics, resources, culture and traditions in some detail. Many of the factors that determined the path taken by Japan have parallels elsewhere, but some are unique to Japan.

Like all nations tempted by imperial adventures – including the ancient empires of the past and those of modern Europe – many twentieth-century Japanese leaders were motivated by a strong sense of their superiority as a race. The ingrained denial that China – its giant neighbour across the *Nihon Kai*, the Sea of Japan – was the origin of much of Japan's culture, language and religion, created a powerful conviction of invincibility within the Japanese mentality. When the Western powers began to circle around Japan for profit and territory, their condescension, at best – and overt racism, at worst – created a powerful backlash among the Japanese, which soon turned into a barely disguised xenophobia. After centuries of stubborn isolation, Japan set itself on a course that would become a holy war.

The purpose of this account is to offer, through a chronological journey, a thoughtful insight into the complexities of Japan's long history, insofar as it reveals what led Japan into four wars of expansion in less than fifty years. It will then provide a detailed analysis of the four extraordinary years from the presumed success of Pearl Harbor in 1941 to the catastrophic events of 1945. Throughout the story, the events will be described through the voices of the Japanese, whether they were victims, perpetrators or those ordinary people who were caught in the maelstrom of a terrible war. This book contains both stories and first-hand accounts that are sometimes very difficult to read.

Even though there is a significant body of objective evidence in Western histories of the Asia-Pacific War, much of it is disputed in Japan, even eighty years after the events. The areas of divergence are well known: for example, the behaviour of Japan's occupation troops, the Nanking Massacre, 'comfort women', the treatment of POWs and the culpability of Emperor Hirohito. On the other hand, many Japanese believe that the West was the historical 'oppressor' in Asia, that Japan's 'encirclement' by the West gave them no choice other than to strike at Pearl Harbor, and that the treatment meted out to Japan by firebombings and atomic weapons was disproportionately cruel.

Thus, there remain strongly held views within Japan about the war, which are at odds with opinions outside Japan. These are differences which, sadly, despite the efforts of many, are largely irreconcilable. Accounts of the Asia-Pacific War require great sensitivity and careful handling.

With one early exception, all the witness material in this book is exclusively Japanese. My task has been to find an objective and balanced collection of accounts: letters, diaries, autobiographies and oral evidence which reflect all shades of opinion from Japanese society at the time. In that context, my hope is that what follows challenges pre-conceived positions and allows the collective voice of the Japanese people, in all its timbres, nuances and complexities, to tell their nation's story.

1

THE WAY OF THE WARRIOR

It is difficult to know when to begin the story of Japan's Holy War. Japan has a long and uniform history. It had never been invaded until American forces arrived in 1945, and it has existed in relative isolation for almost all of its history. Britain lies just twenty-one miles from its neighbours on Continental Europe, whereas Japan is 120 miles from its nearest neighbour, Korea, while the sea crossing from Osaka (Japan) to Shanghai (China) is over 850 miles. Not only that, Japan's western coast – which faces mainland Asia – is rugged and remote, while the vast majority of its population lives on its east coast, looking out on the endless expanse of the Pacific. In fact, about 40 million, a third of all Japanese, live in the mega-city that is the Greater Tokyo Area.

However, in contrast with its isolation, Japan has few natural resources, so that, when it began to modernise, it had to look way beyond its borders and to its Asian neighbours for the materials to develop a modern economy. That blunt fact would prove to be a major catalyst in shaping Japan's future in the twentieth century.

Although much influenced in its origins by mainland Asia, Japan's long periods of isolation have led it to develop a unique cultural heritage. It has a complex melange of cultural norms, from its Shinto religion – a belief system without founder or prophets or a major text which outlines its faith – to its rigid social etiquettes of politeness, service and ubiquitous bowing. However, at the beginning of an account of Japan's Holy War, perhaps the best place to start is with a discussion of the Japanese *bushi* – 'warrior', better known as 'samurai' – and of the concept that defined them, *bushidō* – the 'way of the warrior'.

The early seventeenth-century historian and philosopher Razan Hayashi defined the philosophy of *bushidō* as:

Heaven is above and earth is below [. . .] in everything there is an order separating those who are above and those who are below [. . .] [and] we cannot allow disorder in the relations between the ruler and the subject [. . .] The separation into four classes of warrior (samurai), farmers, artisans and merchants [. . .] is part of the principles of heaven and is the Way which was taught by the Sage Confucius. To know the way of heaven is to respect heaven and to secure humble submission from earth [. . .] There is a differentiation between the above and the below. Likewise, among the people, rulers are to be respected and subjects are to submit humbly. Only when this differentiation between those who are above and those who are below is made clear, can there be law and propriety [. . .] The more the rulers are respected, and the more the subjects submit humbly, and the more the differentiation is made clear-cut, the easier it is to govern a country.

Sokō Yamaga, a samurai scholar and contemporary of Hayashi, explained that a samurai, as a 'superior man':

[. . .] is one who does not cultivate, does not manufacture, and does not engage in trade, but it cannot be that he has no function at all as a samurai [. . .] The business of the samurai consists in reflecting on his own station in life, in discharging loyal service to his master [. . .] and, with due consideration of his own position, in devoting himself to duty above all [. . .] [He] confines himself to practising this Way [. . .] [and] upholds proper moral principles in the land [by punishing any who transgress against them].

The Samurai Code is captured by the following list of well-known quotations.

I know nothing about surpassing others. I only know how to outdo myself.

Knowledge becomes really such only when it is assimilated in the mind of the learner and shows in his character.

Chivalry is itself the poetry of life.

Dishonour is like a scar on a tree, which time, instead of effacing, only helps to enlarge.

Human life has sorrow, they who meet must part, he that is born must die.

A samurai was essentially a man of action. He carried a distinctive curved sword – the *katana* – which was a symbol of power, strength and respect. But the code has also been influenced by many thinkers, including leading samurai.

Victory is reserved for those who are willing to pay the price.
Sun Tzu, Chinese general and philosopher

Strategy without tactics is the slowest route to victory. Tactics without strategy is the noise before defeat.
Sun Tzu

Engage in combat fully determined to die and you will be alive, wish to survive in the battle and you will surely meet death.
Kenshin Uesugi, sixteenth-century Japanese daimyo

Ultimately you must forget about technique. The further you progress, the fewer teachings there are. The Great Path is really no path.
Morihei Ueshiba, nineteenth-century martial artist and founder of aikido

Loyalty and devotion lead to bravery. Bravery leads to the spirit of self-sacrifice. The spirit of self-sacrifice creates trust in the power of love.
Morihei Ueshiba

Study hard and all things can be accomplished. Give up and you will amount to nothing.
Tesshū Yamaoka, a samurai of the final years of the Edo era, who played an important role in the Meiji Restoration

As a samurai I must strengthen my character, as a human being
I must perfect my spirit.
  Tesshū Yamaoka

Honour may not win power but it wins respect. And respect
earns power.
  Mitsunari Ishida, a seventeenth-century Japanese samurai and military commander

There is also a remarkable longevity to Japanese history. Its emperor – 'Tennou', 'Heavenly Ruler' – currently Naruhito, is now the only monarch in the world who holds the title of 'Emperor'. Naruhito, who presides from his Chrysanthemum Throne, is said to be the 126th emperor in a lineage going back to 660 BCE. However, modern historians believe that there is much mythology about the early emperors and that the true lineage did not begin until Emperor Ōjin in the fourth century CE. Even so, the ancestry of Japan's emperors predates the surviving monarchies of Europe by several hundred years.

Although Japan's emperors were powerful in name, that was not always the case in reality. From their traditional seat in Tokyo, successive emperors – some determined, many less so – found it difficult to rein in their many powerful warlords. Called shoguns, officially *Sei-i Taishōgun* ('Commander-in-Chief of the Expeditionary Force Against the Barbarians'), they were the military leaders of Japan during most of the period from 1185 to 1868. Although appointed by the emperor, shoguns were the de facto rulers of the country who, with the support of their samurai (warriors) and daimyo (vassal lords), ruled their clans and domains with a ferocity that led the period from 1467 to 1603 to be called the *Sengoku Jidai* ('The Warring States Period'). It was a time marked by social unrest, political intrigue and almost endless warfare when successive emperors in Kyoto were all but impotent. However, during this chaotic era, three figures emerged who would change the course of Japanese history: Nobunaga Oda, Hideyoshi Toyotomi, and Ieyasu Tokugawa.

Known as *San'nin no idaina tōitsu-sha* ('The Three Great Unifiers'), they managed to forge the fragmented daimyo domains into a unified nation. Their military prowess, political savvy and unrelenting ambition laid the foundations for the *Edo Jidai* ('Edo Period') from 1603 to 1868, which represented over two centuries of peace, high culture and growth, an era that has been called 'Japan's Golden Age'.

It was Ieyasu Tokugawa who would become the most powerful man in Japan after Hideyoshi died in 1598. Ieyasu disregarded promises he had made to respect Hideyoshi's successor, Hideyori. He was determined to become the absolute ruler of Japan. In the Battle of Sekigahara in 1600, Ieyasu defeated the Hideyori loyalists and, in 1603, he was appointed shogun by the emperor and established his government in Edo (Tokyo). What then became known as the 'Tokugawa Shogunate' continued to rule Japan for a remarkable 250 years.

It was Tokugawa who formalised the crucial relationships that underpinned the Japanese social structure, relationships that were still central to Japanese life in the twentieth century.

Whether there is order or chaos in the nation depends on the virtues and vices of everyone. First, the emperor, with compassion in his heart for the needs of the people, must not be remiss in the performance of his duties, from the early morning worship of the New Year to the monthly functions of the court. Secondly, the shogun must not forget the possibility of war in peacetime and must maintain his discipline [. . .] the true master of the way of the warrior is one who maintains his martial discipline even in time of peace. Thirdly, the farmer's toil is proverbial – from the first grain to a hundred acts of labour. He selects the seed from last autumn's crop and undergoes various hardships and anxieties through the heat of the summer until the seed grows finally to a rice plant. The rice then becomes sustenance for the multitudes [. . .] Fourthly, the artisan's occupation is to make and prepare wares and utensils for the use of others. Fifthly, the merchant facilitates the exchange of goods so that the people can cover their nakedness and keep their bodies warm.

Even though the Tokugawa Shogunate remained relatively stable over many decades, its power steadily declined. There were several reasons. A weakening of the finances of the government led to higher taxes and subsequent riots among the rural population. Japan experienced frequent natural disasters which, coupled with years of famine, generated more riots and further financial problems for the country. The social hierarchy began to break down as the merchant class grew increasingly powerful and several groups of samurai became financially reliant on them. Subsequently, corruption, incompetence and moral decline within the ruling hierarchy exacerbated the social tensions.

By the end of the eighteenth century, international pressure became a new and ever more serious issue for Japan when Tsarist Russia tried to establish trade, but without success. They were followed by other European nations and the Americans in the nineteenth century. Eventually, in 1853 and again in 1854, under orders from Washington, American naval officer Commodore Perry arrived to persuade the Japanese, using whatever methods necessary, to open up to international trade. Many in Japan realised that, although their country preferred to live in isolation, it was impossible to keep an encroaching world at arm's length. Powerful nations were greedy for conquests and raw materials and had built steam-powered navies to help them feed their appetites.

Kaishū Katsu, born into a samurai family, was trained as a naval engineer by the Dutch and became a prominent statesman in later life. As a visitor to Europe and America, he warned that Japan had to change: '*By the end of the Tenpou era [1817–1846, Emperor Ninkou] our country had enjoyed peace and prosperity for more than 240 years. Popular customs were lapsing more and more into luxury, the people became all the more indolent, and there were few who considered the possibility of upheaval during those peaceful times. Still more, people throughout society, the high and the low, paid no attention to things abroad, and were not at all concerned that our country might be thought of contemptuously or encroached upon by the rest of the world.*'

Even prominent daimyos like Nariakira Shimazu, lord of Satsuma – a domain deep in the south of the country, on Kyushu, a Japanese island closest to China and Korea – was aware of his country's need to look westwards. His words, referring to Western dominance in China, were spoken in the late 1850s: *'We must take the initiative [otherwise] we will be dominated. We must prepare our defences with this thought in mind. Considering the present situation, it behoves us first to raise an army, seize a part of China's territory, and establish a base on the Asiatic mainland. We must strengthen Japan without delay and display our military power abroad. This would make it impossible for England or France to interfere in our affairs despite their strength.'*

Japanese ports did not open immediately, but change was in the air in the country. Anti-government attitudes hardened, demands for the restoration of the emperor's ancient authority emerged, and many of the new economic elite recognised the benefits of embracing the science and technology of the West through an open-door policy to trade. A vibrant urban culture emerged, especially in Kyoto, Osaka and Edo (Tokyo), enjoyed by merchants growing rich through commerce, reinvigorated samurai, and increasing numbers of townspeople, rather than nobles and daimyos, the traditional patrons. Consequently, in 1867, two dominant anti-Tokugawa clans, the Chōshū and Satsuma, united to overthrow the shogunate and declared an 'imperial restoration', the Meiji Restoration, in the name of the fourteen-year-old Prince Mutsuhito who became Emperor Meiji. The word *meiji* means 'enlightened rule' and the ambition was to combine 'modern advances' with traditional Eastern values.

The Meiji Constitution of 1889, which would remain the constitution of Japan until 1947, created a Diet (parliament), a lower house elected by the people with a prime minister and cabinet appointed by the emperor. Prince Hirobumi Itō, a Chōshū clan samurai, was Japan's first prime minister and chaired the committee which wrote the country's first constitution. Notably, some of its 76 articles, grouped into seven chapters, offer a telling insight into the antiquated attitudes prevalent in Japan at the time and illustrate how ripe the country could be for authoritarian rule in the future.

The Sacred Throne of Japan is inherited from Imperial Ancestors and is to be bequeathed to posterity; in it resides the power to reign over and govern the State [. . .]

ARTICLE I. The Empire of Japan shall be reigned over and governed by a line of Emperors unbroken for ages eternal.

[. . .]

ARTICLE III. The Emperor is sacred and inviolable.

ARTICLE IV. The Emperor is the head of the Empire, combining in himself the rights of sovereignty, and exercises them, according to the provisions of the present Constitution.

ARTICLE V. The Emperor exercises the legislative power with the consent of the Imperial Diet.

[. . .]

ARTICLE XI. The Emperor has the supreme command of the Army and Navy.

ARTICLE XII. The Emperor determines the organisation and peace standing of the Army and Navy.

Also, significantly for the future, the peace and stability of the Tokugawa Shogunate, and the economic growth it cultivated, was the springboard for the rapid modernisation that took place after the Meiji Restoration. There was fundamental social, political and economic change, including the abolition of the feudal system and a major investment in military hardware and personnel, which would soon place Japan in the spotlight on the world stage.

As Japan modernised, its growing economic strength led newly empowered radical elements in Japan to cast envious eyes westwards. Asia was a vast sphere of opportunity too tempting to resist. During the last decades of the nineteenth century, the modern world was closing in on East Asia. Tsarist Russia was expanding into the vast far east of its empire, and the royal dynasties of Korea and China were attempting reform, but with little success. Both had become power vacuums.

After altercations between Japanese traders and locals in Korea, the Ganghwa Treaty was signed on 26 February 1876, which opened Korea to Japanese trade. It was a coup for those in Japan seeking a foothold on the mainland, and it brought Korea an ally against the growing influence of Russia. In a show of force, a Japanese warship, the *Un'yō*, was dispatched to the Korean coast. The new Japan was on the move.

Japan's influence in Korea grew, and by the early 1880s it became associated with reformists within the Korean government, which put it at odds with China, who continued to support the royal family. In 1884, a group of pro-Japanese reformers attempted to overthrow the Korean government, but Chinese troops under General Yuan Shikai rescued King Gojong, killing several Japanese legation guards in the process. Warfare was only avoided between Japan and China by the signing of the Li-Itō Convention, in which both countries agreed to withdraw troops from Korea. Although Japan had to withdraw, the convention put China and Japan on an equal footing in Korea.

Historian Saburō Ienaga summarised the likely progression of events.

> When Japan began to modernise, the Western powers had completed the imperialistic division of Asia and Africa. Japanese leaders, looking around for territory to seize, found only Korea. Japan perceived the modern international arena as a dog-eat-dog struggle where the devil and colonialism took the hindmost.

Ten years later, Kim Ok-Kyun, the pro-Japanese Korean leader of the 1884 coup, was assassinated in Shanghai, probably by agents of General Shikai. His body was put on a Chinese warship and sent back to Korea, where it was quartered and displayed as a warning to other rebels. There was outrage in Japan.

Matters worsened a year later when the Donghak Peasant Revolt broke out in Korea. At the behest of the Korean king, the Chinese government sent troops to put down the rebels. Japan regarded the Chinese intrusion as a violation of the Li-Itō Convention and sent

8,000 troops to Korea. When the Chinese tried to reinforce their own forces, the Japanese sank the British steamer *Kowshing*, which was carrying the reinforcements, which further exacerbated the crisis. War was inevitable.

The first Sino-Japanese War was finally declared on 1 August 1894. Chinese forces outnumbered Japan's forces, but the Japanese were better equipped and prepared and had overwhelming success on both land and sea. By March 1895, Japan had invaded Shandong province and Manchuria and controlled the sea approaches to Beijing. The Chinese sued for peace.

The resulting Treaty of Shimonoseki in 1895 required China to recognise the independence of Korea, to cede Taiwan, the Pescadores Islands and the Liaodong (the southern Manchurian peninsula) to Japan, to open the ports of Shashi, Chungking, Suzhou and Hangzhou to Japanese trade, and to pay an indemnity of 200,000,000 taels to Japan. A tael was equivalent to 1.3 ounces of silver, so the value of the indemnity in today's money was $2.6 billion.

The war had cost Japan 1,132 deaths in battle and a further 12,000 fatalities from disease and wounds, but it had significantly increased its territory and sphere of influence. In short, it had become a new imperial power in Asia. *Bushidō*'s ancient hold on Japan's psyche was not waning with age and the dramatic changes brought about by modernisation, but on the contrary, it was growing stronger.

The war had hardened Japanese contempt for its neighbours until it became overt racism, as historian Ienaga explained.

The Sino-Japanese War changed the Japanese image of China as a great centre of classical culture, a powerful nation. The writer Naka Kansuke, an elementary school student during the war, recalled the jingoistic mood in his classroom: 'After the war started my friends would talk of nothing else but the "brave Japanese, the cowardly Chinks". The teachers urged us on like a pack of puppies whelping after a Chinese bone. We repeated it at every chance, "brave Japanese, cowardly Chinks, brave Japanese, cowardly Chinks".'

It is difficult to know how and why national pride begets nationalism, or how the flush of victory evolves into naked aggression, but Japan's military successes favoured the prevailing view of international relations as tests of strength, to be decided by a code of 'might makes right'. The subsequent humiliation of Tsarist Russia in its war of 1904–1905 would serve to further galvanise the nation.

2

A NATION GALVANISED

This new war was a strategic inevitability, driven by Russian expansionism eastward, the rapid growth of Japan's military muscle, and the martial ambitions of its military elite. Significantly, much to the fury of the Japanese, its victory in the Sino-Japanese War of 1894–1895, and the subsequent addition of the Liaotung Peninsula in Manchuria, had led to an alliance of Russia, France and Germany, which put pressure on Japan to give back the peninsula in return for increased reparations.

In 1897, Russia started to build a railway across Chinese territory to open it to commercial and industrial development, much to the chagrin of Tokyo. Tensions increased further when Russia founded the Russo-Korean Bank, a thinly disguised ploy by Russia to grasp economic control of Korea. Russia then moved troops into Manchuria in response to the 1899 Boxer Uprising in Beijing, during which Japan stood shoulder-to-shoulder with the troops of seven other imperial powers – Britain, Russia, France, Germany, Italy and Austria-Hungary – to defeat the rebels.

Despite that brief interlude of cooperation, tension between Japan and Russia soon boiled over into armed conflict. On the night of 8/9 February 1904, Japanese destroyers launched a surprise attack on Russian warships at Port Arthur in Manchuria and Chemulpo (Incheon) in Korea. The next day, immediately after the attacks, Japan declared war.

The war was short-lived and produced a humiliating defeat for the forces of Russia's Tsar Nicholas II and a glorious victory for Japan's Imperial Army and Navy. On 13 April 1904, a mine sank the Russian flagship *Petropavlovsk*, taking its crew of 662 to the bottom of the Yellow Sea. The Russian navy was soon disgraced yet further, on 27 and 28 May 1905, in the final large-scale encounter of the war. The Battle of Tsushima led to the sinking or capture of twenty-six Russian ships, including eleven battleships, and the death or capture of 11,000 Russian sailors.

On land, the Russians fared little better. In February 1904, Japan had advanced into Manchuria, driving back a much larger Russian army. At the end of April, the Battle of the Yalu River took place on the boundary between Korea and Manchuria. It resulted in a Russian retreat, their withdrawal from Korea, and the surrender of part of the Russian army. Only days later, the Japanese Imperial Army landed unopposed north of Port Arthur on the Liaotung Peninsula. At the Battle of Nanshan, the Russians abandoned the port of Dalny and the outer defences of Port Arthur, which the Japanese besieged until it surrendered on 3 January 1905. In February and March 1905, at Mukden, the two armies fought one of the largest land battles of modern history up to that point. The battle was ferocious and cost both sides a third of their forces, before Japanese troops took the town.

In August 1905, peace negotiations began in the United States, and the Treaty of Portsmouth was signed in September 1905. It recognised Japanese rights in Korea and ceded Port Arthur, Dalny and the adjacent territory to Japan, which also gained control of the South Manchurian Railway.

The war came at a great cost in men and materiel on both sides, which led to domestic unrest in both countries. In Japan, which suffered over 80,000 dead, the peace settlement, in which reparations were not granted, was regarded as an insult, which only added to the trauma of the death toll. Riots lasted for days in several Japanese cities. Martial law was declared and over 2,000 people were arrested. Opponents of the war included liberal aristocrats like Prince Hirobumi Itō but also radicals among the emerging socialist parties which, inspired by European ideology, had developed in the 1870s. Shūsui Kōtoku was one of them and established a *People's Weekly* (*Shūkan Heimin Shimbun*) during the Russo-Japanese war to promote his anti-war position.

One of his anti-war articles, 'Against the War-Time Tax', was published in March 1904.

The phrase, 'for the sake of war', is a powerful narcotic. With this phrase, the sagacious loses his sagacity, the clever loses his clarity, the wise loses his wisdom, and the courageous loses his courage. How much more so will the present political parties be who are not sagacious, clever, wise or courageous! All the political parties in the Diet are drugged by the phrase, 'for the sake of war' [. . .] They discard their common sense, abandon their rationality, and forget the spiritual power given them as political parties. They are now reduced to a mere machine. What kind of machine is it? It is a machine to produce more taxes. And the government skilfully manipulates this automatic machine to levy a burdensome tax of sixty million yen on our rice. Our military might may be known all over the world, but the people do not get one extra suit of clothing. Many of our fellow countrymen are exposed to the dangers of the battlefield, and the families they left behind cry because of hunger. As I see our people unable to understand these simple and clear-cut facts and truth, and while repressing tears bear the pain and unhappiness 'for the sake of war', more than ever, I am convinced of the important role I must play as a socialist.

Unfortunately for left-wing sentiment in Japan and for the political well-being of the country, the views of radicals like Kōtoku fell on deaf ears. Not only that, increasingly repressive government policies strangled the growth of radical opinion. The Japan Socialist Party, founded in January 1906, was a loose coalition representing a wide range of socialist beliefs but was unstable, and collapsed after only a year. Small, short-lived political parties then appeared, many of which came under police scrutiny and were suppressed under increasingly restrictive laws. Significantly, Shūsui Kōtoku and twelve others were arrested and hanged for 'high treason' in 1911 for their alleged involvement in a bomb plot to assassinate the

Emperor Meiji. It was a severe blow to the early socialist movement; the following years became known as 'the winter years' of socialism in Japan as its political activity all but disappeared, and it played no part in Japanese politics until 1945.

Japan's victory in the war against Russia was a watershed in global and world history. The existing major powers looked on in amazement as a new country joined their ranks.

The transformation in Japan's structure, both economic and social, had been profound. Much of the impetus for significant change in Japan began with the 1871 Iwakura Mission. Consisting of forty-eight senior government officials and academics, it was supported by fifty-three students and administrators. Its mission was to travel to Europe and the United States to make a comprehensive study of their modern industrial, political, military and educational systems and structures, and to determine how they could be applied to Japan. The findings of the mission were to prove crucial to Japan's future growth.

In a vital move, the Meiji government initiated a series of reforms to foster capitalism in Japan. The feudal system of post stations, merchant guilds and goods checkpoints – all barriers to industrial development – were abolished. New infrastructure projects began, including the first telegraph line between Tokyo and Yokohama, in 1869. In 1871, a modern postal service replaced the former courier system; post offices were established around the country, and Japan joined the Universal Postal Services in 1877. In the same year, the import of telephones began.

In 1872, the first rail services started between Tokyo and Yokohama, and by the end of the century, a railway network had spread across the whole of the major island of Honshu. Similarly, major road networks were improved and through government patronage, private enterprises like Mitsubishi, Mitsui and Ono were established to compete with Western companies in the international marketplace.

Silk production, previously a famous Japanese cottage industry, was transformed into large-scale industrial production. The

Tomioka Silk Mill in the Gunma Prefecture was built in 1872 and had 300 silk reeling machines imported from France. The mill workers were taught how to use the machines by French technicians, who then passed on their knowledge across the country.

All in all, by 1898, a thriving capitalist economy had been established in Japan. Japan had become a country transformed, driven by a dichotomous mix of emotions. It had embraced what it admired in the West – technology, military prowess, social modernity – yet it resented the disdain shown by the Western powers towards Asian people, including the Japanese. It had rejected aristocratic shoguns but restored the emperor to his position as god-ruler. It had embraced democratic institutions, yet retained its devotion to traditions of honour and discipline. And it had cast out the samurai, yet still revered them.

Writing in 1905, just after Japan's defeat of Russia, academic and diplomat Inazō Nitobe wrote one of the most influential accounts of the power of *bushidō* and how, despite the dramatic changes, it was still at the core of Japanese life.

> An unconscious and irresistible power, *Bushidō* has been moving the nation and individuals for centuries.
>
> *Bushidō* was and still is the animating spirit, the motor force of our country [. . .] for *Bushidō*, the maker and product of Old Japan, is still the guiding principle of the transition and will prove the formative force of the new era. The influence of *Bushidō* is still so palpable [. . .] The universal politeness of the people, which is the legacy of knightly ways, is too well known to be repeated anew. The physical endurance, fortitude and bravery that 'the little Jap' possesses, were sufficiently proved in the China-Japanese war [. . .] 'Is there any nation more loyal and patriotic?' is a question asked by many; and for the proud answer, 'There is not', we must thank the Precepts of Knighthood.
>
> On the other hand, it is fair to recognise that for the very faults and defects of our character, *Bushidō* is largely responsible [. . .] Our sense of honour is responsible for our exaggerated

sensitiveness and touchiness; and if there is the conceit in us with which some foreigners charge us, that, too, is a pathological outcome of honour.

Etsu Inagaki Sugimoto was born in 1874, the daughter of a high-ranking samurai, and as a young girl experienced life in the *bushidō* tradition: '*Since the absence of bodily comfort meant inspiration of mind, of course I wrote in a room without a fire. Japanese picture-writing is slow and careful work and I froze my fingers that morning without knowing it until I looked back and saw my good nurse softly crying as she watched my purple hand. The training of children, even of my age, was strict in those days, and neither she nor I moved until I had finished my task.*'

The necessity of this rigid discipline was never questioned although, as a delicate child, Sugimoto was aware that this enforced regime of study caused her mother some uneasiness.

'*Once I came into the room where she and Father were talking. "Honourable Husband," she was saying, "I am sometimes so bold as to wonder if her studies are not a little severe for a not-too-strong child." My father drew me over to his cushion and rested his hand gently on my shoulder. "We must not forget, Wife," he replied, "in the teaching in a samurai home, we must remember the lioness, who pushes her young over the cliff and watches it climb slowly back from the valley without one sign of pity, though her heart aches for the little creature. So that it can gain strength for its life work."*'

Almost inevitably in a country that had denied itself 268 years of modern history, there was a backlash against this brave new world and Japan became a boisterous youth intent on causing mayhem. On his death in 1912, Emperor Meiji was succeeded by his son, Yoshihito, whose rule was named the Taishō Era.

When the Great War began in Europe, Japan allied itself with the Allies but made no aggressive moves against Germany or its allies. However, it grasped the opportunity to use the political and military vacuum to further its own interests in Asia. In 1915, with Britain, France, Germany and Russia engaged in ferocious fighting in Europe, with the United States preoccupied with the conflict and China remaining neutral, Japanese troops moved to occupy the German-leased territory of Kiaochow.

Even as early as 1871, Japan had flexed its nascent military muscles. As Japan industrialised, so its military prowess blossomed with a similar momentum. In December of that year, a ship had been shipwrecked on Taiwan and the crew massacred. In 1874, using the incident as a pretext, Japan sent a military expedition force to Taiwan to assert Japan's claims to the Ryukyu Islands, a group that extends from the southern tip of mainland Japan, including Okinawa, all the way to Taiwan. As the expedition set sail after being ordered to postpone, it was the first instance of the Japanese military ignoring the orders of the civilian government – an ominous portent of events that would come to pass in future decades.

A new generation of Japanese warriors soon emerged. Aritomo Yamagata, born in 1838, was one of them. The son of a middle-ranking samurai, in the Chōshū Domain, he became the chief architect of Japan's reactionary military ideology and, as the nation's first army chief of staff, has been called the 'father' of Japanese militarism. Even though he died in 1922, he was the driving force behind the modernisation and enlargement of the Imperial Japanese Army, especially through the introduction of national conscription. His loyal supporter General Tanaka Giichi believed that industrial-age warfare required a militarised populace. In 1915, he wrote:

> The outcome of future wars will not be determined by the strongest army, but by the strongest populace. A strong populace is one which has the physical strength and spiritual health; one which is richly imbued with loyalty and patriotism, and one which respects cooperation, rules and discipline.

The Japanese military played an increasingly central role in Japan's expansion abroad, as it and many in the government believed that Japan had to acquire its own colonies to compete with the Western colonial powers.

There was dramatic growth towards an industrial economy. Both the Japanese government and private entrepreneurs adopted

Western technology and knowledge to build factories to manufacture a vast range of goods. By 1912, the majority of Japan's exports were manufactured goods. Some of Japan's new businesses and industries were huge family-owned conglomerates called *zaibatsu* (literally 'family clique'), such as Mitsubishi and Sumitomo, and a number have survived into modern times in the form of companies like Kawasaki, Nissan and Toyota. The phenomenal industrial growth sparked rapid urbanisation, so that the proportion of the population working in agriculture shrank from 75 per cent in 1872 to 50 per cent by 1920.

The strong economic growth and increasing wealth meant that most people lived longer and enjoyed healthier lives. The population boomed from 34 million in 1872 to 52 million in 1915.This emboldened the Japanese to begin to extend their influence in China.

In January 1915, the Japanese minister to Beijing issued what was called 'The Twenty-One Demands'. The demands were divided into five groups: three were concerned with the extension of Japanese rights in Shantung (Shandong), Manchuria and Fukien, and one with the control of Han-Yeh-Ping Company, the chief supplier of iron ore in China. The fifth group, if accepted, would have made China virtually a protectorate of Japan. As a consequence of Japan's military presence, and because of the inability of the Western powers to intervene, China had no choice but to accept the first four groups within five months. The Japanese demands were a stark illustration of their future ambitions for an empire in Asia.

GROUP I. The Japanese Government and the Chinese Government, being desirous to maintain the general peace in the Far East and to strengthen the relations of amity and good neighbourhood existing between the two countries, agree to the following: i) Japan's dispositions on German territories in China, ii) no Chinese territories will be ceded to any other power, iii) the building of a railway line linking Chefoo to Kiaochou-Tsinfu, iv) China opens its cities in Shantung to foreigners.

GROUP II. The Japanese Government and the Chinese Government, in view of the fact that the Chinese Government has always recognised the predominant position of Japan in South Manchuria and Eastern Inner Mongolia, agree to the following: i) agree to the lease of Port Arthur and Darien and its railways for ninety-nine years, ii) Japanese subjects in South Manchuria and Eastern Inner Mongolia to lease or own land, iii) Japanese subjects shall have the right to conduct business in South Manchuria and Eastern Inner Mongolia, iv) Japanese subjects shall have the right of mining in South Manchuria and Eastern Inner Mongolia, v) Japanese subjects shall have the right to construct railways in South Manchuria and Eastern Inner Mongolia, vi) Japan will have first refusal should the Chinese government need political, financial or military advisers in South Manchuria and Eastern Inner Mongolia, vii) agree to the running of the Kirin-Changchun Railway for ninety-nine years.

GROUP III. The Japanese Government and the Chinese Government, having regard to the close relations existing between Japanese capitalists and the Han-Yeh-Ping Company [a Japanese-controlled coal and iron company] and desiring to promote the common interests of the two nations, agree: i) that the Han-Yeh-Ping Company shall be made a joint venture concern of the two nations, ii) that no mines in the vicinity of the mines of the Han-Yeh-Ping Company shall be permitted to exist.

GROUP IV. The Japanese Government and the Chinese Government, with the object of effectively preserving the territorial integrity of China, agree that: i) the Chinese Government agree not to cede or lease to any other Power any harbour or bay on or any island along the coast of China.

Group V of the demands included a wide range of claims that would have ceded almost total control of South Manchuria and Eastern Inner Mongolia to Japan, a group of demands that China was able to resist. Even so, Japan's objectives were clear.

For a few years thereafter, internal social unrest led the Japanese government to pursue a more liberal set of policies; the right to vote was extended, and Japan joined the League of Nations in 1920. Moreover, driven by the influence of the *zaibatsu* (financial elites of industrialists and bankers), a more moderate foreign policy was followed for a while. However, the brief period of what became known as the 'Taishō Democracy' ended with Yoshihito's death on Christmas Day 1926, when his eldest son, Hirohito, the Emperor Shōwa, ascended the Chrysanthemum Throne.

As in many parts of Europe, economic and social pressures were feeding a groundswell of unrest and a rising tide of nationalism and aggressive militarism. It would take a while for the toxic brew to ferment but by 1931, Japan and the Japanese would be ready to meet their destiny and launch their Holy War.

3
HIROHITO

Michinomiya Hirohito was born at the Aoyama Palace in Tokyo on 29 April 1901, and would live to become the longest-reigning monarch in Japanese history, a rule of almost eighty-eight years. He was the son of the Taishō emperor and grandson of the Meiji emperor, and his era became known as 'Shōwa' ('Enlightened Peace', or 'Radiant Japan'). In his enthronement address, which was read to his people, Hirohito explained what he hoped his era would come to be: *'I have visited the battlefields of the Great War in France. In the presence of such devastation, I understand the blessing of peace and the necessity of concord among nations.'*

Sadly, only after 1945 did his era became peaceful. Before that, it was the very antithesis of peaceable.

Studious and curious, he developed an interest in marine biology and, in later life, wrote books about it. In 1921, he visited Europe and became the first Japanese crown prince to travel abroad. When he returned, he became prince regent when his father, who had never enjoyed good health, was unable to rule because of mental instability. Hirohito married the princess Nagako Kuni three years later. Following the death of his father, he became emperor on 25 December 1926.

Early in Hirohito's regency, he faced an issue, the consequence of which would illustrate ominous predilections hidden beneath the surface of Japan's social and political fabric. During his father's Taishō period, there had been several moves towards a more liberal society. The franchise had been widened, the status of women improved, and there were healthy debates in politics, the arts and culture – to the point that, although he played no role in it, his reign has been called the 'Taishō Democracy'. However, that brief period of modest liberalism did not survive for long.

On 1 September 1923, the Great Kantō Earthquake, the deadliest earthquake in Japanese history, struck Japan, leaving the Tokyo-Yokohama area totally devastated. Its epicentre was in the shallow waters of Sagami Bay, twenty-five miles south of Tokyo, creating a tsunami which swamped vast areas with waves as high as forty feet. The total death toll from the earthquake and its aftereffects is estimated to have been close to 150,000. Among the predominantly wooden houses of Tokyo and Yokohama, overturned stoves and broken gas mains set off firestorms which claimed 90 per cent of the homes in Yokohama and left 60 per cent of Tokyo's people homeless. The most horrific of the many tragic stories was the fate of 40,000 working-class Tokyo residents who fled to an area of open ground where they believed they would be safe. Flames surrounded them, and a 'wall of fire' 100 yards high engulfed them. Only 300 survived.

In the days that followed, another firestorm struck, one of racist hatred. Embittered survivors searched for a scapegoat, and soon found the ethnic Koreans who were living among them. Rumours abounded that Koreans had started the fires, were poisoning wells, looting ruined homes and planning to overthrow the government. Around 6,000 Koreans, as well as more than 700 Chinese mistaken for Koreans, were hacked and beaten to death. The police did little to stop the murders in what became known as the 'Korean Massacre'. Hirohito eventually put Tokyo under martial law and toured the devastation on horseback in full military uniform.

Only a couple of months later, on 27 December 1923, a young anarchist, Daisuke Nanba, fired a pistol at Hirohito's carriage as he was en route to the Diet to deliver his inaugural address. The bullet shattered the glass, cutting his chamberlain but leaving Hirohito untouched. The day after this incident, the House of Peers held its first secret session in sixteen years. Their focus was on Nanba's motivation, his social background and the need to tighten 'controls over thought'. Diet member Yoshinaga Nakagawa said, *'Once people awaken socially to defects in society and those defects become unbearable, they will erupt, and it will be too late to do anything about it.'*

At Nanba's subsequent trial he said to the judge, *'I've proved the joy of living for the truth. Go ahead and hang me.'* Then, when his death sentence was read, he shouted three battle cries, *'to the proletariat and Communist Party of Japan, to Russian socialism and the Soviet Republic, and to the Communist Internationale.'*

Hirohito's Lord Keeper of the Privy Seal, Nobuaki Makino, wrote in his diary: *'There has been a tremendous change in popular thought. Even concepts connected to the* Kokutai *[body politic] have undergone astonishing change among some people, but I am more worried about the future now that a person has emerged and actually tried to act out his ideas. I fear that the people might lose their presence of mind by witnessing such a great act of lèse majesté.'*

Hirohito's reaction was more considered: *'I had thought that in Japan the relationship between his majesty and his subjects was, in principle, a monarch–subject relationship, but in sentiment a parent–child relationship. I have always devoted myself to the people on that understanding. But seeing this incident, I am especially saddened that the person who dared to commit this misdeed was a loyal subject.'*

Despite Hirohito's paternalistic tones, the horseback appearances in military uniform and the government's reaction to the Daisuke Nanba incident have led most historians to conclude that, even as early as his regency in the 1920s, Hirohito's future rule would not see a continuation of the Taishō Democracy. Japan's Shōwa era would display very different characteristics.

After Hirohito became emperor, an ancient ritual had to be performed, the details of which offer significant insight into the attitudes and beliefs prevailing in Japan at the time – beliefs that harked back to an earlier, more primitive era in Japan's history. The ceremony, *Daijosai*, better understood now, was highly secret in 1928. After an imperial procession from Tokyo to Kyoto, to be given possession of his imperial regalia, sacred dances were performed and two days of banquets were held. *Daijosai* was then performed, which confirmed the status of Hirohito's divinity through his 'descent from the gods in the plain of high heaven'. In a specially constructed compound, he lay wrapped in a quilt in a foetal position on a mat, which embodied the Shinto sun goddess, Amaterasu Ōmikami, thus consummating his marriage to her. He then lay on another mat and made offerings of food to her, to complete the process of his becoming a living god.

Once he became god-emperor, if ever he undertook a trip into his realm, local officials went to extraordinary lengths to ensure his visit was appropriate for a deity.

> To protect and welcome the emperor, to ensure that the crowds who bowed before him remained silent and controlled, that nothing went amiss while he was in the prefecture, local officials, after praying to the gods for strength and guidance, rehearsed every minute detail of his approaching visit. They mobilised all resources, laid out red carpets for Hirohito to walk on, swept and decorated the streets along which his motorcade would pass, disinfected (literally) and purified (ritually) the limousine in which he would ride, his railroad cars and the imperial locomotive, even the stations where he would stop. Sometimes the railroad tracks along his route were scoured and doused with disinfectants, especially where he was scheduled to alight.

Although local officials were usually successful in ensuring that the emperor's visits were as they were supposed to be, there were one or two unfortunate mistakes, the consequences of which also illustrate the predominant mindset of the Japanese in the early 1930s. For example, in November 1934, a motorcycle policeman leading the imperial motorcade through Kiryū City, Gumma prefecture, was supposed to take a left turn at an intersection. Instead, he led the procession straight on, upsetting the itinerary of the tour. Seven days later the erring policeman committed suicide, the governor of Gumma and all the top officials involved in staging the tour were reprimanded, police officials in Gumma had their salaries docked for two months, and the home minister was questioned and severely criticised in the Imperial Diet.

The extraordinary obsessive necessity to make Hirohito's presence pure and invisible – all eyes had to look down, not at him – says much about the Japanese people's concept of themselves and of those who were not Japanese under Hirohito.

Clean against unclean, pure against impure, us against them. From those profound dichotomies would follow an inevitable progression during the 1930s and early 1940s: We Japanese confront the world as a racially pure nation; therefore, our wars are just and holy wars, and our victories will create a 'new order' in East Asia.

That the enthronement of Hirohito was an emotional, even spiritual watershed for Japan is clear in the reflections of court ritualist Teruoki Hoshino: *'The enthronement showed that the emperor had assumed the reins of government with the benevolent heart of his ancestors. In so doing he has renewed the glory that he inherited from their virtuous spirits and become the basis of the belief we have kept in our hearts and minds for thousands of years: namely, that our majesty is a deity* [kamisama] *and a living god* [ikigami].'

Another event in 1928, the 'March 15 Incident', was a portent of how Hirohito's Japan would evolve and how much of a politician he would become; in other words, he would rule as well as reign. Although the Japan Communist Party had been banned as soon as it was formed in 1922, out of public view it was growing in numbers and lent support to socialist and trade union groups. When, in the 1928 general election, left-wing party members grew in number in the Diet, the conservative government of Giichi Tanaka, which had kept its majority by just one seat, ordered the mass arrest of 1,652 communists under the 1925 Peace Preservation Law. Five hundred of them were prosecuted in public trials, and all were found guilty and sentenced to long jail terms. As a consequence of the trials, the Tanaka government was able to pass legislation to add the provision for the death penalty to the Peace Preservation Law, which was quite specific:

Anyone who has formed an association with the aim of altering the *Kokutai* [body politic] or the system of private property, and anyone who has joined such an association with full knowledge of its object, shall be liable to imprisonment with or without hard labour, for a term not exceeding ten years [a potential death penalty].

As a result of the Peace Preservation Law, in 1927 a sub-bureau, the 'Thought Section', had been created within the Criminal Affairs Bureau of the Home Ministry to root out subversive ideologies. Local 'thought police' branches were established throughout Japan to monitor 'dangerous thoughts and ideologies' and a 'Student Section' within the Ministry of Education to monitor subversive thought among academics and students. Within the Ministry of Justice, special 'thought prosecutors' were appointed to suppress 'thought crime'. In fact, until the laws were abolished by the American Occupiers in 1945, over 70,000 people were arrested under the law.

There were other signs of the ominous path that Japan was going to follow in the 1930s and 1940s – a path that would lead the nation to be internationally castigated for its behaviour.

In 1928, the Tanaka government failed to endorse an international protocol banning chemical and biological warfare. The next year the Privy Council, responding to pressure from the military, failed to ratify the Geneva Prisoner of War Convention, signed two years earlier. The privy councillors accepted the argument of the ministers of the army and navy, and of the foreign minister, that the clause concerning the treatment of POWs was too lenient and could not possibly be implemented because the emperor's soldiers would never allow themselves to become prisoners of war.

With little intervention or restraint from Hirohito, the escalating wayward behaviour of rogue elements within the Imperial Army stationed in China was gradually sowing the seeds of a major conflict with its giant neighbour. At the same time, the actions of the Western powers – which were unnerved by Japan's growing strength – only exacerbated the situation. The rapid growth of Japan's population, close to 65 million in 1930, required significant food imports into a country where agricultural land was at a premium. In order to pay for imports, Japan had to be able to export its goods, but restrictive Western tariffs were a major hindrance to exports. Many on the right responded to the dilemma by arguing that armed force was the way to resolve the impasse.

This growing sentiment played out in China, where its own increasing nationalism was focused on Japan's presence within its borders. Radical elements in the Imperial Army wanted Japan to take a harder line in China, leading to Prime Minister Tanaka, with Hirohito's full support, intervening in Shandong in 1927 and 1928. Troops were deployed three times, including 5,000 men to Tsingtao in April 1928. Of course, the presence of large numbers of Japanese soldiers made matters worse, especially when, without approval from Tokyo, General Hikosaki Fukuda took his men inland to Jinan, the capital of Shandong Province, where clashes with the Chinese were inevitable.

Shandong was a stronghold of Chinese leader Chiang Kai-shek and his National Revolutionary Army, a powerful presence. Clashes between the NRA and Fukuda's men were frequent and increasingly violent throughout 1928. Eventually, Fukuda launched a full-scale attack on the Chinese in Jinan on 8 May 1928. Fighting was intense overnight on 9/10 May, with the Japanese using artillery to bombard the old walled city, where NRA troops had sought protection. The civilian population of the old city was not warned in advance, which resulted in many casualties. By morning, the Japanese had gained full control of Jinan, which remained under Japanese occupation until March 1929, when an agreement to settle the conflict was reached between Chiang Kai-shek and Prime Minister Tanaka. Later estimates suggested that over 6,000 Chinese civilians died in Jinan during the conflict. Thanks to the unilateral actions of Fukuda, yet another rung on the 'escalation ladder' towards war with China had been reached.

At home, civilian ultranationalists were dedicated to the dual theme of internal purity and external expansion. They sought to preserve what they thought was unique in the Japanese spirit and fought against excessive Western influence. Big business, which was becoming profitable through trade with the West, was targeted, and a number of business leaders and political figures were killed. There was also a chasm between town and country. Junior military officers, who were largely from rural backgrounds, resented the urban lifestyles of politicians, and became fertile ground for right-wing ideology.

Ikki Kita was one of the many ideologues who exploited the situation. He called for the Meiji constitution to be suspended in favour of a revolutionary regime advised by 'national patriots' and headed by a military government which should nationalise large properties, limit wealth, end party government and the peerage, and prepare to take the leadership of a revolutionary Asia. He opined in a somewhat grandiloquent tone: '*After destroying England [in Asia] and restoring Turkey, after making India independent and China autonomous, the Rising Sun Flag of Japan shall offer the light of that sun to all mankind. The second coming of Christ, prophesied in every country on earth, actually signifies the scripture and sword of Japan [as a new] Mohammed.*'

Kōzaburō Tachibana was another dominant activist. He believed, '*We must sweep clean the dominance of modern Western materialistic civilisation and return to the surviving essence of the founding of the country. Radical change is necessary because the world of national politics is being poisoned by mammon and the gang of corrupt industrialists who sit in the top seats. The corrosion of local politics by dissolute landlords and the sons of liquor dealers must not be overlooked. We have the strength to mobilise our peerless army and navy for the world revolution [. . .] to pulverise American power in the Pacific, sweep away the influence of the Chinese military clique [. . .] liberate India from England, make Russia realise her mistakes [. . .] and rouse the Germans.*'

The political mood in Japan was then made much more volatile by the dire consequences of the Wall Street Crash of October 1929. The impoverishment it caused around the world hit rural Japan particularly hard. Sho Onuma, a twenty-two-year-old fisherman's son, asked, '*How can we farmers survive? We have to borrow money from loan sharks who demand such high interest. Those who work so hard to grow the rice cannot afford to eat it. Japan is becoming an unworthy country in which to live, so I am determined to devote myself to revolution.'*

Onuma joined the League of Blood, which plotted to kill leading businessmen and liberal politicians, and in a wave of terrorist attacks across the country, proceeded to assassinate a government minister outside a school in Tokyo. Onuma was sentenced to life in prison but was released under a general amnesty in 1940 and lived until 1967. Importantly, Onuma's trial gave the League of Blood a platform from which to promulgate their ultranationalist views. Many Japanese sympathised with their aims, and it became harder for courts to deal harshly with extremists, who claimed to be acting in the interests of the emperor, which added to the erosion of the rule of law.

Korekiyo Takahashi, liberal politician and Japan's prime minister from 1921 to 1922, spoke out about the ominous mood in the country: *'If you say anything bad about the army, then the military police rattle their swords or point a gun or threaten you. When a newspaper publisher in Kyushu wrote something bad about the army, they threatened him by having a plane circle and said that they would bomb him.'*

Takahashi would eventually pay the price of speaking out when he was gunned down during the 'February 26 Incident' in 1936, an attempted coup d'état by a group of army officers determined to purge the government of liberals. The coup was led by the Kōdōha ('Imperial Way') Faction, a group of radical young officers, including Captain Shirō Nonka and Captain Ando Teruzo. Several senior figures were assassinated, including two former prime ministers, and most government buildings in Tokyo were occupied. However, the rebellion eventually failed, in part because of opposition to the rebel officers within the army, and also because Hirohito stood firm in opposing the rebellion. The emperor was not yet ready to support the more extreme militarism within the army.

Even so, a volatile brew continued to ferment. In Japan, the mood of oppressive nationalism was darkening, while in China, radical militarists in the Japanese army were in the ascendancy. Despite Hirohito's unease, successive governments in Tokyo did not seem able or willing to control its forces in China, which itself was in chaos and thus ripe for exploitation.

4

CHINA

Japan's Kwantung Army had been formed in 1906 as a security force to protect Japanese interests in China, Manchuria and Mongolia and, over time, became the most respected command in the Imperial Japanese Army. Many of its personnel won promotions to high positions in Japanese military and civil government, including Hideki Tōjō and Seishirō Itagaki, both of whom became minister of war during Japan's Holy War.

With a total troop strength of 14,000 men, the Kwantung Army was composed of an infantry division and a heavy artillery battalion, supported by six garrison battalions acting as railway guards deployed along the South Manchurian Railway Zone. Its headquarters were in Port Arthur and it was administered as a department by the Kwantung government-general. Vital to Japan's foothold in Asia, the zone was a sixty-two-mile-wide strip of land on either side of the South Manchurian Railway, a series of lines that Japan had acquired from Russia after its defeat in the Russo-Japanese War of 1904–05. The lines extended almost 700 miles, with a total land area of 100 square miles. They connected twenty-five cities and towns, and within each destination included warehouses, repair shops, coal mines and electrical facilities.

With Europe's nations preoccupied with fighting one another during the Great War, in 1915 Japan seized the moment and presented China with 'The Twenty-One Demands'. These produced the Sino-Japanese Treaty of the same year. The treaty gave Japan much more control over China, by making provision that Japanese subjects would be free to reside and travel in South Manchuria and engage in business and manufacturing of any kind. They could lease land to erect buildings for trade, manufacturing and agriculture.

Many of the officers of the Kwantung Army, including much of its hierarchy, were determined to expand Japan's position in Asia by force of arms. Direct action in Manchuria began in 1928 with the murder by bombing of Zhang Zuolin, the warlord ruler of Manchuria. Neither the cabinet nor the Diet in Tokyo was strong enough to punish those responsible, which only encouraged the extremists. A new liberal prime minister, Osachi Hamaguchi, attempted to exert control but was mortally wounded by an assassin in 1930 and died of his wounds in August of that year.

At the beginning of 1931, vice-president of the Privy Council, Kiichirō Hiranuma, reflected on Japan's position and issued what was, in effect, a war cry.

Today, the Great Powers openly emphasise the League of Nations while behind the scenes they steadily expand their military armaments. We cannot simply dismiss as the foolish talk of idiots, those who predict the outbreak of a second world war. Our nation must be prepared to serve bravely in the event of an emergency. If other peoples, Europeans and Americans, obstruct world peace and the welfare of mankind, we must be prepared to display our nationalism in a grand way, based on the spirit of the founding of the state [. . .] The depression in the business world is reaching its height. Unemployment is increasing daily. The family is breaking up. Starving people fill the streets. Do you think people are satisfied with this situation? This is the responsibility of statesmen who govern under the auspices of the emperor's will. To ignore this situation is to ignore the emperor's will. Therefore, at the start of this new year [. . .] to hide the reality and pretend that everything is peaceful would be the height of disloyalty. Because I firmly believe that one who respects the imperial house and loves the fatherland would not embellish the situation, I am clarifying here the essence of nationalism.

On 18 September 1931 came the 'Manchurian (or Mukden) Incident', which set Japan on a path of aggression in Asia that would eventually lead to its Holy War. The Kwantung Army claimed (falsely, because its own officers had laid the explosives) that Chinese soldiers had bombed a South Manchurian Railway train, which suffered little damage and arrived at its destination safely. Then, in an unauthorised attack, the army captured Mukden (now Shenyang), followed by the occupation of the whole of Manchuria. The government in Tokyo was unable to recall the army, and when another new prime minister, Tsuyoshi Inukai, tried to bring the rebels to heel, he was assassinated by radical naval officers in yet another attempted coup d'état.

As the Kwantung Army took more and more control in Manchuria, historians differ in their interpretation of Hirohito's actions. While he was concerned that the rebellious officers were undermining Japan's reputation abroad, and with threats of economic isolation, he failed to condemn their actions. Thus, by saying nothing, he acquiesced to each expansion, even though the officers concerned had committed acts of criminal insubordination. Although it was unlikely that he realised what his actions would lead to, he made future acts of military disobedience inevitable. In fact, over the next few years, Hirohito granted awards and promotions for meritorious service in connection with the Manchurian war. Kwantung Army Commander Shigeru Honjō, Imperial Army Minister Sadao Araki and Imperial Navy Minister Mineo Ōsumi were each awarded the title of 'baron'.

The majority of the Japanese population seemed unconcerned by Japan's reputation abroad. In fact, as international criticism of Japan's aggression grew, most people's support of the army hardened, playing into the hands of the nationalists. Journalist Shirō Iwata urged: *'Today's Japan should not confine itself to its own small sphere, nor should it remain in its position in the orient. Japan bears the burden of a global mission. It should advance to lead the entire world.'*

The emperor could see the path that Japan was taking. In an audience held in January 1932, Hirohito asked the Minister to China, Mamoru Shigemitsu, *'Japanese–Chinese amity will be impossible for some time?'* The minister replied, *'As long as the Manchurian issue remains, I believe it will be impossible to achieve better relations.'*

The price of the successful seizure of Manchuria was the enmity of China. In addition, the army's triumph in Manchuria sharpened its appetite for a piece of China proper. The aim was to expand military operations from Manchuria, Mongolia and North China to all of China. Japan became committed to an aggressive war, trapped in a cycle of military intervention and escalation.

Another step towards war happened later in 1932 when the Tokyo government agreed to re-form Manchuria as the 'independent' state of Manchukuo. The last Qing emperor of China, Pu Yi, was declared regent and later enthroned as emperor, in 1934. However, control lay with the Kwantung Army and all key positions were held by Japanese. Pu Yi was humiliated by the Japanese and found himself to be a prisoner in his own palace in Manchukuo's capital, Changchun. (In a somewhat sad aside, when the Soviet Red Army invaded Manchuria in 1945, it captured Pu Yi and he was handed over to China. He then spent ten years before being freed and moving back to Beijing where he spent the rest of his life as a common citizen, working as a gardener and then an editor. When he returned to the Forbidden City, which had been made into a museum, he had to buy a ticket to enter his former home.)

When the League of Nations called upon member states to withhold recognition from the new puppet state, Japan withdrew from the League in 1933 and proceeded to exploit Manchukuo's resources and develop an industrial base for the 'new order' it intended to bring to the Asian mainland. Cast as benign both at home and abroad, in practice it was ruthless and punitive, as one long-time resident recalled: *There were Japanese who rode in horse cabs and then refused to pay. If the driver demanded payment, they beat him half to death. If the Chinaman protested to the police, the authorities always accepted the Japanese's version even if he was in the wrong. These things happened all the time.*

The mistreatment of local Chinese civilians escalated. Labourers were abducted rather than recruited and then manacled to prevent them from escaping. Any who did escape were tortured and killed. Horses for use by the army were stolen, rather than bought, which led many farmers to deliberately blind their horses.

In 1935, Japan enforced the removal of any officials and armed forces that might be opposed to Japan from both Hebei and Inner Mongolia, which put Shanxi and Shandong under threat. Nationalist leader Chiang Kai-shek chose not to oppose Japan's move, preferring instead to fight his Chinese Communist rivals. However, in December 1936 Chiang was seized by forces under the command of his own generals and forced to join with the communists in a 'United Front' against Japan.

Then, in another strategically significant move, in November 1936, Japan signed the Anti-Comintern Pact with Germany and later with Italy, forming an effective alliance against the Communist International. It was replaced by the Tripartite Pact in September 1940, which recognised Japan as the leader of a new order in Asia, and in which Japan, Germany and Italy agreed to assist each other if they were attacked. The text of the pact declared:

> The Governments of Japan, Germany and Italy consider it as the condition precedent of any lasting peace that all nations in the world be given each its own proper place, have decided to stand by and co-operate with one another in their efforts in Greater East Asia and the regions of Europe respectively wherein it is their prime purpose to establish and maintain a new order of things, calculated to promote the mutual prosperity and welfare of the peoples concerned. It is, furthermore, the desire of the three Governments to extend cooperation to nations in other spheres of the world that are inclined to direct their efforts along lines similar to their own for the purpose of realising their ultimate object, world peace.

Full-scale war began in earnest following what became known as the 'Marco Polo Bridge Incident' on 7 December 1937. Small numbers of both Japanese and Chinese soldiers were stationed near the bridge, ten miles southwest of Beijing. The exact circumstances of the incident are not clear, but the Japanese were carrying out training exercises without giving the customary notice, and a few shots were exchanged with the Chinese troops. The Japanese then discovered that one of their soldiers was missing. They assumed that the Chinese had captured him and asked for permission to search for him. Things escalated quickly into a serious armed conflict, with both sending in more troops. The nationalists in the army and back home in Tokyo grasped the opportunity to make the moves they had strived for and anticipated for several years. Hundreds of thousands of troops were mobilised on both sides and a total war ensued, the Second Sino-Japanese War. The conflict would be cruel and vicious with a terrible price, especially for Chinese civilians, who died in their tens of millions.

General Kanji Ishiwara – together with fellow rebel General Seishirō Itagaki – had been the instigator of the 'Manchurian (Mukden) Incident' of 1931. He advocated: *'Let the government do what they will, the army is going to carry this sacred mission, to save China. The last war in human history is approaching, a titanic world conflict, which will be the gateway to a golden age of human culture. The only way for Asia is to advance together.'*

Although Japan faced a 'United Front' in China, Japan's forces were better resourced, better led and were more committed than those of China. Most cities as far west as Hankou and most of the railway network fell to Japan by the middle of 1937.

Hiroko Nakamoto was seven years old when her father was one of over 4 million men of the Imperial Japanese Army who would fight in China over the following eight years. *'At first the war brought only excitement to me. People talked of it everywhere. Little boys at school spoke proudly about their fathers going to China to fight for our country. On street corners women stood making senninbaris for our soldiers. Senninbari means, literally, "a thousand people's needles". Each of these is a strip of white cloth six inches wide and long enough to go around a soldier's waist. Women passing by would stop to make a stitch in red thread and tie a knot. When the senninbari was finished, it was a symbol of thousands of Japanese women's trust and faith. And the soldier fighting faraway was comforted by the kind wishes of the people at home when he wore it.'*

The ferocity of the war was extraordinary from the outset and a portent of what was to come in the years ahead. Teishin Nohara, a squad leader in the Fujii Unit of the Imperial Army's

35th Regiment, was one of the first men in combat as the army approached Nanking.

'We Japanese soldiers simply formed a line and when officers gave the order, advanced. Our Thirty-Fifth Regiment was almost annihilated that way in the early battles. At a terrible place we called Susaku Seitaku, we had our toughest fight. The enemy was under cover, shooting at us through loopholes in walls, so our dead just piled up. We were in the open fields. "Charge! Forward! Forward!" came the orders, so you'd run a bit, then fall flat, calm your breathing, then charge again. Out of two hundred men, only ten or so weren't killed, wounded, or just worn out. Soldiers were expended like this. All my friends died there. You can't begin to really describe the wretchedness and misery of war [. . .] The battles were always severe. There are many watery creeks in Central China. The dead Japanese and Chinese would just fall into them and get tangled up on the surface. Many hundreds at once. It was a gruesome thing. The corpses would block your way. If you pushed at them with a stick, they moved easily, the whole mass floating away. We drew water from those creeks to drink and cook our rice. Cholera soon spread. The men with cholera we'd put in a bamboo grove. The grove was surrounded by a rope and the patients promised not to move [. . .] Many died.'

Tora Yoshida, a Tokyo housewife, was one of millions of wives who would wave their husbands off to war in the coming years. 'When we arrived the brass band was playing and people were shouting banzai. I told my daughter, "Don't cry, wipe away your tears now. See your father off with a smile." I knew that if I showed my tears it would only give more pain to my husband.'

The Battle for Beijing took twenty-four days before the city fell on 29 July. The capture of Shanghai took over three months of vicious fighting, with heavy casualties on both sides – at least 250,000 Chinese dead and wounded, and as many as 100,000 Japanese.

The next target was Chiang Kai-shek's capital, Nanking. In a five-week campaign between 11 November and 9 December, the Japanese army marched at speed from Shanghai to Nanking. As it did so, it came across retreating Chinese soldiers, who were massacred in their thousands. Much the same happened to Chinese civilians who got in the way. To exacerbate the situation, Chinese forces used scorched earth tactics, which only served to infuriate their Japanese pursuers.

Tadashi Kawashima was killed in South China in February 1945, at the age of twenty-nine. He was one of the few Japanese soldiers appalled by the behaviour of his colleagues: '*In the middle of the night at 1.30 a.m. a telephone message came through to our headquarters: at 5.30, we formed into a body for a punitive expedition and set out in the freezing night, trampling over patches of hardened snow. A trooper of the Nakazawa company had stoned a Chinaman. He was covered with the blood pouring from the wound in his head, but the soldier continued to kick him and to throw stones at him. The officers in charge of the company were calmly watching this act of brutality, which seems to have been committed at the command of one of them, the cruel Lieutenant Takagi.*

'*I cannot help thinking about that poor, innocent Chinaman and now I reproach myself for not having gone to his aid. Even if it had been too late, I ought to have done so. I will never allow my son to be a soldier [...] no, he will never be a soldier. Peace – peace for the whole world – that is my only wish. It is surprising that there has not yet been a rising, after all the acts of violence perpetrated by the regiment garrisoned in this town.*'

The war soon had a major impact on Japan's population at home. Hiroko Nakamoto, who was raised by an aunt from a well-to-do family, recalled: '*Rice became rationed. Other foods, too, were rationed or disappeared altogether from the shops. Daily necessities, such as soap, were rationed or not available. We could not order custom-made shoes from the shoemaker anymore. As the war went on, we were taught always to think about the hungry soldiers who were fighting in China. Refreshments were forbidden on school picnics. In winter we were not allowed to wear our warm coats to school, even when it was very cold. By being cold, we were reminded of the soldiers who were fighting for our country in northern China. Also, though we were little children, we were in this way to learn to discipline our bodies to withstand cold weather.*'

Imbued with racist stereotypes about their enemies, most Japanese soldiers were contemptuous of their Chinese counterparts. Private Shirō Azuma wrote in his diary, '*Seven thousand prisoners all in one place. I thought, how could they become prisoners without even trying to show any resistance. They looked like a bunch of homeless people, with vacant expressions on their faces. It felt quite foolish to think we had been fighting to the death against these ignorant slaves.'*

Azuma's diary records the atrocities perpetrated against civilians everywhere in the combat zone. *'When I tried to cut off the first one, either the farmer moved or I mis-aimed. I ended up slicing off just part of his skull. Blood spurted upwards. I swung again [. . .] and this time I killed him [. . .] We were taught that we were a superior race since we lived only for the sake of a human god – our emperor. But the Chinese were not. So we held nothing but contempt for them [. . .] There were many rapes, and the women were always killed. When they were being raped, the women were human. But once the rape was finished, they became pig's flesh.'*

A corporal returning home in 1942 from Hsuchou, in central China, bragged about his exploits: *'While out foraging for supplies we got hold of a pregnant woman. We stuck our bayonets in her huge belly, skewered her like a piece of meat [. . .] I wiped oil on my sword blade so the Chink's blood wouldn't stick and then I cut a coolie's head off with one stroke.'*

Tadashi Kawashima was a student when he was drafted to serve in North China. He saw soldiers *'beat a Chinese with rocks until his skull split and he fell in a pool of blood. Then they kicked him and threw more stones. Officers watched the killing and did nothing. A weeping woman, his wife I suppose, clung to the mangled body.'*

By 9 December, the Japanese had reached the last line of defence, the Fukuo Line, behind which lay Nanking's fortified walls. The general charged with capturing Nanking was Iwane Matsui, commander of Japan's Central China Area, who assumed that the conquest of Nanking would convince the Chinese to capitulate, thus bringing the war to an end. The city was defended by Tang Shengzhi, leading the Nanking Garrison Force, an inexperienced army of local conscripts and the remnants of badly mauled Chinese units from the fall of Shanghai.

Running for over thirty miles around the city, its historic walls were formidable and hampered the Japanese advance – but not for long. Two days of fighting brought the Chinese to their knees, leaving most of the city surrounded, trapping both soldiers and civilians alike. While some units were able to escape, many more were caught in the death trap the city had become.

On 13 December 1937, news was released in Japan that Nanking, had fallen. Schoolchildren were given a day's holiday to celebrate. With the news came reports of atrocities committed by the army. Journalist Shingorō Takaishi, like most Japanese, did not believe the stories: '*I am proud of our Japanese soldiers. I am positive that they will not act in a repulsive way against civilians. There may be pictures showing inhuman acts committed by Japanese soldiers, but it is improbable that what they represent is true.*'

Although the truth of what has become known as the Rape of Nanking has been the subject of dispute for decades – especially in Japan, where denial is still commonplace – almost all objective historians have verified the many stories of unimaginable horror, many of which were captured in photographs. The International Committee for the Nanking Safety Zone – which was organised by neutral foreigners and other unbiased observers and survivors – recorded testimonies and compiled documents that bore witness to a horrifying tale of mass slaughter. Over a six-week period, countless examples of beheading, rape, mutilation and looting were witnessed by Chinese and Western survivors in the city. Civilians – men, women and children – were treated as harshly as military personnel. Homes and businesses were targeted and systematically plundered and burned. As many as 100,000 Chinese may have been murdered. Victims were buried or burned alive, dismembered alive or drowned.

Masatake Imai was a correspondent for the Tokyo *Asahi Shimbun*, and an eyewitness to what unfolded. The military units in Beijing were given orders to clear the city before General Iwane Matsui's triumphal entry. Tens of thousands of Chinese were suspected of being prisoners of war – soldiers who had changed into civilian clothes after first discarding their weapons, now mingling with the general populace. They were seized, lined up at the Hsiakwanch'ien Bridge and machine-gunned: '*The area was filled with crumpled, twisted corpses piled on top of each other in bloody mounds.'* Civilians were forced to work throwing bodies into the river. Then they, in turn, were lined up on the river bank and machine-gunned. An officer who watched the bodies tumble into the river told Imai, *'There are about 20,000 dead Chinese there.'*

Tadanobu Kurosu of the 19th Infantry Regiment was one of several ordinary Japanese to admit that atrocities did take place and to being a participant: *'5,000 prisoners were taken to the Yangtze river to be executed by machine guns. Bayonets were used to finish them off. I felt a demonic excitement as I climbed up the pile of bodies and stabbed them: soldiers, old, young and children. I have never felt anything like it in my life.'*

A *Mainichi Shimbun* reporter watched the soldiers line up Chinese prisoners on a wall near Chungshan Gate and charge at them with fixed bayonets: *'One by one the prisoners fell down the outside of the wall. Blood splattered everywhere. The chilling atmosphere made one's hair stand on end and limbs tremble with fear. I stood there at a total loss and did not know what to do.'*

A Japanese military correspondent recalled what he witnessed: *'On Hsiakwan wharves, there was the dark silhouette of a mountain made of dead bodies. About fifty to one hundred people were toiling there, dragging bodies from the mountain of corpses and throwing them into the Yangtze River. The bodies dripped blood, some of them still alive and moaning weakly, their limbs twitching. After a while, the coolies had done their job of dragging corpses and the soldiers lined them up along the river. Rat-tat-tat machine-gun fire could be heard. The coolies fell backwards into the river and were swallowed by the raging currents.'*

Yukio Omata watched as Chinese prisoners lined up along the river: *'Those in the first row were beheaded, those in the second row were forced to dump the severed bodies into the river before they themselves were beheaded. The killing went on non-stop from morning until night, but they were only able to kill 2,000 persons. The next day, tired of killing in this fashion, they set up machine guns. Two of them raked a crossfire at the lined-up prisoners. Rat-tat-tat-tat. The prisoners fled into the water, but no one was able to make it to the other shore.'*

According to Kōzō Tadokoro, a former soldier in the 114th

Division, '*The women suffered the most. No matter how young or old, they all could not escape the fate of being raped. We sent out coal trucks from Hsiakwan to the city streets and villages to seize a lot of women. And then each of them was allocated to 15 to 20 soldiers for sexual intercourse and abuse.*'

One of the most notorious incidents has been called the 'Hundred Man Killing Contest'. It arose from a newspaper account of a contest between two officers, Toshiaki Mukai and Tsuyoshi Noda, over who could kill 100 people more quickly while using a sword. They were later executed on charges of war crimes. The story became highly controversial in Japan when it emerged in the 1970s. A fellow officer and veteran of the war, Shintarō Uno, wrote about the controversy in his autobiography: '*Whatever you say, it's silly to argue about whether it happened this way or that way when the situation is clear. There were hundreds of thousands of soldiers like Mukai and Noda, including me, during those fifty years of war between Japan and China. At any rate, it was nothing more than a commonplace occurrence during the so-called "Chinese Disturbance"*'.

During his post-war trial for war crimes, Shintarō Uno said, '*One of the essential means of obtaining information was the interrogation of prisoners. Torture was an inevitable necessity. Killing the victims and burying them is a natural consequence. You do it because you don't want it to be discovered. I believed and acted that way because I was convinced of what I was doing. We were doing our duty as we had been taught for the sake of our country and because of our subsidiary obligations to our ancestors. On the battlefield, we never considered the Chinese to be human beings. When you are the winner, the losers seem miserable. We concluded that the Yamato* [Japanese] *ethnic group was superior.*'

By the beginning of 1938, China's nationalist forces were in disarray and no longer able to offer much resistance. However, in rural areas Communist-led forces were still effective. In Tokyo, the military leadership, conscious that a future war with the Soviet Union was likely, hoped to limit the conflict to the areas around Beijing, Shanghai and northern China. However, Tokyo had, to a large extent, lost control of the Imperial Japanese Army in China, and the war continued to rage.

The Chinese capital was moved west to Hankou, but it also fell in October 1938, as did Guangzhou in the south. The Japanese pressed northward and westward along the railway lines into Shanxi and Inner Mongolia. They dominated Shandong and the lower part of the Yangtze valley and had complete command of the sea. The Chinese air force had been destroyed and Japan's air force could bomb China's cities at will.

In November of that year, Japan's prime minister, Prince Fumimaro Konoe, made his country's intentions clear, not only in China but across the whole of Asia.

By the august virtue of His Majesty, our naval and military forces have captured Canton and the three cities of Wuhan; and all the vital areas of China have thus fallen into our hands. The Kuomintang Government exists no longer except as a mere local regime. However, so long as it persists in its anti-Japanese and pro-Communist policy our country will not lay down its arms – never until that regime is crushed.

What Japan seeks is the establishment of a new order that will insure the permanent stability of East Asia. In this lies the ultimate purpose of our present military campaign.

This new order has for its foundation a tripartite relationship of mutual aid and co-ordination between Japan, Manchukuo, and China in political, economic, cultural, and other fields. Its object is to secure international justice, to perfect the joint defence against Communism, and to create a new culture and realise a close economic cohesion throughout East Asia. This indeed is the way to contribute toward stabilisation of East Asia and the progress of the world.

Japan's actions in China were a clear and obvious herald of what was to come in Asia and the Pacific over the next eight years. Although Japan's overt imperialism was all too evident, it concealed its conquests beneath a cloak of 'liberation' with slogans like 'Asia for the Asians'. Despite the mask of propaganda, the Japanese people, and the army in particular, harboured a profound sense of superiority over other Asians. Such sentiments led to an almost complete denial of the rights and privileges of Japan's enemies, making its soldiers and civilians capable of committing shocking and widespread war crimes, which were committed without any sense of remorse.

Shōzō Tominaga was a twenty-five-year-old officer recruit when he was sent to China in the summer of 1941. *'The day after I arrived, a special field-operations training exercise was announced for all twenty-two of the new candidate officers [. . .] We were taken out to the site of our trial. Twenty-four blindfolded prisoners were squatting there with their hands tied behind their backs. A big hole had been dug – ten metres long, two metres wide, and more than three metres deep.'*

The test for Tominaga and his colleagues was a trial of ruthless resolve and swordsmanship. In front of a group of seated senior officers, each of the prisoners was dragged in succession to the edge of the hole and made to kneel. The candidate officers were required, in turn, to carry out a swift execution.

When Tominaga's turn came, *'the only thought I had was "Don't do anything unseemly!" I unsheathed my sword [. . .] and stood behind the man. The prisoner didn't move. He kept his head lowered. Perhaps he was resigned to his fate. I was tense, thinking I couldn't afford to fail. I took a deep breath and recovered my composure. I steadied myself, holding the sword at a point above my right shoulder, and swung down with one breath. The head flew away and the body tumbled down, spouting blood. The air reeked from all that blood. I washed blood off the blade then wiped it with the paper provided. Fat stuck to it and wouldn't come off. I noticed, when I sheathed it, that my sword was slightly bent. At that moment, I felt something change inside me. I don't know how to put it, but I gained strength somewhere in my gut.'*

Tominaga was a sword-wielding officer, but ordinary soldiers had to be trained to kill with a bayonet. He describes the army's training technique used to turn farm boys and office workers into killers.

'A new conscript became a full-fledged soldier in three months. We planned exercises for these men. As the last stage of their training, we made them bayonet a living human. Prisoners were blindfolded and tied to poles. The soldiers dashed forward to bayonet their target at the shout

of "Charge!" Some stopped on their way. We kicked them and made them do it. After that, a man could do anything. The thing of supreme importance was to make them fight. Men useless in action were worthless. Good soldiers were those who were able to kill, however uncouth they were. Good sons, good daddies, good elder brothers were brought to the front to kill each other. Human beings turned into murdering demons. Everyone became a demon within three months. Men were able to fight courageously only when their human characteristics were suppressed. This was the Emperor's Army.'

Shin Hasegawa, a twenty-two-year-old trainee pilot, reflected on what the behaviour of Japanese soldiers showed about humanity: *'I heard a talk given by an infantry officer who had spent a long time on the battlefields of our Central China operation. He talked about how they killed prisoners and women in a way that was so hideous such words as "cruel" and "inhumane" are inadequate. I felt a little relief about having transferred into the Air Corps. Perhaps, in the final analysis, it may be the same thing, but at least I do not have to do any killing by using my own bare hands. Whatever we might call it, the beastly nature, or whatever, in the human being [. . .] I thought very seriously over the fact that it is so deeply rooted in our natures.'*

In Japan, domestic censorship disguised and hid the truth about China, and anyone who voiced opposition was either imprisoned or 'persuaded' to change their view. Progressive thinkers, writers and professors who did not wholeheartedly embrace national policies were immediately attacked. When Imperial Diet member Takao Saito asked for a justification for the nation's enormous sacrifice of men and resources, he was expelled from the house for insulting the spirits of the war dead.

The conflict continued without resolution until it merged into the Second World War. By the time the Japanese army withdrew from China in 1945, the Second Sino-Japanese War had cost over 500,000 Japanese military deaths, over 3 million Chinese military and an estimated 17 million Chinese civilian deaths.

While Japan and China exchanged lethal blows in Asia, Europe was on the brink of a catastrophic war all of its own. Japan's ally Adolf Hitler's overt belligerence had been appeased in the

Rhineland, in the Anschluss with Austria and in the Sudetenland, but when he invaded Poland, on 1 September 1939, Britain and France declared war with Germany two days later. Suddenly, two continents were at war.

The effect on Asia was profound. The subsequent fall of the Netherlands and France in 1940, and Britain's weakened military resources, created a power vacuum in their Asian colonies. With America still staunchly isolationist and Hitler's panzers marauding across Europe, the Axis powers were in the ascendancy.

America and Britain continued to send supplies in support of China along the Burma Road. This, coupled with Washington's overt determination to isolate Japan and deny it the raw materials it craved, was a short road to war.

On 25 July 1941, the US government froze all Japanese assets in the country, an action quickly followed by the British and the Dutch. Their actions led the Japanese military and government to conclude that the goal of eliminating all resistance in China demanded that they wage war across the entire region and take on the whole world.

Conducted under the divine leadership of the Emperor Hirohito, his Holy War was about to begin.

5

THE MIGHTY ESCALATION

Japan's Greater East Asia War began spectacularly. It would end in a spectacular tragedy – but that would be four and a half years later.

As early as 1935, Japan's military strategists had decided the oil reserves of the Dutch East Indies were vital to its war effort in China. This was made more salient as China continued to resist, and the sheer scale of the country and its rugged interior drained more and more men and materiel. By 1940, the war in Europe had made Europe's Asian colonies a part of Japan's strategic mix, and plans were added to include Indochina, Malaya and the Philippines in what became known as the 'Greater East Asia Co-Prosperity Sphere'. In November 1940, *Time Magazine* published a summary of an article in *Hinode* (*Rising Sun*), a popular Japanese magazine. It had put together a panel of Japanese naval officers for a Q&A session.

> *Hinode*: How will 'Greater East Asia' be accomplished?
> Admiral Sankichi Takahashi, former Commander-in-Chief
> of Japan's Combined Fleet: 'It will be constructed in
> several stages. In the first stage, the sphere that Japan
> demands includes Manchukuo, China, Indochina, Burma,
> Straits Settlements, Netherlands Indies, New Caledonia,
> New Guinea, many islands in the West Pacific, Japan's
> mandated islands and the Philippines. Australia and the
> rest of the East Indies can be included later.'
> *Hinode*: 'When will Japan and America fight?'
> Vice-Admiral Yoshijirō Hamada: 'America's participation in
> the European war will automatically involve Japan [. . .]
> Statesmen will try to prevent such a calamity, but the

circumstances are beyond their control. There can be no
settlement until Japan and America have a showdown.'
Hinode: 'Does that mean that Japan has completed
preparations for war with the United States?'
A minor officer: 'We won't answer that question. We simply
smile.'

The *Time* writer went on to quote from the Japanese media.

The Emperor himself paused the pompous celebrations of the
2,600th anniversary of the Japanese Empire to discuss expan-
sionist moves with Army and Navy leaders. The newspaper
Yomiuri defined all this without mincing words, 'The work left
for Japan is to sweep away the remains of the white empire
which so long has held sway in our part of the world.'

As Japan's belligerence intensified, the response of the Western
powers only served to exacerbate the looming crisis. Australia, the
US, Britain and the Dutch government-in-exile ceased the sale of
oil, iron ore and steel to Japan. In Tokyo, far from intimidating
the militarists, the embargoes were seen as an act of aggression.
Imported oil was about 80 per cent of domestic consumption,
without which Japan's economy would collapse, as would the
Imperial Army's ability to wage war. The Japanese media created a
frenzy of anger by referring to the embargoes as the 'ABCD Encirclement' (American-British-Chinese-Dutch) and casting Japan as
the defender of Asia against British and American imperialism and
Chinese communism.

Japan's leaders felt cornered and, rightly or wrongly, impelled
to fight their way out of a predicament imposed upon them.
Fervent nationalist, future prime minister and current army minister Hideki Tōjō believed: *'Two years from now we will have no
petroleum for military use; ships will stop moving. When I think about
the strengthening of American defences in the southwestern Pacific, the
expansion of the US fleet, the unfinished China Incident, and so on, I
see no end of difficulties [. . .] I fear that we would become a third-class
nation if we sit tight.'*

Knowing that they could never fully defeat America, the more sober of Japanese planners prepared for a limited war in which Japan would conquer its main objectives and then establish a defensive bulwark to thwart American counter-attacks. Then, in the medium to long term, Washington would have little choice but to negotiate a peace deal, leaving Japan in control of East Asia and the Pacific and in charge of its destiny. It was an optimistic outlook – to the point of naivety – but angry belligerence is not usually conducive to clear thinking.

Three stages of the war were defined. The first aimed for the occupation of the Philippines, Malaya, Borneo, Thailand, Burma, Rabaul and the Dutch East Indies. This stage would be followed by expansion into the South Pacific: New Guinea, New Britain, Fiji, Samoa and strategic points in the Australian area. Finally, there would be a push further into the Pacific, when Midway and the Aleutian Islands would be captured, thus denying the US fleet any potential Pacific harbour for its fleet beyond Hawaii.

Hirohito was fully aware of the planning. Admiral Sōkichi Takagi was Chief of the Navy Ministry's Research Section and had influence at the Imperial Palace. Takagi was witness to a meeting with the emperor on 5 September 1941, at which Hirohito sanctioned war. Also party to the exchange was General Hajime Sugiyama, the army's de facto commander-in-chief, and Osami Nagano, chief of the Imperial Japanese Navy.

> Emperor: 'In the event we must finally open hostilities, will our operations have a probability of victory?'
>
> Sugiyama: 'Yes, they will.'
>
> Emperor: 'At the time of the China Incident, the army told me that we could achieve peace immediately after dealing them one blow with three divisions. Sugiyama, you were army minister at that time.'
>
> Sugiyama: 'China is a vast area with many ways in and many ways out, and we met unexpectedly big difficulties.'
>
> Emperor: 'Didn't I caution you each time about those matters? Sugiyama, are you lying to me?'

> Nagano: 'If Your Majesty will grant me permission, I would like to make a statement.'
> Emperor: 'Go ahead.'
> Nagano: 'There is no 100 per cent probability of victory for the troops stationed there [. . .] Sun Tzu says that in war between states of similar strength, it is difficult to calculate victory. If we waste time, let the days pass, and are forced to fight after it is too late to fight, then we won't be able to do a thing about it.'
> Emperor: 'All right, I understand.'

With no wise voices cautioning restraint, Japan was rushing headlong into war. All opposition had been silenced. Writing in the 1950s, Saburō Ienaga commented:

> The Imperial Army and Navy enjoyed virtually unlimited freedom of action. And their modes of action reflected the remarkably irrational and undemocratic character of the military. It was typical of the Japanese military mind to charge recklessly into an unwinnable war and continue it to the point of national destruction [. . .] The military went into the Pacific War still clinging to the concept of fighting spirit as decisive in battle. The result was wanton waste of Japanese lives, particularly in combat with Allied forces whose doctrine was based on scientific rationality.

Ienaga's observation was all too accurate. The 1908 army criminal code contained the following provisions:

> A commander who allows his unit to surrender to the enemy without fighting to the last man or who concedes a strategic area to the enemy shall be punishable by death. If a commander is leading troops in combat and they are captured by the enemy, even if the commander has performed his duty to the utmost, he shall be punishable by up to six months confinement.

Although public dissent was almost impossible, many people expressed their opposition and anxieties in private diaries or under the guise of anonymity.

Home minister Kiichirō Hiranuma received an anonymous letter in 1941: '*Get rid of the Emperor and set up a republic. Demolish all the Imperial tombs and convert the areas to farming land [. . .] End the China Incident now. If we grab China, only the military and a few businessmen with political connections will profit from it. To us ordinary folks it doesn't matter if Japan loses. We want peace now.*'

Graffiti appeared on a public toilet in Oita Prefecture: '*Assassinate Premier Konoe. End the war and restore peace.*'

Another anonymous letter addressed to the home minister said, '*Citizens of Tokyo! I think you are all stupid. I'll tell you why: you're giving your lives for that fool who lives for free in the big mansion right in the middle of Tokyo. He should be got rid of, chased out of Tokyo. We should revolt and make a free country like America. Isn't the Emperor a human being just like the rest of us?*'

Yōichi Yanagida, a twenty-three-year-old conscript, wrote in his diary on July 12, 1941: '*Draftings into the service have been very heavy lately. And, more than ever, I sense that this is a time of national emergency. Every second we seem to be on the brink of falling into an abyss. When will that fatal second arrive? It could be right now. A huge and invisible storm is brewing. An indeterminate something is surrounding my body like a whirlpool. It pushes me up to the world of the unknown. What sort of time are we living in? What on earth is humanity, like being tossed about in an angry sea. I can hear the wheels of a wagon drawn by phantom horses. I ask again: What is history? What is humanity? And what in the world are they going to do with me?*'

On 18 October, Hideki Tōjō, ultranationalist and powerful advocate of war, became prime minister. Although Tōjō's elevation was another step on the road to war, it was far from inevitable. That the two major powers either side of the Pacific Ocean might at some point in the future come to blows had been seen as a possibility since the 1920s. After all, both had ever bigger muscles and were inclined to use them if needed. American expansion in the Pacific, in Hawaii and the Philippines, had unnerved Japan. At the same time, Japan's analysis of the Great War in Europe had shown that modern wars would be long, would require mass mobilisation and demand economic self-sufficiency. Given that Japan's growing population needed to be fed beyond its domestic output and that its military needed iron, oil and coal, it feared being stung by trade embargoes and economic encirclement.

Despite the mutual anxieties and mistrust, the relationship between Japan and the US remained relatively cordial, and they had continued to trade through the 1920s. Tensions only began to grow with Japan's invasion of Manchuria in 1931. As Japan's war in China escalated into full-scale war, Washington became ever more wary about what the future might bring. At the same time, in Tokyo, the escalating costs of the war on the mainland made Japan's need for vast quantities of scarce resources even more obvious.

The situation had worsened in 1937 when a US Navy gunboat, the USS *Panay*, was bombed on China's Yangtze River at the cost of three American lives. Later, during the Japanese occupation of Nanking, the American consul at the US Embassy in Nanking was struck in the face by a Japanese soldier. That, coupled with the stories emerging of the atrocities in the city, swung US public opinion against Japan. In 1938, following an appeal by President Roosevelt, American companies had stopped providing Japan with implements of war.

Another major escalation had occurred in September 1940, when in order to prevent China from receiving arms and fuel through Indochina, Japan invaded and took control within four days. The United States immediately halted shipments of aeroplanes, parts, machine tools and aviation fuel to Japan. In mid-1940, President Roosevelt had moved the US Pacific Fleet from San Diego to Pearl Harbor in Hawaii and ordered a military build-up in the Philippines, which convinced the Japanese strategists that a devastating pre-emptive strike against the US Pacific Fleet was the only way to thwart the American plans in the area. Finally, the United States ceased oil exports to Japan in July 1941, which convinced Tokyo to proceed with plans to invade the oil-rich Dutch East Indies.

Japan and the United States engaged in extensive negotiations during 1941, attempting to improve relations. By making peace with China's Nationalist government Japan offered to withdraw from most of China and Indochina. Washington rejected the proposal.

Japanese Prime Minister Konoe then offered to meet Roosevelt, but Roosevelt insisted on reaching an agreement before any meeting. The American ambassador to Japan repeatedly urged Roosevelt to accept the meeting, warning that it was the only way to preserve the conciliatory Konoe government and peace in the Pacific. However, his recommendation was not accepted. The Konoe government collapsed in October, when the Japanese military rejected a withdrawal of all troops from China.

Japan's final proposal, delivered on 20 November, offered to withdraw from southern Indochina and to refrain from attacks in Southeast Asia, so long as the United States, United Kingdom and Netherlands supplied 1 million US gallons of aviation fuel, lifted their sanctions against Japan, and ceased aid to China. The American counterproposal six days later required Japan to completely evacuate China without conditions.

By the time the American offer arrived in Tokyo, the Japanese task force had already set sail for Pearl Harbor.

•

Admiral Isoroku Yamamoto was the commander of Japan's Combined Fleet. He had been opposed to the invasions of China in 1931 and 1937, and to the Tripartite pact with Germany and Italy. Even so, like most of his generation, he was a loyalist to his emperor and his nation.

'To die for Emperor and Nation is the highest hope of a military man. After a brave hard fight, the blossoms are scattered on the fighting field. But [. . .] the fighting man will go to eternity for Emperor and country. One man's life or death is a matter of no importance. All that matters is the Empire. As Confucius said, "They may crush cinnabar, yet they do not take away its colour; one may burn a fragrant herb, yet it will not destroy the scent." They may destroy my body, yet they will not take away my will.'

Yamamoto had planned the attack against the US Pacific Fleet in great detail. The logic was clear: with the US fleet out of action, Japan would have free rein for the conquest of the whole of Southeast Asia and the Indonesian archipelago. Planning had begun early in 1941, and was in full swing by early spring. Pilots were trained, equipment prepared and adapted, and, most importantly, intelligence gathered about Pearl Harbor, its fleet and its air defences. Besides Yamamoto, there were two key planners: Rear Admiral Kusaka Ryūnosuke, who was an accomplished swordsman, and Commander Minoru Genda, who had travelled to Europe to study German air defences and those of Britain during the Battle of Britain.

Hirohito did not give 'in principal' approval for the attack until 5 November – after the third of four Imperial Conferences to discuss the attack – and gave final approval on 1 December.

On 26 November, the task force departed from the Kuril Islands, 800 miles north of Hokkaido, Japan's most northern island. From there, Vice Admiral Chuichi Nagumo led a fleet – including six aircraft carriers, two battleships, three cruisers, and eleven destroyers – to a point some 275 miles north of Hawaii. The attack was then carried out by 360 planes launched from the carriers. The first wave was to be the primary attack, while the second wave was to attack carriers as its first objective and cruisers as its second, with battleships as the third target. The aircrews were ordered to select the highest-value targets, battleships and aircraft carriers. Dive-bombers were to attack ground targets, and fighters were to destroy as many parked aircraft as possible.

The diary of Hirohito's naval aide, Eiichirō Jō, offers us a detailed first-hand account of the fateful day of 7/8 December 1941 and also makes it clear that Hirohito was central to the entire operation.

'*4am.: Japan issued a final ultimatum to the United States. 3:30am: the Hawaiian surprise attack was successful. 5:30am: Singapore bombed. Great results. Air attacks on Davao, Guam. Wake. 7:10am: all the above was reported to the emperor. The American gunboat Wake was captured on the Shanghai front. The British gunboat Petrel was sunk. From 7:15 to 7:30 the chief of the Navy General Staff reported on the war situation. At 7:30 the prime minister informally reported to the emperor on the imperial rescript declaring war. Cabinet meeting from 7am. At 7:35 the chief of the Army General Staff reported on the war situation. At 10:45 the emperor attended an emergency meeting of the privy council.*

At 11:00am. the imperial rescript declaring war was promulgated. At 2:00pm, the emperor summoned the army and navy ministers and bestowed an imperial rescript on them. The army minister, representing both services, replied to the emperor. 4:30pm: the chiefs of staff formally reported on the draft of the Tripartite [Germany-Italy-Japan] Military Pact. At 8:30pm, the chief of the Navy General Staff reported on the achievements of the Hawaii air attack [. . .] Throughout the day the emperor wore his naval uniform and seemed to be in a splendid mood.'

It is hardly surprising that Hirohito was in a 'splendid mood' that day, and it can only have become even more euphoric as his forces launched a tsunami of men and machines across Asia and the Pacific. The surprise carrier-based air strike on Pearl Harbor, in Hawaii, crippled the US Pacific Fleet and put eight American battleships out of action, destroyed 188 aircraft and killed 2,403 Americans. Japan lost fifty-five pilots and nine submariners, who manned midget submarines in the attack.

As Japanese soldiers sailed from home to begin the emperor's Holy War, they must have been comforted by the propaganda pamphlet they were given – 'Read This Alone, And The War Can Be Won' – a simple guide to how easy their task would be.

> Motor vehicles get through by determination. Force your way ahead, even if you have to carry the thing on your shoulders. Westerners – being very superior people, very effeminate, and very cowardly – have an intense dislike of fighting in the rain or the mist, or at night. Night, in particular (though it is excellent for dancing), they cannot conceive to be a proper time for war. In this, if we seize upon it, lies our great opportunity.

The pamphlet seemed to ring true in the coming weeks and months. Like dominoes, Japan's conquests after Pearl Harbor followed in quick succession.

When the Japanese invaded Thailand on 8 December 1941, Thailand's prime minister, Plaek Phibunsongkhram (Phibun), was forced to order a general ceasefire after just one day of resistance and allow Japan to use the country as a base for its invasions of Burma and Malaya. Phibun, who modelled himself on Italian dictator Benito Mussolini, signed a military alliance with Japan on 21 December. A month later, Phibun declared war on Britain and the United States. Subsequently, Thailand committed 35,000 troops to Japan's attack on Burma.

Hong Kong was attacked on 8 December and fell on Christmas Day. The vastly outnumbered British and Commonwealth garrison of just 10,000 faced a Japanese army 27,000 strong. The Hong Kong garrison consisted of British, Indian and Canadian troops supported by Auxiliary Defence Units and the Hong Kong Volunteer Defence Corps. Of the three territories of Hong Kong, the defenders abandoned the two mainland territories of Kowloon and New Territories within a week. Less than two weeks later – with their last territory, Hong Kong Island itself, untenable – the colony surrendered.

During the attack, the Japanese Army committed several massacres of prisoners of war. The worst was against forty-seven Allies. Some of the victims of the massacres were women, and there were widespread incidents of looting and rape. Reprisals against Hong Kong's civilian population were exceptionally brutal. An estimated 10,000 were killed, while many more were assaulted, tortured or mutilated. Commonwealth forces suffered at least 2,000 missing or killed during the battle for Hong Kong. A further 10,000 were taken as prisoners of war and subjected to horrendous treatment throughout the remainder of the war, which many did not survive.

The deed was done. Hirohito and his nation had launched Japan's Holy War; its *Seisen* ('Crusade') – called a 'Day of Infamy' by US President Roosevelt. It was the beginning of a Pacific War that would be brutal in the extreme, and one that Japan would bitterly regret.

6
PACIFIC EXPANSION

The British colony of Penang fell on 19 December 1941. US bases on Guam and Wake Island were lost at the same time. Two major British warships – the battlecruiser HMS *Repulse* and the battleship HMS *Prince of Wales* – were sunk off Malaya on 10 December, in an attack by a swarm of Mitsubishi G38 and G4M bombers of the Imperial Japanese Air Force and became the first capital ships to be sunk solely by air power on the open sea.

The fall of Penang during the Malaya Campaign illustrated the extent of Japan's pre-war planning. Intelligence from what would become its future conquests was conveyed to its Taiwan-based Japanese Military Affairs Bureau Unit 82 by secret agents: Japanese embassy staff, disaffected locals, Japanese and Taiwanese 'merchants' who operated businesses, as well as 'tourists' and Allied traitors. In fact, there were several British and American secret agents working for Japan before the war. Unit 82 was headed by ultranationalist Isamu Chō, and was responsible for the detailed planning of the Asia-Pacific War. (Chō would later commit suicide on Okinawa, in 1945. When his body was found, lying next to it was his *yukata* (dressing gown), on which was written: 'With bravery I served my nation. With loyalty I dedicate my life.')

The conquest of Penang was another illustration of the weakness of Allied defences in the Far East, and of the Allied betrayal of the local populations and many of its own citizens. After the city's Butterworth Airbase and oil tanks were devastated by bombing attacks on 15 December, the base was abandoned. That allowed Japanese bombers to dive-bomb George Town, Penang's capital, during which they machine-gunned civilians, leaving behind piles of dead bodies. Buildings were burned to the ground and civil servants and policemen fled, allowing looters to roam freely. The last British and Commonwealth troops destroyed and abandoned the Batu Maung Fort. Despite being offered the chance to be evacuated together with the Europeans, none of the local Penang civilian population took up the offer, because the evacuation of their family members was not guaranteed by the British. This act of discrimination was later seen as one of the British Empire's cruellest betrayals.

Finding themselves abandoned, a group of local leaders established the 'Penang Service Committee'. It decided immediately that its first task was to take down the Union Jack flying on the city's Esplanade and to free Japanese civilians, getting them to write messages on large pieces of cloth which would be raised over the Esplanade. The committee also commandeered Penang's radio station, over which an appeal was broadcast to the Japanese.

This is Penang calling. Penang calling the Japanese Headquarters in North Malaya. Penang has been evacuated by the British. There are no more troops or any defences whatsoever in Penang. Please refrain from bombing Penang.

When Penang finally fell, Allied troops captured during the Malaya Campaign were forced to sweep the city's streets in front of local onlookers. It was a ritual humiliation intended to destroy the aura of invincibility that the British had enjoyed in Southeast Asia during the previous century and a half.

In January 1942, Japan also invaded Burma, the Dutch East Indies, New Guinea and the Solomon Islands and captured Manila, Kuala Lumpur and Rabaul. The capture of Rabaul on the northeastern tip of the island of New Britain was the beginning of the long and bitter New Guinea Campaign, a struggle which would last until the end of the war. Rabaul overlooks Simpson Harbour, an important natural anchorage of strategic importance. It was to become a vital naval base for the Imperial Navy and became known as Japan's 'Pearl Harbor of the South Pacific'. It would soon be well defended by 367 anti-aircraft guns and five airfields, two of them pre-war, and three that would be built by Japanese sappers and defended by army units. An effective early-warning radar system provided up to sixty minutes' notice of an Allied attack. The elaborate defences were crucial as both Simpson Harbour and Rabaul were subject to significant Allied air raids. By 1943, there were over 100,000 Japanese personnel based in Rabaul.

It took just over two months for Japanese forces to conquer Malaya. The invasion is renowned for Japan's use of 'bicycle infantry', which allowed troops to carry modest loads of equipment and move quickly through thick jungle terrain. Japan had used 50,000 bicycle troops in its 1937 China campaign, so knew how to deploy them. However, because of concerns that a lack of heavy weapons would slow up its amphibious attacks, the Japanese army was under orders not to embark for Malaya with bicycles. Even so, they knew from intelligence that bicycles were plentiful in Malaya, so, as soon as they landed, they systematically confiscated bicycles from civilians and retailers. Using bicycles, the Japanese troops were able to outflank the retreating Allies. The speed of the Japanese advance, usually along plantation roads, native paths and over improvised bridges, surprised Allied forces defending the main roads and river crossings, by attacking them from the rear.

Although British and Commonwealth forces destroyed over a hundred bridges during a calculated retreat in Malaya, it did little to delay the Japanese. Singapore was the great prize at the tip of the Malayan peninsular. An apparently impregnable fortress and a symbol of the might of the British Empire, it was called 'Gibraltar in the Far East', a strategically vital military base that protected Britain's possessions in the Far East. British troops stationed in Singapore were told that the Japanese were poor fighters; competent against soldiers in China who themselves were poor soldiers, but of little use against the might of the British Army. Its military planners were certain that Japan would launch an amphibious attack on the colony, so its key defensive facilities faced south, out to sea. It was thought impossible for the island city to be attacked from the north, through the jungle and mangrove swamps of the Malay Peninsula. But that was exactly the route the Japanese took.

As the Japanese army moved at speed through the peninsula, its troops were ordered to take no prisoners as they would slow up the advance. A pamphlet issued to all soldiers stated:

When you encounter the enemy after landing, think of yourself as an avenger coming face to face at last with his father's murderer. Here is a man whose death will lighten your heart.

The Allied army defending Singapore was 90,000 strong: British, Indian and Australian troops. Led by General Tomoyuki Yamashita, the Japanese force was 65,000 men who had fought in the Manchurian/Chinese campaign and were battle-hardened. Many of the Allies' 90,000 men had never seen combat. The Japanese attack was based on speed, ferocity and surprise and overwhelmed the Allied defenders. Wounded Allied soldiers were killed where they lay. Those who were not injured but had surrendered were also murdered – some captured Australian troops were doused with petrol and burned to death. Locals who had helped the Allies were tortured before being murdered.

On 31 January 1942, the British and Australian forces withdrew across the causeway that separated Singapore from Malaya. On 8 February the Japanese attacked across the Johor Strait. Spread too thinly across a seventy-mile coastline, most Allied men were too remotely located to have any impact on the battle and 23,000 Japanese soldiers were able to march into Singapore. At the Alexandra Military Hospital, Japan's soldiers murdered the patients they found there. General Yamashita demanded an unconditional surrender and on 15 February, the Allies capitulated and about 80,000 men became prisoners of war, to add to the 50,000 taken in Malaya. Many of the prisoners died of neglect, disease or forced labour thereafter.

Three days after the surrender, the Japanese began the Sook Purge, killing thousands of civilians. By the time Japan captured Singapore, it had suffered almost 15,000 casualties; Allied losses totalled over 130,000, including estimates of at least 8,000 killed, 11,000 wounded and 120,000 missing or captured. (General Yamashita, who became known as the 'Tiger of Malaya', was convicted of war crimes after the war and was executed in the Philippines in 1946.)

From early February 1942, the Japanese navy began to gradually eradicate Allied naval dominance in Southeast Asia and the western Pacific. The US and Australia had become relatively recent naval powers in the area, but Britain and the Dutch had held sway for centuries. As their colonies were conquered, their control of the high seas was neutralised.

At the first Battle of the Java Sea, in late February and early March, the Imperial Navy inflicted a resounding defeat on the Allies, leading to the surrender of Java and Sumatra. On 28 February, in the Sunda Strait, an Allied force encountered the main Japanese invasion fleet heading for West Java and was attacked by at least three cruisers and several destroyers. In a ferocious night action that ended after midnight on 1 March, the Allies lost one heavy cruiser (sunk), one light cruiser and a destroyer. Over 1,000 sailors were killed and over 600 taken prisoner.

Two days later, the Second Battle of the Java Sea occurred on 1 March, which saw the end of Allied warships operating in the waters around Java, allowing Japan to complete its conquest of the Dutch East Indies unhindered. By the end of the battle, a Dutch destroyer and two American destroyers were either scuttled or sunk as they attempted to escape to Australia. The main ABDA (American-British-Dutch-Australian) naval force had been almost totally destroyed: ten ships and approximately 2,173 sailors had been lost. The Battles of the Java Sea ended significant Allied naval operations in Southeast Asia in 1942, and the Japanese army landed on Java on 28 February. The Dutch fleet was all but annihilated in Asia, and Holland would never reclaim full control of its colony. By conquering the Dutch East Indies, Japan gained control of one of the most important food-producing regions in Asia and the fourth-largest oil producing area in the world at the time. The surviving remnants of Allied forces in Asia beat a hasty retreat to Australia, leaving some Dutch troops to hold out for a week before a full surrender was declared on 9 March.

Japan had destroyed Allied power in Southeast Asia. The Japanese Air Force had been able to make a devastating attack on Darwin on 19 February, which killed at least 243 people. Over the following nineteen months, Australia was attacked by air almost 100 times, and in late May 1942, Sydney was attacked when Japanese midget submarines raided Sydney Harbour. Just a few days later, two Japanese submarines briefly shelled Sydney's eastern suburbs and the city of Newcastle.

In March and April, a Japanese carrier force attacked the British Royal Navy in Ceylon (Sri Lanka), sinking the aircraft carrier HMS *Hermes* and forcing the British to withdraw to the western Indian Ocean. That cleared the way for a Japanese assault on Burma and India, and on 8 March, the Japanese occupied Rangoon. *Hermes* and destroyer HMS *Vampire* were spotted off the coast of the city of Batticaloa in eastern Ceylon by a Japanese reconnaissance plane from the Kongō-class battleship *Haruna*. Eighty-five Aichi D3A dive-bombers, escorted by nine Mitsubishi A6M Zero fighters, were launched at the two ships. At least thirty-two attacked them and sank them within twenty minutes.

Hermes sank with the loss of 307 men. Miraculously, *Vampire* lost only nine of her men. Most of the survivors of the attack were picked up by the hospital ship *Vita*. Japanese losses in total were four D3As lost and five more damaged. On 6 May, the Japanese landed on Corregidor and the Americans surrendered. So overwhelming had been Japan's onslaught, many in the military, as well as civilians at home, thought the Holy War would soon be over, leaving their divine emperor with an empire to rival any in history.

Shigenori Tōgō, Japan's foreign minister, was concerned about what would be the consequences of the euphoria of victory.

'Not only the soldiers at the front, but all classes in Japan, filled with the exhilaration of victory, felt that Japan was invincible. There was no thought now but of destruction of the enemy, and it was asserted ever more truculently that no diplomacy was wanted during the war. [...] The intoxication with victory was no less apparent in the Diet. In February 1942, at a meeting of the Budget Committee of the House of Representatives, one of them demanded a statement of the attitude of the Foreign Minister towards peace. I replied that it was natural and necessary to stop war and re-establish peace, and that I was consequently prepared to that end. This drew protests from the members that the purpose of war

was to destroy the enemy and that the Foreign Minister should not be heard to say that he was preparing for peace, and they demanded that I retract my statement. I refused. Even within the Cabinet there was the opinion that the Representatives were right, and that Japan might well, if she kept on at the present pace, occupy Washington!'

Shigeru Nambara was another who was not celebrating: *'Against common sense, against scholarly sense, it's happened: Japan's at war with the world. Japan attacks the US and Britain: that alone explains the deep sadness on the train, the morning of the eighth.'*

•

As the tsunami of conquest became known to the rest of the world, the news of seemingly unstoppable conquest was met with both incredulity and fear. There would also have been revulsion if Europe and America had been aware of what had been happening in China. The atrocities had begun, but it would be three years before the awful stories were revealed. Following the capture of Singapore, Japanese forces arrested more than 70,000 overseas Chinese. They were suspected of carrying out subversive activities and were slaughtered in their thousands, allowing no time to establish their guilt. According to a Japanese account, *'The executions were carried out in a heinous way. A large number of Chinese were tied together, loaded on a boat, taken out to sea, and pushed overboard.'* To the people of Singapore, this must have seemed a strange kind of liberation; their English colonisers had been replaced by summary Japanese justice and vicious reprisals.

Having conquered a vast Pacific and Southeast Asian empire in just five months, Japan's momentum began to slow. With enormous lines of communication and supply, and massive commitments of men and materiel in China, ambition had to succumb to reality. It was still vital to cut off Australia and New Zealand from US supply lines, but that was easier said than done.

On 7 March the Liaison Conference (Imperial General Headquarters –Government Liaison Conference) defined the key strategy of the rapidly expanding Pacific offensive in a new policy document. This made it clear that the final objective of the emperor's

Holy War was to build an Asia-Pacific empire that could become permanent by bringing the Allies to the negotiating table at which they would concede most of Japan's conquests. It was clearly a misguided ambition, given the depth of pride and fortitude within the peoples of the Allied nations. Even so, the first article of the document declared:

> In order to force Britain to submit and the United States to lose its will to fight, we shall continue expanding from the areas we have already gained; while working long-term to establish an impregnable strategic position, we shall actively seize whatever opportunities for attack may occur.

The next day, Lae and Salamaua in New Guinea were occupied.

Two days later, with the army advancing throughout the whole of the Central and South Pacific, Privy Seal Kido wrote in his diary that Hirohito, '*Was in a more pleasant mood than usual and smilingly said to me, "We are winning too quickly." The enemy at Bandung on the Java front, he continued, had announced surrender on the seventh, and we are about to force total collapse in the entire Dutch Indies. The enemy forces at Surabaya have also surrendered. Rangoon on the Burma front has fallen. The emperor was obviously delighted. I could only express congratulations.*'

By April 1942, the Japanese had captured strategic points in the remote Andaman and Nicobar Islands, territory belonging to British India and running from the Malacca Straits all the way to the mouth of the Indian Ocean.

The second phase of Japan's war strategy required attacks much further east and south, including New Guinea, Midway, Fiji and Samoa, and the Imperial Navy even considered advances into Australia. However, with large numbers of troops fighting in China and Manchuria, the Imperial Army did not have the manpower needed. So, in an attempt to isolate Australia, the decision was taken to attack New Caledonia and then move on to Fiji. However, naval reverses at the battles of Coral Sea and Midway effectively ended Japan's Pacific expansion.

Ominously for Japan's dream of imperial greatness, the first US troops arrived in Australia in April 1942 and the Doolittle Raid of 18 April became a portent of the dreadful retribution that would soon be unleashed by the Allies. Admiral Isoroku Yamamoto, the architect of the attack on Pearl Harbor, who had voiced serious doubts about waging war against America, had said during the planning of Japan's war in the Pacific, '*Should hostilities break out between Japan and the United States, it would not be enough that we take Guam and the Philippines, nor even Hawaii and San Francisco. To make victory certain, we would have to march into Washington and dictate the terms of peace in the White House. I wonder if our politicians who speak so lightly of a Japanese American war have confidence about the final outcome and are prepared to make the necessary sacrifices.*'

After Pearl Harbor, Yamamoto was even more anxious: '*In the first six to twelve months of a war with the United States and Great Britain I will run wild and win victory upon victory. But then, if the war continues after that, I have no expectation of success.*'

The Doolittle Raid of 18 April 1942 was of little strategic significance, but it was a psychological shock and a harbinger of doom for the Japanese population. In the aftermath of Pearl Harbor, US president Franklin Roosevelt, demanded that his military leadership find a way to strike a retaliatory blow against Japan that would unnerve the Japanese and boost morale at home. With Japan in control of the entire western Pacific, any attack on Japan would have to be an audacious, carrier-based bombing raid. An experienced aviator, aircraft engineer, air racer and stunt pilot, James 'Jimmy' Doolittle, was chosen to lead the raid. He recruited experienced pilots to fly sixteen B-25 Mitchell medium bombers, each with a crew of five. The planes had to be heavily modified to reduce weight and increase fuel capacity.

The raiders flew as low as possible before climbing to 1,200 feet bombing height when they reached Tokyo. Fourteen tons of bombs were dropped, with the crews claiming hits on virtually all of the assigned targets. On the ground, the raid killed about fifty people and injured 400, and damage to Japanese military and industrial targets was slight, but it did have the desired psychological effect, both at home and in Japan. Chief of the Imperial Japanese Navy

General Staff, Marshal Admiral Osami Nagano, a witness to the attack, wrote, '*This must not be happening!*'

The Japanese press played down the impact of the raid and suggested that its targets were civilian: '*Enemy bombers appeared over Tokyo shortly after noon for the first time in the current East Asia War. Heavy and telling damage was inflicted on schools and hospitals.*' The report went on to minimise the death toll, and stated that nine of the sixteen planes had been shot down. The aftermath of the raid was, however, a mixed blessing.

First of all, shaken by the attack, Yamamoto advanced his plans to attack Port Moresby at the southern end of New Guinea and to launch a naval assault on the isolated Mid-Pacific Island of Midway, both of which would be watersheds in the conflict. Secondly, although most of Doolittle's crews survived, several were held captive, three were killed in crash landings in China and eight were captured by Japanese forces in China. Of those eight, four lived to be rescued, one died of disease in brutal captivity in solitary confinement, and three were executed. Stories of their pre-execution torture are widespread and varied but lack clear verification. Fearing American retaliation against Japanese living in the United States – a not unreasonable concern – General Tōjō initially opposed death sentences for the American prisoners. However, to decrease the likelihood of further air attacks, Sugiyama and the Army General Staff insisted on executing all eight. Hirohito decided to intervene and commute the punishments of five. Why he allowed the others to die in violation of international law is a question that is impossible to answer because all records and documents pertaining to prisoners of war were destroyed by the Japanese at the end of the war.

Finally, realising that mainland China was a 'blind spot' for future air attacks on Japan, and in straightforward acts of revenge, the Japanese military launched air and land attacks on the eastern seaboard of China. Anyone discovered to have helped the US raiders was executed, and thousands of civilians were killed in bombing raids and in rampages by Japanese troops, including biological warfare campaigns by Unit 731, the secret bacteriological warfare group. The unit tested 'plague bombs' by dropping disease-infected weapons over cities to see whether they would cause infections, which led to many thousands of deaths.

The emperor was particularly keen to complete the campaign in China. He knew that until China was defeated, the war would be a huge strain on Japan's manpower and resources. On several occasions during 1942, he pressed Sugiyama for a solution, '*Can't you find a way somehow to put an end to the China situation?*' As a result, Sugiyama planned a major offensive, Operation Go-gō, with fifteen divisions to destroy China's forces in Szechuan Province and capture Chungking. Over 140,000 Japanese troops were committed, with the support of 300 tanks and 500 planes. They faced a Chinese army over 200,000 strong. The basic plan of Operation Go-gō was to make breakthroughs on several fronts towards Sichuan in Central China. Heavy aerial support and the bombing of Chungking was to support the advance of the Japanese Army, while Japanese Navy patrol boats on the Yangtze River were to provide further bombardment.

The invasion phase was to involve Japanese units first occupying Wanxian, from where they could advance to Chungking. However, in subsequent battles, the Japanese suffered defeats at the hands of the Nationalist Chinese armies. As a result of the defeats, and after heavy losses in the Battle of Changde in Hunan, Japan abandoned Go-gō and moved its focus to Yunnan. Even so, the bombardment of Chungking continued at the cost of tens of thousands of civilian casualties.

Many more Chinese cities were extensively bombed, with major loss of life, although accurate casualty figures for the conflict are unknown. In the end, Chinese resilience, the support of the US along the Burma Road, and the sheer scale of the Chinese mainland, continued to thwart Japan's desire to conquer its giant neighbour. Indeed, what was soon to become clear was the stark contrast between Japan's ambition in China and the reality of the sheer scale of the undertaking. Despite the ruthless efficiency of Japan's armed forces, they were fighting in a vast land of extraordinary geographical contrasts, against a people with a population of close to 300 million – well over 10 per cent of the global population.

7

THE TURNING POINT

Japan also faced other problems. Its whirlwind of expansion had been impressive, but was its vast new empire sustainable? Did it have the resources to govern its new subjects, did it have the military muscle to defend its borders? It had firm control of the land it occupied and some strength in the skies, but did it have the naval power to rule the huge expanses of the Pacific and Indian Oceans within its imperial boundaries?

The Battle of the Coral Sea, which lasted for four days from 4 May 1942, was a unique naval encounter, the first naval action in which the opposing fleets neither sighted nor fired upon one another. The battle was fought entirely from the skies by planes launched from aircraft carriers. The battle took place in the open seas between Australia, New Guinea and the Solomon Islands, with awesome materiel statistics: between the two fleets there were five carriers, seventeen cruisers, twenty-nine destroyers, twenty-nine support vessels and 267 aircraft. Japan's ultimate objective was to expand its empire far enough southwards to ensure that Australia was isolated from any support from the United States. It probably acknowledged that an invasion of Australia was beyond its reach, but the ability to weaken it by naval blockade was very appealing. Conversely, the Allies knew that access to Australia was vital to any plans to win back Asian territory lost to Japan.

Unfortunately for Japan's Imperial Navy, the Americans had been warned in advance of the plan in April when US naval code breakers unscrambled ULTRA intelligence. Extensive preparations were made to counter the attack by the deployment of a large Allied naval task force. The encounter began with a Japanese invasion of Tulagi, a small island in the Solomons, which preceded the naval encounter. Once the two fleets found one another – about seventy miles apart – the carrier-based aerial battle began in earnest. The outcome was inconclusive, with both sides claiming victory. However, for Japan, it was an unexpected setback with the loss of two aircraft carriers and seventy-three experienced aircraft pilots – men and materiel which could not, therefore, participate in the crucial Battle of Midway a month later. The strength of the combined US-Australian Allied fleet surprised the Imperial Japanese Navy, which had faced only token opposition in the past. The invasion fleet poised to attack Port Moresby was recalled, and Japan's hierarchy had to come to terms with the fact that the first of its major offensives at sea had been halted. At this point, the huge empire that had been created by the ambition of Japan's Holy War had reached its greatest extent.

If Coral Sea's stalemate was a setback for the Japanese, the next major battle was an unmitigated disaster for them. The battle for the tiny (just 2.4 square miles) but strategically vital atoll of Midway began on 4 June 1942. It was an even mightier encounter than Coral Sea. The two fleets consisted of seven carriers, thirteen heavy cruisers, two light cruisers, nineteen destroyers, twenty-nine submarines, thirty-one other vessels and 608 warplanes. Without too much exaggeration, Midway has been judged the most decisive victory in naval warfare history.

Before the attack on Pearl Harbor, the US navy had begun work on a major air and submarine base on Midway, an island that the Americans had claimed as their own since 1859. By the following year, Midway had three runways, while Sand Island housed a seaplane hangar, a small garrison, a power plant and radio facilities. Tokyo had long realised that control of the atoll would be critical for any control of the central Pacific, with Hawaii located just 1,100 miles to the southeast. Not only that, the supply lines between the United States and Australia could be cut, with major naval and air power based on Midway.

Admiral Yamamoto was convinced that Midway would give Japan a secure perimeter in the middle of the Pacific and also be a lure that would entice the US fleet's aircraft carriers – vessels that had not been in dock at Pearl Harbor – into a trap. Once snared, they could be systematically destroyed, leaving Japan in total control of the Pacific. Yamamoto sent out the bulk of his *Kidō Butai* (Mobile Force), a massive carrier battle group under the command of Vice Admiral Chuichi Nagumo. It included four heavy aircraft carriers – *Akagi*, *Hiryū*, *Kaga* and *Sōryū* – along with two light aircraft carriers, two seaplane carriers, seven battleships, fifteen cruisers, forty-two destroyers, ten submarines, and various support and escort vessels. It was an enormous armada. Yamamoto's orders were clear: engage and destroy the American fleet, and invade Midway.

However, since his masterstroke at Pearl Harbor, times had changed. Poor planning and battlefield mistakes – not all of his doing – led to a catastrophe. Most importantly, the surprise factor that had been critical at Pearl Harbor had gone. US cryptographers had been able to discover the date and location of the planned attack, allowing the US Pacific Fleet to set its own trap.

After a diversionary attack on the Aleutian Islands off the coast of Alaska, Yamamoto planned a three-part strategy for Midway. First would be an aerial attack, launched from his major carriers, Second, an amphibious force led by Vice Admiral Nobutake Kondō would capture the island. Finally, once the anticipated American reinforcements from Pearl Harbor arrived, Nagumo's forces and Yamamoto's own fleet, which would be waiting 600 miles to the west, would launch a counterstrike.

After the Japanese attack on the Aleutian Islands on 3 June, US B-17 bombers flew from Midway to attack Kondō's land invasion force, with little success. A second attack, early on the morning of 4 June, was also unsuccessful. Admiral Nagumo initiated the first phase of Japan's assault on Midway as planned, launching 108 Japanese warplanes from his four aircraft carriers. They inflicted significant damage but left the airfield still useable and the US anti-aircraft defences still viable. As Nagumo was rearming Japanese planes for a second air attack, a Japanese reconnaissance plane spotted portions of the US fleet, including USS *Yorktown*, to the east of Midway. Nagumo switched tactics, ordering planes that were still armed to prepare to attack the US ships.

But an hour later, as the Japanese refuelled and rearmed their planes, another wave of US carrier-launched bombers struck, hitting the Japanese carriers *Akagi*, *Kaga* and *Sōryū*, and setting them ablaze. In response, Japan's surviving carrier, *Hiryū*, launched two waves of attacks on *Yorktown*, which had to be abandoned but remained afloat. US dive-bombers returned to attack *Hiryū* and set it ablaze as well, putting all four Japanese carriers out of commission. That evening, *Kaga* and the *Sōryū* both sank, while *Akagi* and the *Hiryū*, both of which had managed to remain afloat through the night, were scuttled. Rear Admiral Tamon Yamaguchi chose to go down with *Hiryū*, his flagship, and was accompanied by Rear Admiral Tomeo Kaku. Their actions deprived the Imperial Japanese Navy of one its finest flag officers as well as one of its most experienced naval aviators.

The airborne battle produced a decisive victory for the Americans, such that on 6 June, Yamamoto ordered his ships to retreat. Japan had lost 3,000 men, including most of its most experienced pilots, nearly 300 aircraft, one heavy cruiser and, crucially, four aircraft carriers. As a result of the defeat, Japan abandoned its expansion plans in the Pacific and, in effect, put itself into a defensive posture for the rest of the war. In contrast, the outcome had the reverse impact on the US and its Allies. Japan's seemingly invincible tidal wave of victories had become a spent force.

In Japan, there was no public reaction to the defeat, simply because the citizens were never told. A cabinet minister was appointed to control the concealment of facts. The injured were treated clandestinely in secure hospital wards, then sent back to sea, and the circumstances in which combatants died were hidden from their families. Hirohito clearly knew about the naval setbacks, but his subsequent mood is a surprise. Kōichi Kido, Lord Keeper of the Privy Seal, discussed the Battle of Midway with the emperor on 8 June.

'I had presumed the news of the terrible losses sustained by the naval air force would have caused him untold anxiety, yet when I saw him, he was as calm as usual and his countenance showed not the least change. He said he told the navy chief of staff that the loss was regrettable but

to take care that the navy not lose its fighting spirit. He ordered him to ensure that future operations continue to be bold and aggressive. When I witness the courage and wisdom of the emperor, I am very thankful that our imperial country Japan is blessed with such a sovereign.'

The next telling setback for Japan was known as the Battle of Guadalcanal in the Solomon Islands. However, it was not a single battle but a prolonged campaign that lasted over six months. Even so, like Coral Sea and Midway for the Imperial Japanese Navy, Guadalcanal was the fulcrum on land that broke the back of the Imperial Japanese Army. Beginning on 7 August 1942, in the first major Allied offensive of the war, the Allies committed 60,000 men – US marines and army – against a Japanese occupation force of 32,000. The outcome was devastating for Japan. The imperial forces lost almost 20,000 men on land and thirty-eight ships at sea, including a light carrier, two battleships, three heavy cruisers and eleven destroyers, as well as 683 aircraft. American losses were significant – with over 7,000 dead, 7,800 wounded and twenty-nine ships lost – but the tide had turned.

Most importantly, the US was able to replace its losses of both men and materiel at almost twice the rate of Japan. In simple terms, as Yamamoto predicted, if the Americans' will to win remained resolute, Japan was, from mid-1942 onwards, fighting a losing battle. It took three major land battles, seven large naval battles, five night-time surface actions and two carrier battles, plus almost daily aerial battles, before Japan abandoned its efforts to retake Guadalcanal and evacuated its forces on 7 February 1943. From then on, the Allies went on the offensive and seized the strategic initiative in the Pacific.

One of the Japanese pilots in the dogfights over Guadalcanal was Zero ace Saburō Sakai, who ended the war with sixty-four kills. Like his fellow soldiers, sailors and airmen, he was disciplined mercilessly in training, which began when he was sixteen: *'Petty officers would not hesitate to administer the severest beatings to recruits they felt deserving of punishment. Whenever I committed a breach of discipline or an error in training, I was dragged physically from my cot by a petty officer. "Stand tall to the wall! Bend down, Recruit Sakai!" he would roar. "I am not doing this because I hate you, but because I like you and want you to make a good seaman. Bend down!" And with that he would swing a large stick of wood and with every ounce of strength he possessed would slam it against my upturned bottom. The pain was terrible, the force of the blows unremitting. There was no choice but to grit my teeth and struggle desperately not to cry out. At times I counted up to forty crashing impacts into my buttocks. Often I fainted from the pain. A lapse into unconsciousness constituted no escape, however. The petty officer simply hurled a bucket of cold water over my prostrate form and bellowed for me to resume position, whereupon he continued his "discipline" until satisfied I would mend the error of my ways.'*

After the war, Sakai became a Buddhist and vowed never to kill another living thing, even an insect. Nevertheless, his previous discipline was unrelenting: *'Had I been ordered to bomb Seattle or Los Angeles in order to end the war, I wouldn't have hesitated. So I perfectly understand why the Americans bombed Nagasaki and Hiroshima.'*

Throughout the gruesome attritional battles for Guadalcanal – what the defenders called the 'Island of Death' – Hirohito continued to press his high command to defend territory, or to retake lost ground. In doing so, he not only pressured the more realistic of his generals not to accept the inevitable defeat, but also added to the prolonged suffering of his loyal forces on the ground.

Hirohito intervened again on the Guadalcanal front after the Imperial Army launched another unsuccessful offensive there on 23–24 October. This was followed a few days later by a second major sea battle in which the Imperial Navy engaged the American fleet, sinking the aircraft carrier *Hornet* and a destroyer. The diary entry of Matome Ugaki, Vice Admiral and Chief of Staff of the Combined Fleet, for 29 October recounts that Hirohito issued an imperial rescript addressed to Combined Fleet Commander Isoroku Yamamoto, which said, *'We are deeply pleased that this time in the South Pacific the Combined Fleet has inflicted great damage on the enemy fleet. However, we believe the war situation is critical. Officers and men, exert yourselves to even greater efforts.'*

Ugaki went on to write that a separate radio message came to him later that evening saying that after the emperor had handed

Nagano the rescript intended for Admiral Yamamoto, his majesty had cautioned him, '*What I want to tell you now concerns the latter part of my rescript. Guadalcanal is the focal point of the war and an important base for the navy. So don't rest on small achievements. Move quickly and recapture it.*'

When the emperor's rescript and verbal warning to Nagano were radioed to the Combined Fleet Headquarters on Rabaul, Ugaki immediately replied, '*We are dismayed by the concern our failures on Guadalcanal have caused the emperor. Only the quickest possible achievement of our goals can excuse us before his majesty.*' The navy was unable to improve on its 'small achievements', and within two weeks it lost the battleships *Hiei* and *Kirishima* to an American battle group in the third great engagement in the Solomons.

Throughout the bitterly fought ground and sea battles for Guadalcanal, the emperor put constant psychological pressure on his naval commanders to recapture the island, and on three different occasions he pressed the army high command to throw in more troops and planes to assist the hard-pressed navy. At first General Hajime Sugiyama was reluctant, partly because army pilots were inexperienced, but also because he planned to reinforce the army in China. However, the emperor's persistence forced his senior generals to relent. After his second request for army air force participation on the Solomons front, Sugiyama reported to Hirohito the next day that the army had decided to deploy its air power to New Guinea and Rabaul. This change in an ongoing operation had been opposed by both upper- and middle-echelon officers. Hirohito, nevertheless, forced the change.

Despite the fact that his men on the ground were dying from famine and disease, even as late as December 1942, Hirohito demanded of his general staff, '*What I want to know is how they propose to force the enemy to submit. The situation is very grave indeed. I believe we should now convene an imperial conference in my presence, and it makes no difference whether we hold it at the end of this year or the start of next. I am ready to participate at any time.*'

The situation on the island was unbearable. A communiqué dated 23 December, sent from Lieutenant General Harukichi

Hyakutake, the commander of the Japanese Seventeenth Army on Guadalcanal, seemed to tip the balance in Tokyo: '*No food is available and we can no longer send out scouts. We can do nothing to withstand the enemy's offensive. Seventeenth Army now requests permission to break into the enemy's positions and die an honourable death rather than die of hunger in our own dugouts.*'

While Tokyo pondered, Hyakutake's men had developed a survival formula.

'*He who can rise to his feet – 30 days left to live.*

'*He who can sit up – 20 days left to live.*

'*He who must urinate while lying down – 3 days left to live.*

'*He who cannot speak – 2 days left to live.*

'*He who cannot blink his eyes – dead at dawn.*'

When the imperial conference was held on New Year's Eve and the generals asked for permission to withdraw from Guadalcanal at the end of January, it took four days for a decision to be made. Eventually Hirohito agreed, but insisted, '*It is unacceptable to just give up on capturing Guadalcanal. We must launch an offensive elsewhere.*' As had been the case for several years, Hirohito's words were not those of a benign emperor, concerned with the welfare of his armed forces or of his people, but rather the words of a warrior leader intent on prosecuting an increasingly bloody war.

Hirohito continued to pressure his commanders. When the 2,500-man garrison on Attu Island in the Aleutians was destroyed at the cost of all but twenty-eight men of the entire garrison, he wrote on 29 May: '*No matter how good an agreement between the army and the navy may be, if it isn't carried out, that's worse than no promise at all. The way we're waging war now raises the enemy's morale and we're causing China to puff its chest up. Isn't there some way, some place, where we can win a real victory over the Americans?*'

In the same month the *Asahi Shimbun* ran a competition to write a song to honour the 'glorious defeat', entitled 'The Bloody Battle Heroes of Attu' who, it was claimed, had killed 6,000 American attackers. Not only did the song falsify the story, but it asked its readers to sacrifice themselves, 'for the Glory of the Emperor's Army', so that 'Virtue may Endure Forever'.

Two days after the disaster on Attu, journalist Kiyoshi Kiyosawa questioned the wisdom of 'heroic' sacrifice: *'Yesterday there was a report that the entire Japanese Army on Attu died with honour. It was a public announcement by the Imperial Headquarters at 5:00 p.m. When one looked at this morning's newspapers it was stated that at the end around 150 or 160 survived; the wounded killed themselves, and those still able fought savagely and died [. . .] Why were they left isolated and helpless just as they were, without any prior or later assistance in this regard? For an army renowned throughout the world for its incomparable courage, is not this total destruction a defeat in terms of strategy?'*

Sei Ito, a translator of English literature, was among many shocked by the defeat: *'Our forces on Attu have been wiped out. The 2,000 and some hundreds more of our men were surrounded by 20,000 of the enemy and in the end were destroyed. On the night of the 29th, the wounded and ill committed suicide. More than a hundred of the survivors made a final charge under the command of Colonel Yamazaki Yasuyo and perished [. . .] I don't know of any more tragic event. What can one say? It has finally come to this. The war has at last shown its true face nakedly. I feel as if I have just wakened from sleep.'*

Twenty-three-year-old Tokuro Nakamura was mobilised in October 1942. By May 1943, he was totally disillusioned: *'We Japanese are often like the frog who contemplates the universe from the bottom of a well. We must see further and reflect on the things of which we could really be proud. I am sick of this unflagging self-adulation. We must set aside all boastfulness which is so meaningless. It is only by great efforts that we will acquire true capability. Will we never cease to think of Japan as invincible? If we were to study history a little more closely, we could not indulge in these complacent dreams, and we would get rid of our childish vanity. Nothing is more dangerous than this kind of dream. A vainglorious nation is never a prosperous nation.'*

By August, Hirohito had become increasingly frustrated with his army chief of staff. A telling exchange between Sugiyama and the emperor took place on 11 September, during which Hirohito spoke not as a divine leader to whom God had entrusted the welfare of his subjects, but as a commander-in-chief. He interrogated his chief of staff regarding arrangements for shipping supplies to Rabaul and western Papua New Guinea, which was vital to the navy. On the question of logistics and transport, and despite Sugiyama's reassurances, the emperor insisted: '*I'm not going to tolerate another, "Our men fought bravely, then died of starvation.*"'

As in all other incidents of bad news, the disaster of Guadalcanal was hidden from the Japanese people but some of the survivors brought their memories home with them. Kashichi Yoshida was a non-commissioned officer who survived the battle and wrote a collection of *Poems from the Battle of Guadalcanal*. In it he describes the events of 31 December 1942, the same day as Hirohito's imperial conference. He begins with a telling observation: '*No matter how far we walk / We don't know where we're going.*' Then he talks of the horrors of Guadalcanal, of '*eating roots and grass*' and of having '*no cloth to bind our wounds*' and describes how he often thought of suicide.

The word *gyokusai* (describing suicidal loyalty as a 'shattered jewel'), from the song 'Bloody Battle Heroes of Attu', was perfect for propaganda purposes. In February 1944, Hideki Tōjō used it in his call to the nation for '100 million shattered jewels'. However, Japan's population was only seventy-three million at the time, so to muster 100 million it would have needed to enlist 30 million subjects from its empire. Although his arithmetic was wayward, his message was clear: the emperor required his people to fight to the death to protect their homeland.

When they went to the battlefield, a significant proportion of his people did fight to the death. However, more than a few of his devoted followers took their devotion to extreme limits. Ken Yuasa was a junior army doctor: '*In late 1942, at the time of the battle for Guadalcanal, I asked the doctor who was about to administer a lumbar anaesthesia if he wasn't going to disinfect the point of injection. "What are you talking about? We're going to kill him." After a while, a nurse struck the man's legs and asked him if it hurt. He said it didn't, but when they tried to get him to inhale chloroform, he began to struggle. We all had to hold him down. First, there was practice in removing an appendix. That was carried out by two doctors. When a man has appendicitis, his appendix swells and grows very hard. But there was nothing wrong with this man, so it was hard to locate. Next a doctor removed one of his arms. You must know how to do this when a man has shrapnel imbedded in his arm. You have to apply a tourniquet, to stanch the flow of blood. Then two doctors practised sewing the intestines. If the intestine or stomach is pierced by bullets that kind of surgery is a necessity.'*

After the end of the war, further stories emerged of Japanese medical experiments which used human vivisection, with and without anaesthesia, to find ways of testing human capacities and in the training of doctors in battlefield surgical techniques. The victims were either captured military personnel or civilians.

American success on Guadalcanal coincided with the Wehrmacht's surrender to the Red Army after the horrors of the Battle of Stalingrad. There were similarities between events on the two fronts, both strategically and psychologically. Both the German army and Japan's Imperial Army would fight on for many months, but their defeats at the beginning of 1943 were watersheds in the war from which there was no real recovery for either of the Axis powers.

8

A 'TRULY GRAVE' SITUATION

By March 1943, Japan's Holy War was beginning to create consequences that did not seem possible just twelve months earlier. Among both the military and civilians, the exigencies of warfare were beginning to bite, and bite hard.

Hiroko Nakamoto recorded that, *'Everywhere the war brought great changes. Soldiers came in train loads, shiploads. They filled the city. From our Ujina Harbour, soldiers were packed into boats and headed for combat against the Americans in the South Pacific. The city was full of soldiers. Some of the young officers were cruel. Often, we saw elderly private soldiers made to stand stiffly at attention to be preached at. Sometimes we saw them slapped by young soldiers of higher rank because the older men had not saluted them quickly enough.'*

The shortages that had begun with the invasion of China were beginning to be severe: *'Meantime, there was less and less food for us civilians. We had no meat, no vegetables, no fruits, no fowl, no fish. These foods were sent to the armed forces. People were near starvation. We were hungry all the time. At the factory, on the night shift, after standing for hours, we were marched into a dining hall where we had our supper. It was a bowl of weak, hot broth, usually with one string of noodle in it and a few soybeans at the bottom. We would gulp it down, then go back to the factory. It was very cold there. Because of the war there was no fuel available. Finally, a few empty oil cans were brought in, and small pieces of charcoal were burned in them. Seeing the glow of the little pieces of charcoal, smelling the smoke, we felt warmer. At nine o'clock at night each of us was given a little cake made out of weeds. But the taste of the cakes was so terrible that hungry though we were, we could not eat them. We would take them over to the oil cans and burn them on the charcoal and then eat them. That way we tasted a burned taste, which was better than the weed taste.'*

These witness accounts were written in the spring of 1943. There would be two more years of agonising deprivation to endure, towards the end of which would be added the utter devastation of firestorms and atomic weapons.

•

The Battle of the Bismarck Sea had begun on 2 March, when aircraft of the US Fifth Air Force, supported by the Royal Australian Air Force, attacked a Japanese convoy transporting troops to Lae in New Guinea. The Bismarck Sea sits southeast of the Bismarck Archipelago, north of East and West New Britain and east of Papua New Guinea. The day before, US reconnaissance planes had spotted sixteen Japanese ships en route to Lae and Salamaua in New Guinea. The Japanese were trying to hold on to the island with 7,000 reinforcements, supplies of aircraft fuel and food and other provisions. A three-day bombing campaign ensued, which destroyed eight Japanese troop transports and four Japanese destroyers. More than 3,000 Japanese troops and sailors died, and the supplies sank with the ships. Of 150 Japanese planes that attempted to engage with the American bombers, 102 were shot down. Among the losses was transport ship *Kyokusei Maru*, with the loss of 700 of the 1,500 men on board.

It was another demoralising defeat for Japan. Of the 6,900 troops bound for New Guinea, only about 1,200 made it to Lae. Masatake Okumiya, a senior staff officer, assessed the damage: *'Our losses for this single battle were fantastic. Not during the entire savage fighting on Guadalcanal did we suffer a comparable blow.'* Abandoning their effort to stop Allied offensives in New Guinea, Japan made no further attempts to reinforce Lae.

•

The diary of probational officer Toshihiro Ōura offers a vivid picture of the fate of hundreds of thousands of ordinary Japanese soldiers stranded in far-flung outposts of Asia and the Pacific. As food, weapons and ammunition began to become scarce, they were left with little except their honour and their duty to die for their emperor. Ōura kept a diary for just twenty-five days. His entries begin on 29 June, in an optimistic tone.

'*I wonder if they will come today. I have become used to combat, and I have no fear. In yesterday's raid our air force suffered no losses, while nine enemy planes were confirmed as having been shot down and three others doubtful. Battle gains are positively in favour of our victory.*'

Writing the following day, his belief in the invincibility of the Imperial Japanese Army remains firm.

'*At last, the final decisive battle has come. [. . .] At 4:10 this morning rain clouds hovered over us. At Rendova, four cruisers, two destroyers, two transports, and countless boats appeared. At 8 a.m. our planes finally came. About 20 planes kept watch from the sky at all times. At 2 p.m., some planes came from the west [. . .] 30 medium attack planes are sure a sight. We are moved to tears and wave our hands, saying, "We're counting on you; we're counting on you."*'

Under bombardment from US naval gunfire on 2 July, Ōura admitted to being scared for the first time and by 4 July, the conditions they were enduring meant that he and his fellow men were suffering from acute diarrhoea. Four days later, Ōura had the comfort of a letter from home.

'*Last evening, I received my first and possibly last mail from home. It appeared that they haven't received my letters yet and are somewhat doubtful as to whether I'm still alive or not. They learned that I was on New Georgia. They will really worry if the news of the enemy landing on New Georgia is announced in the newspapers. Father repeated in his letter that I must fight to the last as an honourable warrior. I will fight to the last, always for the emperor. I will show them that we will fight to the last.*'

The shelling increased as the days passed and, by 13 July, Ōura's position was increasingly precarious.

'*Sergeant Takagi died last night in the naval shelling. The dead already amounted to 6 to 7 men. Lance Corporal Ito and four men, who were handling rations, are missing. 2nd Lt. Imura was killed and a total of four wounded today. This morning's shelling was a shelling of all shell-*

*ings. [. . .] Shells are hitting close by right now, so we can't go outside.
[. . .] No one back home would ever think that we are living in a crater.'*

By 22 July, Ōura's ordeal was coming to its inevitable conclusion.

*'If I am to die, there is nothing I can do about it, so I just lay in my
dugout, smoking a cigarette and listening to the wild American-made
music of "rat-tat-tat" and "boom-boom-boom". Just think: I haven't
washed my body or my face nor have I brushed my teeth for a month
already. One of my upper front teeth has been broken off. My body smells
like that of a wild dog. Only by staying in the dugout can I say that I'm
still alive. Friendly forces! Please come to our aid! Show them the might
of the Japanese army.'*

Ōura made his final diary entry on 23 July.

*'Battle Situation: Nothing aside from annihilation. No cooperation
from the navy. Our mountain artillery positions were knocked to pieces
by enemy tanks. We are encircled, so they say, and about to be overrun?
We are positively fighting to win, but we have no weapons. We stand with
rifles and bayonets to meet the enemy's aircraft, battleships, and medium
artillery. To be told we must win is absolutely beyond reason. [. . .] If I
die, it will be a hateful death. How regretful!'*

Ōura's fate is unknown. His diary was found on the battlefield,
but not his body. Given the small number of prisoners taken and
the handful of Japanese who escaped from New Georgia, it is
unlikely that he survived. A week after Ōura's final entry, Japanese
forces withdrew to Kolombangara and other islands. US forces
continued their advance, and the airfield at Munda Point – a major
Allied objective – fell on 5 August 1943.

Admiral Yamamoto had always wanted the Solomons to be
a killing ground, where the terrain, heat and jungle would cost
American lives in large numbers. The attritional nature of their
losses would demonstrate the enormous price in terms of both men
and materiel they were going to have to pay to regain every inch of
Japanese territory, which in turn would persuade them to negotiate
a peace deal on grounds favourable to Japan. The plan seemed to
be working. It had taken the Americans far longer than planned
to take New Georgia; a far superior Allied force had found it very

difficult to overcome a much smaller Japanese force of men lacking food, heavy artillery and reinforcements.

However, for the Japanese defenders, the situation was dire, with only discipline holding them together. First Lieutenant Toshiro Kuroki described the conditions they faced.

'We have an army, a division and an area army, with a commander-in-chief, a divisional commander, a chief of staff, a director of intelligence and what have you, but in the front line we have to contend with a rotten supply situation and live a dog's life on potatoes. You will not find many smiling faces among the men in the ranks in New Guinea. They are always hungry; every other word has something to do with eating. At the sight of potatoes their eyes gleam and their mouths water. The divisional commander and the staff officers do not seem to realise that the only way the men can drag out their lives from day to day is by this endless hunt for potatoes. How can they complain about slackness and expect miracles when most of our effort goes into looking for something to eat!'

On 30 September 1943, the Imperial General Headquarters in Tokyo endorsed a plan to reduce Japan's defence perimeter. The new perimeter went from Burma through Dutch New Guinea, the Caroline Islands and, finally, to the Marshall Islands. Although it made strategic sense to consolidate conquests and to shorten supply lines, it was ruthless in the extreme. It meant the abandonment of 300,000 Japanese troops outside of the perimeter – from where evacuation was out of the question because of superior Allied air and naval power – leaving the men to fend for themselves. A total of 120,000 Japanese were based in eastern New Guinea, many of whom were running out of food and supplies. Many more were isolated on smaller islands and in remote garrisons throughout the southern Pacific. Apart from fending for themselves, they were all expected to continue to resist the enemy and to fight to the last when the time came.

Atsushi Tsutsui was stationed on East New Britain on New Guinea. He wrote to his wife, Taiko, on 30 September 1943.

'As soon as we arrived at our destination, Rabaul, we found out that we were heading for New Guinea. Right now, it is the most important area in the war and where the hardest fighting is going on. Additionally,

and before they even get there, our forces are decimated by the horrendous combined might of the enemy submarine fleet and their air power. The enemy makes bombing runs here too all the time. We will be leaving shortly. I feel certain that my life will not be spared much longer, and I have readied myself psychologically for that eventuality. I hope that you will prepare yourself for it too, just so you will be able to conduct yourself in the best possible way at that worst possible time. Everyone here, with tragic and heroic hearts, seems to be glaring in the direction of the faraway skies over America and Britain. Now that the situation has reached this point I have, as I said, summoned up a certain resolution and readiness for the worst, but still, when I think of it, I feel as though there were many things that I should have taken better care of.'

Tsutsui was reported missing in action in February 1944.

A journalist writing about the tragic fate of Japan's abandoned troops criticised the use of the expression 'lost troops', by a fellow journalist: *'The words flashed into my mind and stuck there. Faced with unexpected, grave developments in the situation, the Imperial Headquarters had no longer any time to think of the troops they had sent out to New Guinea. Poor fellows [. . .] [They were] mostly non-career officers and men who had been called to the colours from among common people engaged in peaceful occupations. Were they not children of Japan just as any Japanese was?'*

One of the most critical outcomes of the Battle of the Bismarck Sea was the depletion of Japan's air power. In 1940, the US was producing 3,500 aircraft per annum. In 1943, it made 53,183. In fact, by the end of the war, Japan had produced 85,600 aircraft, but the US had made well over 300,000. Not only that, Japan soon diminished its pool of experienced pilots and was unable to replace the missing expertise as quickly as the Americans could.

First Lieutenant Uchimura of the 41st Division wrote in his diary: *'In air superiority [. . .] we are about a century behind America [. . .] This present war is termed a war of supply. Shipping is the secret to victory or defeat in this war of supply in countries thousands of miles across the sea [. . .] To have regular shipping lanes, air superiority is essential. Ah, if only we had air superiority [. . .] If only we had planes.'*

Uchimura had highlighted a crucial point that Admiral Yamamoto, with his detailed knowledge of the United States and its resources, had known since the start of the Pacific War. In 1941, Japan's chosen enemy had a population of over 130 million, whereas Japan had only 73 million. Its Gross Domestic Product was $192 billion, unlike that of its giant foe, whose GDP was $943 billion. One does not need to be a macro economist to appreciate the implications of those huge disparities. For example, the US Naval Construction Battalions (Seabees) and the US Army Engineer Battalions, collectively employing over 325,000 tractor drivers, carpenters, masons, dynamiters, electricians, shopfitters and machinists, were able to effectively transfer US combat power 5,000 miles across the Pacific. For the first time in modern warfare, logistical elements arrived with or immediately behind the assault troops, thus guaranteeing a ready supply of firepower, ammunition and food. Bulldozers could follow a successful US forces' attack within forty minutes, to begin airstrip construction and defences that would be usable within hours.

When Japan attacked Pearl Harbor at the end of 1941, it had grabbed a tiger by its tail and shaken it violently. The tiger was surprised and ran off into the undergrowth, where it lay quietly for a while, its pride hurt. But after a while, the tiger emerged in search of its aggressor. It wanted revenge and to punish its attacker. By the end of 1943, the tiger's day of reckoning was getting ever closer.

9

BURMA: A PORTENT OF THINGS TO COME

The Campaign in Burma, in the far west of Japan's new empire, was a unique conflict within the Asia-Pacific War. Fought in monsoon conditions and often in mountainous terrain, it was notable for the length of the conflict (almost four years), its long periods of stalemate, and the use of guerrilla tactics. The lack of useable roads meant that supply by air was critical and that the Japanese, in particular, had to live off the land. Japan's adversaries were predominantly British, Commonwealth, Chinese and Indian forces. The losses in the Burma Campaign were at least 200,000 Allied personnel and a similar number of Japanese and its Thai and other allies. There were also at least half a million Burmese civilian casualties.

For the Japanese frontline troops, Burma became a sorry tale. The initial euphoria of victory and conquest soon became a bitter war of attrition, during which their resources and morale were slowly strangled. Corporal Buhachiro Nakai of the 55th Mountain Gun Regiment, 55th Division, was advancing to Tavoy in southern Burma. As the Japanese advanced, huge numbers of people moved westwards to escape, provoking one of the biggest mass migrations in history to that point. Even in the early days of stunning victories, Nakai soon had a taste of what was to come: *'We took small boats going up the River Keonoi and arrived at a small village near the Burma-Thailand border on 7 January 1942. Here we were told to send back to the rear all spare materials and unnecessary personal belongings [...] it was thought important to carry as much ammunition as possible, so the amount of food we could bring with us was limited.'*

The harsh reality of war soon hit home for Nakai, just a farm boy from Kofu, Honshu: *'The forced march through the jungle was very, very hard. I tried my best to keep up with the group [...] there was not any road, just a narrow animal track. We could make only 2 or 3 kilometres per day, and ran out of rice on the eighth day. Finally it was decided to eat one of the oxen carrying ammunition [. . .] Its meat was too tough and after two meals my gums were swollen and ached, so I could take only beef soup.'*

The Japanese advance was relentless during January and February. They attacked over the Kawkeriek Pass and captured the port of Moulmein, then advanced northwards, outflanking successive British defensive positions. Burma's capital, Rangoon, could not be defended, and the city was evacuated on 7 March, after its port and oil refinery had been destroyed.

Lance Corporal Koji Kawamata was with 3rd Company, 1st Battalion, 214 Infantry Regiment, 33 Division, as it approached Rangoon: *'Every day we walked from sunset until dawn. During the daytime we slept in the dense forest, which was still dark and also humid, as little air circulated and mosquitoes assailed us. At sunset on 7th March, we were ordered to go on an even worse forced march. [. . .] Almost everybody in the platoon had developed blisters. The forced march was the hardest I had ever experienced. Late in the night we heard the sound of heavy firing close on our left, but our company continued the forced march without a halt. At last we entered the city of Rangoon. It was 8.50 in the morning of 8th March 1942. We could not see a single enemy soldier. We had expected to fight in the streets.'*

Lance Corporal Masakichi Kanbayashi was also part of the 33rd Division, in 7th Company, 2nd Battalion, 215 Infantry Regiment. He was also there when Rangoon fell and clearly enjoyed one of those interludes that soldiers on the battlefield yearn for.

'We marched a long way from Thailand and on 8th March 1942 raced into Rangoon, which had just been deserted by the British army. We stayed in a school building near Lake Victoria in the suburbs of Rangoon. We had a completely free time for about ten days: no duty, no sentry assignments and no service work. A paradise for soldiers, the first I enjoyed in my military life. We had canned food, coffee, cocoa, milk, butter, cheese, corned beef, jam, cigarettes. [. . .] We had parties every night and sang cheerfully, danced, ate and drank enough. We really enjoyed

ourselves. We lacked fresh vegetables so when fried leech was served it tasted good. A comrade made tasty doughnuts.'

His ten days in heaven over, Kanbayashi's soldiering duties resumed. He and his colleagues were greeted as liberators from colonial rule, a mood that would continue until the harsh realities of the Japanese presence emerged: *'After a very relaxing ten days we were told to advance north to chase the retreating British. We crossed the great Irrawaddy River by small boats and arrived at Henzada, where we stayed for a few days. Burmese people who lived along the road welcomed us enthusiastically day and night as we passed. They cried "Dopahma! (Hurrah for the independence of Burma)" and offered us fruits and water continually; their hearty reception impressed us greatly.'*

Further east, motorised troops of the Japanese 56th Division almost destroyed the Chinese 6th Army and advanced northward through the Shan States, outflanking the Allied defensive lines and cutting off the Chinese armies from Yunnan. With the effective collapse of the entire defensive line, there was little choice for the Allies other than an overland retreat to India. A period of relative stalemate followed during much of the rest of 1942 and 1943. Japanese priorities lay elsewhere, and chaos and famine in Northeast India meant that reorganisation and logistics were severely hampered.

A period of military stalemate did not mean a respite of peace and calm. Tokuhei Miura had been called up in the spring of 1940 and joined the Kokura 114th Regiment where he was assigned to the 7th Company of the regiment's 3rd Battalion. He had fought in Malaya and Singapore, was stationed in Northern Burma and had begun to learn the Burmese language. After a successful Allied attack on Miura's unit, in which several of his comrades were killed, his commanding officer, insisting that the local Burmese must have helped the Allies, ordered Miura to round up the local villagers, including the children. He offered them a jar of rice and a can of salt.

Suffering from a shortage of food, the villagers, twenty-seven of them, gathered with smiles on their faces. The unit first pulled out five people and shot them. One man fled but they fired on him, killing him. Then they threw a hand grenade at them and shot the two or three people who managed briefly to escape. Miura was stunned. He had not realised that he was rounding up the inhabitants for mass murder. He had participated in the execution of prisoners before, but this was the first time he was complicit in the killing of local inhabitants with no hostile intentions.

'*It was too much; I got goose bumps over my entire body. Up to now we'd cut off POW's heads, blown enemies to bits with hand grenades, put bayonets through the chests of enemy soldiers begging for mercy. But these were all things that happened in the confusion of battle [. . .] Because if you didn't, you'd lose your own life. But this time is different. It goes against everything. Now we would see people killed who have no hostility and harbour no hatred, who've committed no crime. Yet now that things have come to this there's no way to stop it [. . .] An indescribable feeling pounded in my chest.*'

Beginning in December 1943, the strategic balance in the Burma campaign shifted decisively. Improvements in Allied leadership, training and logistics, together with greater firepower and growing air superiority, gave them a significant strategic advantage. Training, equipment, health and morale of Allied troops under Lieutenant General William 'Bill' Slim was improving, as was the extensive use of aircraft to transport and supply troops. Slim was a soldier's soldier, much loved and one of Britain's forgotten military heroes.

While the Allies reorganised, the Japanese created the Burma Area Army under Lieutenant General Masaka Kawabe who took command of the 15th Army and the newly formed 28th Army. The new commander of 15th Army, Lieutenant General Renya Mataguchi, was determined to launch an invasion of India. Mutaguchi, who had been one of the successful commanders in the Malaya Campaign, was a highly political commander with strong links to Tokyo's ultranationalists.

'*I started off the Marco Polo Bridge Incident, which broadened into the China Incident, and then expanded until it turned into the Great East Asia War. If I push into India now, by my own efforts, and can exercise a decisive influence on the Great East Asia War, I, who was the cause of the outbreak of the war, will have justified myself in the eyes of the nation.*'

Although full of risks because of the terrain and the length of the supply lines, Imperial General Headquarters approved Mutaguchi's idea, 'Operation U-go'. Mutaguchi was the polar opposite of Slim. Called a 'reckless fanatic' by historians, he provided his soldiers with only twenty days of food for the invasion. Captain Shosaku Kameyama, 3rd Battalion, 58th Infantry Regiment, 31st Division, took part in the invasion.

'We were told Operation U-go was a necessity for the defence of Burma [. . .] This was the first time we had fought with the British-Indian forces, which was very different from our experience of fighting the Chinese army who had inferior weapons to ours. Our battalion commander ordered an attack during the coming night. From our experience in China, we were confident of the success of the night attack, but a mass of bullets from the overwhelming enemy automatic weapons resulted in great casualties. Under a strong counter-attack the commander and most soldiers were killed or wounded. Though we wanted to advance we could not even lift our heads because of the heavy fire which we had never before experienced.'

Like his comrades before him, Kameyama had discovered that the experience of defeat in battle is very different from the experience of victory.

'The rule of the battlefield is "If you do not kill the enemy, you will be killed." This is why war is a vice. It is war that forces us to do the killing. In the war my comrades were killed in rapid succession, and I may happen to be killed next. Despite that we had to advance towards the enemy [. . .] It is the war which forces human beings into such a dreadful environment; an environment that turns human beings evil.'

Kameyama was soon experiencing the ignominy of retreat: *'Although we kept fighting it was very lonely and miserable [. . .] winning seemed too remote. We ran out of ammunition and food, so sometimes we went out to attack an enemy position at night, and when the enemy ran away after firing several rounds, we collected rations, bullets and grenades, and used them the next day. In this way we held out stoutly day by day, but inevitably someone got hurt or killed, so only a few, maximum seven to eight, men defended a position [. . .] Still, we did not give up and never thought of running away. In fact, our unit was not beaten off in the fighting, but by the decision of Lt General Kotoku Sato, Commander 31st Division, who ordered us to retreat from the Kohima hills on 13th May, and from the Aradura hills on 3rd June. We walked over the muddy mountains, drenched in rain, exhausted and hungry, and got back to our base on the River Chindwin in the latter part of July 1944.'*

The key battle of the Burma Campaign had taken place around Imphal and Kohima, beginning in March 1944. Operation U-Go – the invasion of India by a Japanese army 85,000 strong – was launched when it crossed the Burmese border at the Chindwin River on 8 March and poured into India. By April, the Japanese had reached Imphal, where the Allies' 14th Army – a mix of British, Indian and East and West African men – made its stand. The Japanese quickly surrounded the defenders but, thanks to being supplied by air, the Allied defenders held their ground. The fighting was brutal, and it became a vicious fight for survival.

Sixty miles north of Imphal, at the highest point of the pass through the impenetrable mountain jungles to Dimapur, a small Allied garrison held the town of Kohima. If Kohima fell, Dimapur would follow, and the vital airborne supplies for the defenders of Imphal would cease. On 3 April, a Japanese force of 15,000 attacked Kohima. Of the 2,500-strong garrison at Kohima, only half were combat troops. After two weeks of constant bitter fighting, the garrison held only 400 square yards. Few Allied men were not wounded, many were all but starving, and water supplies were exhausted.

At dawn on 18 April, with the Japanese in their trenches about to make a last charge, the exhausted Kohima garrison was about to fall. At that moment shells began falling on the Japanese positions, and the tanks of a relieving force could be seen arriving. The garrison was saved, and Kohima was secured. The Japanese, however, fought on, trying to hold the many ridges and hills surrounding Kohima. But four weeks later, in mid-May, the starving Japanese men were finally forced to withdraw.

With the road to Dimapur secured, on 22 June the defenders of Imphal linked up with reinforcements advancing from Kohima. Under constant air attack, and with their supply lines mercilessly assaulted by Chindit forces and air strikes, the last Japanese attacks at Imphal launched in late June had no success. On 3 July, after nearly five months of fighting, the surviving Japanese forces fell back. More than 8,000 Allied servicemen were wounded, killed or missing, but of the 85,000-strong Japanese force that had crossed the Chindwin River in March, less than a third returned. The battles had been fierce, but it was starvation and disease that had caused most of the Japanese losses. It was by far the worst Japanese land defeat of the war to that point.

The invasion and its key battles at Imphal and Kohima proved a catastrophe for the Japanese Army. Lieutenant General Hikosaburo Hata of the General Staff had made a tour of inspection of Southern Army's headquarters in late April. When he returned to Tokyo, he reported pessimistically on the outcome of the operation at a large staff meeting in front of Prime Minister Hideki Tōjō. Hata's concerns were dismissed, and Imperial Headquarters sent messages urging that the operation be fought to the end.

Lieutenant General Kawabe had travelled north from Rangoon to see the situation for himself on 25 May. Several officers remained confident of success but concealed the seriousness of the situation. At a meeting between Mutaguchi and Kawabe on 6 June, because neither of them wanted the responsibility of ordering a retreat, both used *haragei* (literally, 'stomach language'), an unspoken form of communication using gesture, expression and tone of voice, to express their view that success was impossible. Although Kawabe became ill with dysentery, he nevertheless ordered more attacks, and Mutaguchi instructed the 31st Division, which had retreated from Kohima when facing starvation, to join the 15th Division in a renewed attack on Imphal from the north. Being in no condition to obey, neither division carried out the order. When he realised that none of his orders were being obeyed, Mutaguchi finally ordered the offensive to be broken off on 3 July.

Reduced in many cases to a rabble of broken men, the Japanese fell back to the Chindwin River, abandoning their artillery transport, and leaving behind many soldiers too badly wounded or sick to walk. The Allies recovered Tamu at the end of July and found 550 unburied Japanese corpses, with over 100 more severely wounded soldiers slowly dying amongst them.

Senior Private Manabu Wada, Transport Section, 3rd Battalion, 138th Infantry Regiment, 31st Division had been part of Japan's invasion and then its humiliating retreat. His regiment had been tasked with spearheading the rapid advance across the rugged Arakan Mountains to attack British and Indian forces, and capture Kohima.

'Conditions were hard, well-nigh impossible. Our cattle and horses fell down the mountainside, taking our provisions with them; the slopes were so steep we couldn't go down to retrieve anything, but at last we reached the summit and could see, to the west beyond the boundless sea of clouds, Tibet and the Himalayas. After many days of bitter fighting we captured ridges north of Kohima but 138th Regiment had no rations left. By 5th April our rations were exhausted.'

What had started so well for Wada, had become the soldiers' nightmare of no food and no ammunition. Defeat was only a matter of time.

'The enemy's heavy and medium artillery opened up on us as a prelude to their infantry attacks. For our part, we were limited to reply with just a few shells each day, while the British shells rained down on us in hundreds and thousands in great barrages. In this storm of fire, we had to run to seek shelter and could barely hold Kohima. It is not possible to express our terror as shrapnel burst upon us with tremendous force so that officers and men were cut to pieces by jagged splinters that tore into the head, the abdomen, arms, legs. We watched as enemy reinforcements arrived by truck with more and more arms and ammunition to be thrown immediately against us. [. . .] Our soldiers fought bravely, but they had no rations, no rifle or machine-gun ammunition, no artillery shells for the guns to fire. And, above all, they had no support from rear echelons [. . .] We felt we had arrived at the very limit of our endurance.'

Inevitably, Wada's regiment suffered terrible casualties: *'At the beginning of the Imphal Operation the regiment was 3,800 strong. When our general gave the order to withdraw to the east we were reduced to just a few hundred still alive. Without shelter from the rains, with boots that had rotted and had to be bound with grass, we began to trudge along the deep mud paths carrying our rifles without ammunition, leaning on sticks to support our weak bodies. The bodies of our comrades who had struggled along the track before us lay all around, rain-sodden and giving off the stench of decomposition [. . .] we fell amongst the corpses again and again as we stumbled on rocks and tree roots made bare by the rain and attempted one more step, then one more step in our exhaustion.'*

Stationed in Burma, Kinpei Matsuoka, fearful about the consequences of Japan's adventure in Burma, wrote home long before the calamities at the end of the Burma Campaign: *'Older soldiers, and my own generation as well, are all getting killed or injured in the effort to build up Greater Asia and to ensure our own nation's peace and tranquillity. Someone has said that a war is easy when you are winning but becomes very difficult once it turns into a defensive struggle. Speaking out straightforwardly, I should ask the government whether or not this war, in which Japan is now engaged, is being fought with any probability of winning? Cannot it be that the government is forever fighting on with only an empty dream of victory? Can they tell us citizens with any degree of certainty that Japan will definitely win?'*

Nurse Hideko Nagai was part of the 490th Relief Squad (Wakayama) of the Japan Red Cross in Rangoon in 1944. She described her experiences: *'We disembarked at a station short of Rangoon at midnight on 20th February 1944. Our team and the Kumamoto team went to Rangoon Military Hospital [. . .] We worked busily at the hospital, but many of us were infected by dengue fever and had to rest with high temperatures, stomach pain and loss of appetite. [. . .] On 18th January 1945, we were transferred to 118th Base Hospital located at Paungde, a town on the River Irrawaddy [. . .] close to the battlefields. Everybody felt sad by the transfer, as we knew the miserable situation of the front lines from the conditions of patients carried into the hospital. The wounded were extremely undernourished, in poor spirits, just like living skeletons, and their uniforms were worn to shreds with sleeves hanging down. I was often shocked and wept secretly in sympathy with these new patients when they asked solemnly, "May I eat all of this?" as I put boiled rice in their mess kit.'*

Staff Sergeant Yasumasa Nishiji witnessed the horrors of Japan's harrowing retreat from Burma. He was one of a dozen healthy men selected to operate the boats ferrying soldiers across the Yu River during the heavy monsoon rainfall. The river crossing was followed by an arduous trek through muddy mountain passes: *'In increasing numbers our soldiers fell, physically emaciated and crippled, yet mentally alert [. . .] One soldier gave his money to his mates and, light-heartedly, told them to buy something to eat when they got away from the front. After a while, he crawled to the foot of a tree, holding a grenade. Without any sign of hesitation, he activated the grenade. In our position at the very rear of the retreating troops I saw many exhausted men unable to keep up with their units, and their comrades too weary to help them. [. . .] Almost all of them, tens of thousands, perished. We called the road the "Human Remains Highway". What happened here was beyond the bounds of acceptable human behaviour. It was a vision of hell.'*

In June 1944, Corporal Takashi Sakimoto was with the Communications Unit of the Miyazaki Detachment of the 31st Infantry Group when it was ordered to cover the withdrawal from Kohima. Just 700 men were asked to hold the road between Kohima and Imphal, a feat that an entire Japanese division had been unable to achieve. After six days of resistance, the few survivors of the Miyazaki Detachment pulled out and Sakimoto was put in charge of a group of stretcher-bearers. As a result, he and his team became isolated.

'Along the way, many soldiers fell by the wayside. The master sergeant distributed hand grenades to those who could not walk, ordering them to kill themselves. The road from Ukhrul to Fumine was strewn with countless bodies of those who had died of starvation. The soldiers came to call it "The Bleached Skeleton Highway". The entire bodies of soldiers who'd died of hunger or disease were draped in black by bluebottle flies, the countless eggs that came out of their rear ends turning instantly into maggots. You grew horrified at the sight of them crawling around, but you encountered them everywhere. As a result, the heads became like skulls in an instant, some of them with hair and beards still attached. Their limbs were covered only with leather, with each one of their bones visible. Their clothes were covered in mud – it was a completely hellish vision. Hundreds, thousands of soldiers were dying like this. If the dead had even the smallest thing that might be of use on them, be it an undershirt,

underpants, boots, it was stripped off. At one point I witnessed an officer pulling off boots.'

With the complete collapse of his offensive, Renya Mutaguchi was relieved of command on 30 August and recalled to Tokyo. The Imperial Japanese Army had descended from an all-conquering, unstoppable juggernaut into a pitiful shadow of its former self. The death toll was over 164,000 dead, with 56,000 wounded.

As in all wars where glorious conquest turns into humiliating defeat, Burma became one of Japan's most agonising memories. The pain subsided on the mainland, as it suffered its own traumas. But for the veterans who managed to return to their homes, as evidenced by the above accounts, the scars remained raw for the rest of their lives.

10

A FEROCIOUS DEFENCE

In 1943, with stalemate in China and 300,000 men stranded beyond its new defensive perimeter, Japan was facing the slow, lingering death of its empire and hundreds of thousands of its people. Its Holy War would soon be over. It was only a matter of time. How long that would take would depend on the adherence of its people to its long-held martial traditions. Central to those traditions was their divine emperor, Hirohito. Would he save his people from the death and destruction that awaited them or invoke the spirit of *bushidō* – the way of the samurai warrior – and fight to the death?

When, on 13 November 1943, US forces attacked the north-ernmost Gilbert Island, Makin Atoll, it was defended by 798 men. These comprised 284 troops of the 3rd Special Base Force, Makin Detachment, as well as 100 aviation personnel, 138 members of the 11th Construction Unit and 276 men of the 4th Fleet Construction Unit. They were all commanded by a very junior officer: Lieutenant, Junior Grade, Seizō Ishikawa. Most of the aviation and labour troops had no combat training and were not assigned weapons or a battle station. The number of actual combat troops to defend Makin numbered no more than 300 men. What became of Ishikawa is not known, except that he did not survive.

One of the defenders kept a diary which was found when the atoll was cleared two days later. The body of the diarist was never found and there was no name contained in the diary. Barely a handful of Japanese survived the attack, so it is highly likely his remains are still on the atoll, today a part of the island nation of Kiribati. Like so many of his stranded countrymen, the unknown diarist seemed to be resigned to his fate.

'*November 12th. We know we are going to die, so we have no fear of anybody, and everyone is high-spirited. Even though we are alive we figure we will only live about 2–3 days. All of us put the muzzle of the gun to our throats several times but, however, eventually we will die so why not just stick it out to the finish?*'

By 24 November, the majority of the Japanese had been captured and the Americans' Seabees were preparing a landing strip. However, hidden on the atoll, the diarist survived and remained uncaptured after the initial assault. For Japanese soldiers, being captured – or surrendering – was regarded as the greatest dishonour. Suicide, not surrender, was the honourable option in their martial tradition.

The diarist and his fellow defenders had few resources to withstand an American invasion force over 6,000 strong, supported by tanks, naval artillery and fighter planes. Small-arms sniper fire and machine-gun positions were the only weapons available to them. The Japanese snipers had stored rifles and gourds of sake in the fronds of palm trees. Significantly, one of them was a crack shot and killed the commander of the 165th Infantry Regiment, Colonel Gardiner J. Conroy, who was shot between the eyes while rallying his men.

'*November 26th. Paid respect to the place where the commander was killed* [presumably, Ishikawa]. *Got about twenty enemy hand grenades* [. . .] *waited for them all day but we did not see them* [. . .] *We can hear some gun fire from all directions and our morale goes up. Today we filled ourselves up for the first time on chocolate, beef, sugar, and bread which was left by the enemy* [. . .] *The whole day passed but we did not see friend or foe.*'

With the Americans sweeping the atoll with tanks and infantry, the diarist and others built rafts and canoes to travel from island to island to evade capture and wait for hoped-for reinforcements.

'*December 2nd. We are determined and plan to battle against the tanks if we do not see our forces come in by December 8th's anniversary of the beginning of the war* [. . .] *It seems that the Americans are giving a lot of false propaganda, that American forces have landed in the Marshalls and will soon invade Japan. They have told them* [the natives] *that 10,000 landed at Tarawa and also they told them that if Japanese soldiers come to the village to tell them to give up, don't make me laugh [. . .] We can die anytime.*

'*December 3rd. We are still in high spirits but there is little food left and we are determined to make it last until the 8th. We would like to stick it out until the end a little more and let our forces know the courage of the commander and subordinates. As our last hope we are waiting for the power of god [. . .] The place where a soldier dies is very important.*'

The diarist had joined men from another unit and, as they moved from island to island, they encountered American forces. One morning, after a breakfast of coconuts, the diarist, carrying a hand grenade, left to use the latrine. As he returned, he heard shots and several people shouting.

'*December 4th. Hurriedly I came back but it was too late [. . .] Atobe was left behind and shot off five rounds and reloaded another clip and tried to commit suicide, and I said, "Wait! There is more ammunition." [. . .] We opened a can of food and ate it and with rifles and ammunition we went out to the beach. At that time, Engineer Nakada was not quite dead and was suffering so we finished him off with one round, which shows our love for a comrade, that he will not be taken prisoner.*'

The Americans had declared the island secure by the end of November, but the resourcefulness and determination of the diarist and others had kept them alive.

'*December 7th. This morning the weather is good and ten of us finished breakfast in high spirits [. . .] two enemy tanks approached the island. Everyone was separated. I and two others from the 14th Air Unit were hiding in the entrance of an air raid shelter and they passed us three times about three metres distance from us. The tanks stayed on the island from 6:00 am until sundown. We swam for about two hours and due to the large waves, we were completely exhausted and thinking it was impossible we turned back. Finally, the end has come and it is impossible to commit suicide [. . .] Enemy tanks with infantry came up about fifty metres away. Don't know why but the four got up and ran into the sea. The tanks opened up with their guns [. . .] Maybe the four were either killed or were out of range. God has saved me again. I am all alone and it is pretty lonely.*

'*December 8th. Today is the 2nd anniversary of the great Asiatic war [...] I looked around for signs of others being killed but did not find any, so my morale went up when I thought they were still alive. Ate coconuts and rested on the beach. Waited for my shirt, trousers, and socks to dry [...] I went around the island looking for others, but did not find them and finally determined to commit suicide. When I started to go back, someone called and it was Komatsu, Atobe, and Nozuchi. They had finally completed a raft and were about to start out. It must have been the help of the good god. I regained my courage again.*'

For the next five days, they roamed from island to island, evading capture from American troops. The diarist wrote how weak he was and that, between them, he and his remaining comrades carried one rusty rifle. Waiting for the weather and tide to work in their favour, they hoped to sail to a nearby island. His last entry was on 13 December. He had survived for three weeks on Makin and its smaller atolls, an area of just two and a half square miles, which was occupied by 6,400 Americans.

'*December 13th. Terrific squall in the morning. Spent whole day in a hut. Departure to be tomorrow. For the first time we wash our face and hands with soap. Plan to go to Kuma* [nearby island] *in the night.*'

It is thought that only five Japanese soldiers survived. The diarist was not one of them. What became of him will never be known. At least, unlike many thousands of other loyal Japanese soldiers, a record of his bravery has survived.

One hundred miles to the south of Makin a ferocious battle was taking place on Beito, the Tarawa Atoll's main port. It had begun on 20 November where, yet again, the Japanese fought to all but the last man. Japan's defenders consisted of 2,636 troops and 2,200 Japanese and Korean labourers, facing an American invasion force of 53,000. In a battle that lasted just seventy-six hours, only seventeen Japanese, one officer and sixteen men, and 129 Koreans survived. Although suicide charges and individual suicides were commonplace among the defenders, the casualty figures – especially among the Korean labourers – suggest that the Americans took few prisoners.

Despite the increasing setbacks, most Japanese, like poet and writer Sei Ito, remained steadfast. He wrote in his diary: '*Our men on Tarawa and Makin have all perished. They have made this sacrifice for the Imperial Land and for our race. The land of Japan, where as autumn turns into winter the beauty of Fuji becomes visible, is protected by the blood of these men [...] Will the Anglo-Saxon race, which has established on the American continent the biggest materialistic culture, turn Asia into colonies under its rule, or will the Yamato race, devoted to the Asian ideal of the finest men dying for their country, lead the billion Asians of every belief and defend Asia to the end? The race is living through a fearful, decisive battle. The Americans excel at manufacturing, but when it comes to fighting, no people are the match of the Japanese. The manner in which the Japanese are now fighting is succeeding.'*

Rear Admiral Keiji Shibazaki, commander of the Japanese garrison and veteran of the China Campaign, had boasted to his men that '*it would take one million men one hundred years*' to conquer the island. Unfortunately, Shibazaki and all his senior officers were killed in action on the first day of the battle. Apparently, while they were walking to a secondary command post, they were killed by the airburst of a 5-inch naval shell, fired from a US destroyer. Shibazaki was posthumously promoted to vice-admiral.

Typically, as Japan's Holy War crumbled, Sei Ito's resolve hardened.

'People like myself feel intuitively that it would be better to die than to live as members of a defeated country. This for a Japanese is instinctive; so if the Americans and British think of us in the same way they think of the Italians, they will find they have made a big mistake [...] The Yamato race faces a genuine crisis. I believe in the eternity of the Divine Land and there has been no change in my absolute confidence in the invincibility of the Imperial soldiers, but we face increasing hardships; the bombing of our capital can be foreseen; and our allies in Europe are little by little being subjected to pressure on all sides, causing us further problems. How can we break through this impasse? Yamato race, bestir yourself! This is the moment to use our full strength, carrying our lives to their ultimate objective of ensuring the honour and destiny of the land of our ancestors.'

Despite the mounting setbacks and the conditions being faced by his troops in far-flung islands in the Pacific, Hirohito, safe and secure in his residence in Tokyo's Imperial Palace, demanded, '*Defending isn't enough. We have to do the attacking.*'

However, despite his exhortations, there was no respite for Hirohito and his people. The 'island hopping' of the Americans continued apace with Kwajalein Atoll in the Marshall Islands. Facing a US invasion force of over 46,000, there were only 166 survivors from a Japanese garrison of about 5,000 in a battle that lasted only three days. The rest of the Marshall Islands fell to the Americans within a month.

The noose was tightening, and the next climactic battle would be yet another portentous watershed as the horror and hatred intensified on both sides.

11
GYOKUSAI

It had taken a mighty armada of 535 US ships and 127,000 troops, including 77,000 marines, to take the Marshall Islands. With the Solomon Islands, eastern New Guinea, western New Britain, the Admiralty Islands and the Gilbert and Ellice Islands already captured, the next objective was the volcanic Mariana Islands, a pivotal strategic fulcrum in the Central Pacific. Capture of the Marianas would isolate Japan from its resource-rich southern conquests and put its mainland within striking distance of strategic attacks by US forces' new long-range B-29 Superfortress bombers. Three of the Marianas were critical: Guam, Tinian and Saipan, which would be first.

Saipan, the largest of the Mariana Islands, had, under a League of Nations mandate, been under Japanese rule since 1919. The island had a garrison of 30,000 Japanese troops and an important airfield at Aslito. The invasion plan estimated that Saipan would be taken in three days, after which US forces would seize Guam and Tinian. However, American intelligence had greatly underestimated Japanese determination to resist at all costs. In fact, it took twenty-four days to defeat the defenders, who paid a terrible price for their resistance.

The invasion of Saipan began on 15 June 1944. Coincidentally, the attack was launched just days after the Allies had established a beachhead in Normandy after the D-Day landings. The American invasion force of marines and infantry was 300,000 strong, supported by 500 ships. Facing them, under the command of Lieutenant General Yoshitsugu Saitō, was a combined Japanese force of over 30,000 army and naval personnel, a force more than twice the size the Americans expected. The naval force was commanded by

Admiral Chūichi Nagumo (who, after becoming trapped by heavy bombardment in a remote cave, would commit suicide on 6 July).

The attack on Saipan was preceded by the naval battle of the Philippine Sea, which took place on 19–20 June. The Americans called the encounter the 'Great Mariana Turkey Shoot'. It was the greatest carrier battle in history and got its name because it was so one-sided. A much larger American naval force with quality pilots, pitted against a much weaker Japanese fleet with inexperienced pilots, it was a no-contest. The Americans had fifteen carriers and 900 aircraft, while the Japanese had nine carriers and 750 planes. The Americans suffered damage to one of its battleships and lost 123 aircraft, but the Japanese lost two fleet carriers, one light carrier, two oilers, six other ships damaged, over 600 aircraft and 3,000 personnel. The defeat was yet another disaster for the Imperial Navy, one from which it never recovered.

In the five major carrier-on-carrier battles – from the Battle of the Coral Sea to the Battle of the Philippine Sea – the Imperial Japanese Navy had lost nine carriers, while the US Navy had lost four. The aircraft and trained pilots lost at the Philippine Sea were an irreplaceable blow to the already outnumbered Japanese fleet air arm. The Japanese had spent the better part of a year rebuilding its depleted carrier air groups, and the Americans had destroyed 90 per cent of their capability in two days.

After failing to stop the American landing, the Japanese army retreated to Mount Tapotchau, the mountain peak that dominates Saipan, where it was able to establish an all but impregnable position. However, after fierce fighting, Tapotchau fell by the end of June, forcing the Japanese to retreat further north.

In early July, the Japanese commander of Saipan, Lieutenant General Yoshitsugu Saitō, retreated to the northern part of the island, where his forces became trapped. The Imperial fleet he had hoped would relieve him had suffered a devastating defeat in the Battle of the Philippine Sea and never arrived at Saipan. Realising he could no longer hold out against the Americans, Saitō apologised to Tokyo for failing to defend Saipan and committed gyokusai, ritual suicide. In an island cave at dawn on 10 July, he disembowelled himself, after which his adjutant shot him in the head. Admiral Chūichi Nagumo, also trapped on Saipan, had already shot himself in the temple on 6 July.

Before his death, Saitō had ordered his remaining troops to launch an all-out, gyokusai banzai attack for the honour of the emperor: '*Whether we attack or whether we stay where we are, there is only death. However, in death there is life. I will advance with you to deliver another blow to the American devils and leave my bones on Saipan as a fortress of the Pacific. There is no longer any distinction between civilians and troops. It would be better for them to join in the attack with bamboo spears than be captured.*'

Obeying orders, early on the morning of 6 July, shouting 'Banzai!', 4,000 Japanese soldiers attacked with grenades, bayonets, swords and knives, waging an assault against a camp of Americans near Tanapag Harbour. Facing howitzers and machine-gun fire, wave after wave of Japanese overran several US battalions. In vicious hand-to-hand fighting more than 1,000 Americans were killed or wounded. It was the largest banzai charge of the Pacific war, in which almost all the Japanese troops fought to their death. However, the attack made no difference to the inevitable outcome, and three days later the US flag was raised over the island.

The Battle of Saipan resulted in more than 3,000 US deaths and over 13,000 wounded. The Japanese losses were horrendous. By best estimates, of the 31,629 Japanese on Saipan when the battle commenced, only 1,485 were alive when hostilities ceased. Even more alarming, on 9 July, when the Americans declared the battle over, thousands of Saipan's civilians, terrified by Japanese propaganda that warned they would be killed by US troops, leapt to their deaths from the high cliffs at the northern end of the island. Another disturbing feature of the battle was the use of flame-throwers by the Americans. Although the use of fire in war was centuries old, when Japanese soldiers and civilians retreated to Saipan's many caves, flame-throwers were used extensively to flush them out, resulting in horrific injuries.

The loss of Saipan stunned Tokyo, marking the first defeat on Japanese territory that had not been added during Japan's invasions in 1941 and 1942. Significantly, General Hideki Tōjō, Japan's prime minister, who had promised that the United States would never take Saipan, was forced to resign a week after the island fell. Because Saipan had been part of Japan, details of the catastrophic defeat reached the homeland, where the reaction was a mix of anger and incredulity.

Aiko Takahashi, a fifty-year-old woman living in Tokyo, recorded in her diary on 18 July 1944: *'Last night the heat was oppressive, and it was a sleepless night. Yesterday a change of navy ministers was announced, and it made us wonder whether something terrible was about to happen. Just as we were thinking that, we heard the sad report that our troops on Saipan had committed gyokusai and were annihilated. Apparently for six or seven days after the decisive battle, the survivors hid in trenches before deciding to commit gyokusai. As the stepping stones leading to Japan are occupied one by one and the hand-to-hand fighting comes closer, our unease is unbearable. Although this is what we feel, the reports in newspapers and magazines boast that giving up these islands is a tactic for drawing in the enemy and that the enemy is doing what we want. No matter how favourably you look at the war situation, it's been impossible to imagine that Japan enjoys the advantage. Hearing about our troops' gyokusai on Saipan makes us angry. We should have the courage come hell or high water to give up the fight.'*

Journalist Kiyoshi Kiyosawa was a liberal who opposed Japanese militarism. He was censored for his views in 1941 and was forbidden to speak in public. Even so, he kept a diary from 1942 to 1945, until his death just before the end of the war.

'19 July 1944. The fact that there was the sacrificial death of all the Japanese on Saipan presents us with problems hereafter. Is not this style of death a dog's useless death? Is it in the interests of Japan? Of course, living under the current military leadership, there are difficulties in finding any other path, but in the end, it is as if we're fighting just to die.'

The defeat on Saipan brought an end to Hideki Tōjō's government.

'20 July 1944. The Tōjō Cabinet has completely resigned. The cabinet that had the responsibility for plunging Japan into misery collapsed. According to a story of Kasahara, there were a great many anonymous

complaints, and even a secret policeman said that if Tōjō had committed suicide, it would probably have been alright, but if he lives on in shame it may be that he will be killed. If the war becomes unprofitable, the people will necessarily express their discontent. Here is the turning point of the Greater East Asian War. July 20 will probably be a day that will be remembered.'

On 19 August, details of the aftermath of the Battle of Saipan appeared in the *Asahi Shimbun*. Kiyosawa wrote in his diary: '*Young boys died and women died. The soldiers and noncombatants on Saipan died in this manner. It was a sacrifice to feudal ideology. It is slavish submission to military leadership. I hope this kind of dying will be brought to an end.'*

Two weeks after the capture of Saipan, the Mariana Island of Guam was the next American target. Commander Masatake Okumiya admitted, '*They [the Japanese pilots] never had a chance against the determined defence of the Hellcat fighters and the unbelievable accuracy and volume of their ships' anti-aircraft fire.'*

Writing in 1955, he would later conclude, '*I am firmly convinced that the Pacific War was started by men who did not understand the sea and fought by men who did not understand the air.'*

Guam was a prize catch. It had an excellent harbour and several airfields. The attack on Guam, codenamed Operation Stevedore, was intended to start only days after the landings on Saipan. However, it was delayed so that an effective naval bombardment and air attacks could prepare the ground. General Takeshi Takashina commanded 19,000 Japanese defenders who had built an elaborate network of bunkers and artillery fortifications.

The American attack commenced on 21 July on the west coast of the island. Despite fierce night attacks and banzai charges by the Japanese over the first few days of the battle, the US forces soon had a strong beachhead. By then, much of the Japanese strength had been undermined and Takashina himself had been killed. Surviving Japanese units fought on for another two weeks, gradually moving north and inland. Organised resistance eventually ceased, but Guam's particularly mountainous terrain allowed a few diehards to hold out. Some small units fought on until after the end of the war, causing occasional US casualties. Remarkably, one solitary veteran, Sergeant Shōichi Yokoi, emerged from the jungle to surrender and return to Japan in 1972, eight years after two other comrades had died in a flash flood.

Born in Aichi Prefecture, Yokoi was an apprentice tailor when he was conscripted in 1941. A veteran from Manchukuo, he had served with the 38th Regiment on Guam. For the last eight years before his discovery, he lived alone and survived by hunting, primarily at night. He also used native plants to make clothes, bedding and storage implements, which he carefully hid in his home, one of the island's many caves. In January 1972, Yokoi was discovered alongside a small river, by two locals who were checking their shrimp traps. Yokoi said later that he expected the local men to kill him but was surprised when, before turning him over to the authorities, they fed him hot soup at their home. His diet included wild nuts, mangos, papaya, shrimp, snails, frogs and rats and when he was examined, he was in relatively good health, although slightly anaemic due to a lack of salt in his diet.

'It is with much embarrassment that I return,' he said upon his return to Japan in March 1972. He had known since 1952 that the war had ended, but feared coming out of hiding. 'We Japanese soldiers were told to prefer death to the disgrace of getting captured alive.' After a whirlwind media tour of Japan, Yokoi married and settled down in rural Aichi. He became a popular television personality and an advocate of modest living. He eventually received the equivalent of US$300 in back pay, and a small pension. Although he never met Hirohito, while visiting the grounds of the Imperial Palace, Yokoi offered him a message via reporters: 'Your Majesty, I have returned home [. . .] I deeply regret that I could not serve you well. The world has certainly changed, but my determination to serve you will never change.' Yokoi died in 1997 of a heart attack, at the age of eighty-two.

Guam had lost 81 per cent of its defenders when it fell on 10 August, leaving most of the Marianas in American hands. One of the few survivors on Guam, a young soldier, witnessed the gravity of Japan's position. 'The enemy, circling overhead, bombed our airfield the whole day long. When evening came our carrier bombers returned, *but the airfield had been bombed and they could not land. Having neither fuel nor ammunition, the fifteen or sixteen planes were unable to land and had to crash. It was certainly a shame. I watched with tears in my eyes. The tragedy of war was never so real.'*

As it was on Saipan and Guam, so too on Tinian, an American invasion force of 40,000 struggled to overcome the Japanese defenders. Again, caves became places of refuge for the Japanese and banzai charges were used as last-ditch gyokusai attacks to achieve 'honourable' deaths. Japan lost another 5,000 dead in the futile attempt to hold on to Tinian, the last of the Mariana Islands to fall. Once again, the defenders fought to the death. Only 400 were captured.

Kiyochi Ogata was the commanding officer on Tinian. He was in charge of 4,500 soldiers on the island, while the other troops were led either by the commander of the four airfields on Tinian, Captain Goichi Oie, or the commander of the naval forces, Vice Admiral Kakiji Kakuta. Ogata's defences were poorly prepared, and the Americans made it on to the beaches with little opposition, forcing him into the interior of the island. The Japanese were defeated and the island fell in just eight days. Ogata and Oie committed suicide, while Kakuta and his staff took refuge in a cave on Tinian's east coast and were never seen again. By the end of the battle, 5,745 Japanese defenders lay dead.

The loyalty of the emperor's forces was remarkable, particularly given the way many were treated, both in training and on the battle-front. Kiyoshi Takeda entered the Anti-submarine Defence School at Kurihama in January 1944.

'Tuesday, 7th August. This evening, I felt thirsty and I went to drink tea in the canteen. I saw sailors lined up in the twilight along the sea-front. A quartermaster was giving them a lecture on morale, holding a cudgel of oak against his hip. Then he suddenly began to roar and called one man after the other out of the ranks and struck them on the back with all his might. If a man did not move, he struck harder still.

'Last Sunday, a sailor came back from leave ten minutes before the prescribed time, and a chief petty officer who was waiting for him at the gate struck him in the face, pretending that he was late. [. . .] The

blow took him by surprise, so that he fell backwards on the stony road, moaning with pain. A trickle of dark blood appeared behind his head and then ran along the back of his neck. [...] How am I to interpret such actions? One must not think too much about these things, for the more I think about them the more lost I feel.'

After a calamitous summer in 1944, by the middle of August, calm heads in Tokyo might well have decided that it was time for Japan to count its losses and consider the pursuit of peace. However, no such calm heads existed in Tokyo – and had not for many years. On 26 July, Hirohito had made it clear what he intended for the future of his people by telling his new prime minister, Kuniaki Koiso, that he intended *'to remain in the divine land and fight to the death'*. It was not to be his own death knell, but it was for many of his people.

The next battle in the Marianas was on the island of Peleliu, less than 2,000 miles from Japan. Japan had been at war for over seven years and was fighting the combined forces of China, the British Empire and the United States. Fuelled on both sides by vicious propaganda, the fighting had reached new levels of barbarity. Sub-lieutenant Shin Hasagawa believed, *'Any question of justice is no longer an issue in this war. The whole thing amounts to an explosion of hatred between national groups. Neither side will stop fighting short of their total self-destruction. How shameful.'*

Beginning on 15 September 1944, the heavily outnumbered Japanese defenders put up such a fight, often to the death, in Hirohito's name that Peleliu became known in Japanese as the 'Emperor's Island'. Against an American force of almost 48,000 marines and infantry, 12,033 Japanese soldiers died, with only 360 taken prisoner. Post-war statisticians calculated that it took US forces over 1,500 rounds of ammunition to kill each Japanese defender and that they expended 15 million rounds of bullets, 118,262 hand grenades and 150,000 mortar rounds. US commander William Rupertus predicted that it would take him four days to take Peleliu; in fact, it took him almost ten weeks.

Almost inevitably, Japan and its people would continue to be victims of their past and their unique beliefs and prejudices. There were many who knew the game was up, but their adherence to the traditions of their past prevented them from taking the decisions that would offer a different future. With the Americans preparing their aerial onslaught on Japan's mainland, Prince Naruhiko Higashikuni, commander-in-chief of home defence, knew what the future held: *'The war was lost when the Marianas were taken away. We had nothing in Japan that we could use against the weapons from the air. From the point of view of the Home Defence Command, we felt that the war was lost, and said so. If the B-29s came over Japan, there was nothing that could be done.'*

Despite the dire circumstances that Japan faced, Hirohito remained obdurate. Even though Tokyo was only 1,272 miles from Saipan, well within the range of America's B-29 bombers, Hirohito continued to implore even more effort. In an audience on 17 June, he told Vice Chief of Staff Admiral Shimada to, *'Rise to the challenge; make a tremendous effort; achieve a splendid victory like at the time of the Japan Sea naval battle [in the Russo- Japanese War].'*

Hirohito had warned Prime Minister Hideki Tōjō that if Japan ever lost Saipan, repeated air attacks on Tokyo would likely follow. No matter what it took, Japanese forces had to hold the island. He was told by his chiefs of staff on two occasions that the situation on Saipan had become hopeless. After the island was lost, Hirohito ignored their advice and ordered Shimada to recapture it.

During that perilous summer, there is no record of Hirohito ever expressing gratitude for, or even acknowledging, the extraordinary bravery and loyalty of his armed forces who were sacrificing themselves in their tens of thousands in China, Burma and the Pacific. Neither did he offer his sympathies to his subjects at home, who were suffering significant privations and anxieties and grieving for the loss of their loved ones. On the contrary, through his subordinates, he demanded yet more loyalty, yet more devotion and yet more sacrifice to his cause and that of the empire which his Holy War had created.

12

KAMIKAZE

The first landings in the American attempt to recapture the Philippines took place at Leyte on 17 October 1944, when offshore islands in Leyte Gulf were seized. On 20 October, when the US 6th Army went ashore on the east coast of Leyte, a vast armada of US battleships, carriers, cruisers and destroyers had already pounded the area before the landings.

The Japanese response was Operation Sho, in which four carriers, with just over 100 planes, were to move southward to lure the US task force towards them. At the same time a fleet of Imperial Japanese Navy battleships, cruisers and destroyers was to converge on Leyte Gulf to attack the American landing force. The Japanese army and navy air forces were also ordered to attack the invaders, but their actual strength had been reduced to a mere 212 planes by the time of the landing.

On 23 October 1944, a Japanese naval force was intercepted by US submarines. Two heavy cruisers were sunk and another seriously damaged. On the following day, another group was pounded by US carrier-borne planes, and the *Musashi*, one of the two mightiest battleships of the Imperial Japanese Navy, was sunk. Meanwhile, a group under the command of Vice Admiral Shoji Nishimura was ambushed in Surigao Strait by a force of the US 7th Fleet and all but annihilated.

Vice Admiral Ozawa's force was caught by the main US force, and a total of four carriers, a light cruiser and two destroyers were sunk, causing the navy to abandon its original intention of forcing its way into Leyte Gulf, and withdraw. The Battle of Leyte Gulf was a disaster for the Japanese navy. Operation Sho not only failed to inflict serious damage on the enemy, but resulted in significant losses: three battleships, one large carrier, three light carriers, six heavy cruisers, four light cruisers and eleven destroyers.

Vice Admiral Takijirō Ōhnishi, the newly appointed commander-in-chief of the 1st Air Fleet, finally decided to employ suicide missions to deal with the crisis. He believed he held an ace up his sleeve but, in fact, it was far from hidden; it was in plain view in the skies above the Allied armada. The card, which has acquired almost mythical proportions, is known by various names: 'kamikaze', 'divine wind', 'spirit wind', and, officially, *Shinpū Tokubetsu Kōgekitai* ('Divine Wind Special Attack Unit'). In plain English they were suicide attacks. The word *kamikaze* derives from *kami* ('god', 'spirit' or 'divinity') and *kaze* ('wind'). It originated from *waka* – poetry in classical literature – referring to the wind that dispersed the Mongol-Koryo fleets which invaded Japan under Kublai Khan in 1274 and 1281.

Lieutenant Yukio Seki died in the very first special suicide attack on 25 October 1944, at the age of twenty-three. He was the leader of the Kamikaze Special Attack Corps, Shikishima Squadron, from the 201st Naval Air Group. He led five Zero fighters carrying 250kg bombs, which took off from Mabalacat Airfield in the Philippines. His final letter – addressed to the parents of his wife, Mariko, offers some insight into the extraordinary sacrifice made by the kamikaze pilots.

'*Now standing at the crossroads of victory or defeat for the Empire, I am determined to repay the emperor's grace with my own body. There is nothing that surpasses this as the long-cherished desire of a military man [. . .] I am determined to repay the emperor's grace by carrying out a taiatari* [body-crashing] *attack on an aircraft carrier with my own body for the Empire of Japan.*'

Seki also wrote words of farewell to his wife. They had been married in the spring of 1944: '*I am truly sorry for going to fall without being able to do anything for you. Even without words, I think that you, with readiness as the wife of a military man, are sufficiently able. Please keep in mind to show filial piety to your parents. I write now before my departure while many memories come to me. I hope that Emi* [sister] *and her young boy also will be in high spirits.*'

He also wrote to his students in the 42nd Class of Flight Students at Kasumigaura Naval Air Group where he was an instructor from January to June 1944: '*My students, fall like mountain cherry blossoms.*'

Purpose-built or converted from conventional aircraft, kamikaze planes were, in effect, pilot-guided missiles. Loaded with bombs, torpedoes and other explosives, their pilots attempted to crash into enemy ships in what was called a *taiatari* ('body attack'). About 19 per cent of kamikaze attacks were successful.

Twenty-year-old Masuo Isao wrote a final letter home: '*Dear Parents, please congratulate me. I have been given a splendid opportunity to die. The destiny of our homeland hinges on the decisive battle in the seas to the south where I shall fall like a blossom from a cherry tree.*'

To help the young kamikaze recruits, an eighty-page suicide manual was produced by unit commander Major Hayashino of the Shimoshizu Air Unit in Chiba Prefecture, near Tokyo.

Upon sighting the target, aim for a point at the centre of the ship. As you dive, shout at the top of your lungs, 'Hisatsu' – sink without fail! Just before the collision, it is essential you do not shut your eyes. You will feel that you are suddenly floating in the air. At that moment you will see your mother's face. Then you are no more.

It also included the somewhat bizarre suggestion:

You have lived for twenty years or more. You must exert your full might for the last time in your life. Exert supernatural strength. At the very moment of impact: Do your best. Every deity and the spirits of your dead comrades are watching you intently. Just before the collision it is essential that you do not shut your eyes for a moment so as not to miss the target. Many have crashed into the targets with wide-open eyes. They will tell you what fun they had.

The diary of experienced fighter pilot Yasuo Itabashi describes his journey, one that is typical of so many young men who sacrificed themselves as kamikaze pilots. Slowly but surely, the lure of an honourable death in the service of his emperor and his people overwhelms him.

He writes on 28 November 1944: *'We've made some military gains. Kamikaze units attacked and sank an aircraft carrier and a cruiser. I heard from Superior Flight Petty Officer Nishide, just back from Manila, that my older brother Origasa died recently in an attack on an aircraft carrier. I was quite overcome with emotion and couldn't speak.'*

On 3 January 1945, reacting to news of the gyokusai at Tarawa and Makin and, more recently, Saipan and Tinian, he remains resolute: *'But we are not defeated. We're winning. We are definitely winning this war. Both the army and the navy have formed special-attack units and are continuing the intense and endless battles. I believe that 1945 is the autumn of emergencies when the Yamato race, one million strong, will choose death and make a last stand.'*

In the three-day period from 7 to 9 January, the Americans started to come ashore at Lingayen Bay on Luzon Island, with 350 transport ships and warships protecting them. It was reported that the Allied military forces were four or five divisions strong. In response, Japanese army and navy special-attack units were formed, with young kamikaze pilots transforming themselves into virtual fireballs and mounting frenzied attacks. Writing in his diary on 14 January, Itabashi is inspired by recent news: *'I am full of the spirit that will make it easy for me to become a member of a human bomb special-attack unit. Mine is not empty energy. We cannot not win. To help us prevail, I'd happily see my little five-foot body smashed to pieces.'*

In the face of further military setbacks, Itabashi writes on 22 March: *'It was finally announced that all the members of the Iwo Jima garrison committed gyokusai. This had been predicted, but my blood still boiled. I will avenge them. I definitely will avenge them. We must not let the brave warriors who committed gyokusai die a dog's death. Whether right or wrong, Japan must win!'*

And on 23 March: *'The Yamato people are brothers and sisters. Japanese citizens are united and facing their national crisis together. Japan absolutely cannot be defeated. If the basis for my life is the eternal peace of the Yamato people and progress, how can this little body have any regrets?'*

Finally, on 7 April, he receives the order he's been waiting and hoping for: he will be sent into action on the 9th. He makes his final preparations the day before, and records in his diary: '*The engines of our planes were in great shape, and we were in good spirits. I'll get myself ready, write my last letters, and make arrangements for the things I'll leave behind. In the end, my life will have been twenty-two years long. I'll smear the decks of enemy warships with this teenager's blood. It'll be wonderful.*'

His final letter is addressed to his parents, in which he expresses his fervent commitment to Japan's victory: '*Yasuo is happy and will go off to die laughing. All I can do is aim my aircraft, and it may not be something I can laugh about, but I expect to be laughing at the moment I crash [. . .] Japan definitely will win and I happily go off dreaming of the day of victory. Please put up a good fight until the day of the final victory.*'

Twenty-five-year-old Norimasa Hayashi was called up in September 1943. Writing in his diary on 13 April 1945, he seems clear-sighted about his fate: '*Captain Kuniyasu and Lieutenant Tanigawa Takao have been killed. We are all going to die. The life of the pilot of a suicide-plane is ephemeral. Yesterday I learnt that Sub-lieutenant Yatsunami is dead. He was found on the white sands of Kuju Kurihama. Alas! Dear Yatsunami.*'

Norimasa flew his final mission at the beginning of August, just six days before Japan's surrender. His final words are addressed to his family in a letter dated 9 August 1945: '*I have changed a lot, but I still keep the blue flame of idealism burning in my heart. I have fun with girls, I drink and tell bawdy stories. I have remained an idealist. I shall remain true until I die to the oaths we swore together. In the east the sky has cleared up a little. The breeze that blows into my room is delightful. I am sitting near the window in the twilight. I am writing these lines to you from a bomb-proof shelter, while I am waiting for orders to take off. Farewell, Father, Mother, my brothers and sisters and my family. Keep in good health and live happily. I am off to fairyland, the country of Andersen's stories, and there I shall be a prince. I shall talk with the birds, the flowers and the trees. May Great Imperial Japan remain prosperous for ever!*'

Although hailed as heroes at home, in their private diaries and letters, many kamikaze told a different story. The words of 22-year-old army pilot Yoshi Miyagi leave a bitter taste: '*We the Kamikaze are nothing but robots. If we had listened to those Japanese who really love their country, we would not now be faced with this disaster. I know that my death can no longer serve any purpose.*'

Despite the kamikaze hitting over 300 ships and killing more than 5,000 Allied sailors, the Allied advance towards Japan rolled on. As it did so, young Japanese men continued to sacrifice themselves for their sacred emperor. Though many, like 21-year-old Haruo Araki, may have felt ambivalent about their sacrifice: '*Dear Wife, the happy dream is over. Tomorrow I will dive my plane into an enemy ship. I will cross the river into the other world, taking some Yankees with me. When I think of your future, it tears at my heart.*'

The Cherry Blossom Squadrons were formed to fly newly developed Ohkas (Yokosuka MXY-7), rocket-powered glider bombers. They all flew with a cherry blossom logo on their fuselage, and songs were sung to honour their pilots. Historian Saburō Ienaga, writing in 1979, paints a picture of the kamikaze pilots which is in stark contrast to the rhetoric of heroism that has become legendary.

The special attack pilots were doomed men. A 'successful' mission ended when they blew themselves up against an American ship. The units were glorified as the supreme expression of the Japanese military spirit, and the impression was given that all the pilots were volunteers. However, author Takagi Toshiro's meticulous research has shown the sordid reality behind this cherry blossom myth. The units were organised from 'volunteers' who had joined after intensive psychological pressure. Pilots who returned to base without carrying out their mission because of a mechanical malfunction were derided. They had to face ostracism and comments like 'Why did you come back alive?' and 'A coward who is afraid to die is a disgrace to the special attack unit.' Condemned pilots suffered terrible mental anguish. Many were so desperate that they crashed their planes into the ground or into the ocean just to end it all. Those who tried to carry out their missions did little better because of inferior planes and American air supremacy. No more than 1% to 3% of the suicide pilots actually hit Allied warships; most seem to have crashed short of the target. Legions of promising young men were sent off to meaningless deaths.

Examples of suicide attacks or soldiers deciding to pay the ultimate price in battle are not unique to Japan's kamikaze, but the scale of their attacks and the collective commitment of the young pilots was extraordinary. After the war, Dr Daisetsu Suzuki, philosopher and proponent of Zen Buddhism, reflected on the origins of the kamikaze phenomenon.

The Japanese Army was imbued with certain German ideologies, including the thought that war is destruction. [. . .] Soldiers, therefore, should not be thought of as human beings, but merely as a means of destruction. [. . .] Shrink from nothing that may serve to destroy the war potential of the enemy. There were uttered such specious phrases as 'the highest cause of our country', but thoughtful visions of the utterers were totally blind to the spiritual side of things. It is most regrettable that Japanese military men have consistently been so irreligious in their outlook. Army and Navy men reiterate endlessly such Shinto ideas as 'the Divine Glory of His Majesty', 'The Divine Nation', 'The Holy War', and similar phrases. But they neglect or ignore such truly universal ideas like love, humanity and mercy. Shinto is replete with gods of war, but there are no gods or goddesses of love. These war gods do not give life, only take it. The eternal thought was, 'The essence of life is to die like a true samurai.' Kamikaze attacks were a product of that feudalistic concept.

The last of approximately 3,800 kamikaze pilots to die was Vice Admiral Matome Ugaki, the man charged with using kamikaze tactics to protect Japan's mainland. He had kept a diary throughout the war and wrote his last entry on the day of Hirohito's surrender: *'As one of the officers the throne trusted, I faced this sad day. I've never been so ashamed of myself.*' He then took off his insignia of rank and boarded his plane, bound for Okinawa.

He sent a farewell radio message:

> Despite brave fighting by each unit under my command for the past six months, we have failed to destroy the arrogant enemy in order to protect our divine Empire, a failure that should be attributed to my lack of capability. Yet believing that our Empire will last forever and that the special attack spirit of the Air Force will never perish, I am going to proceed to Okinawa, where our men lost their lives like cherry blossoms, and ram into the arrogant American ships, displaying the real spirit of a Japanese warrior. All units under my command shall keep my will in mind, overcome every conceivable difficulty, rebuild a strong armed force, and make our Empire last forever. The Emperor, banzai!

Ugaki's plane never reached its target. It is thought a mishap may have led it to plummet into the sea or, more likely, it was shot down by American anti-aircraft fire. The next morning, the crew of a US landing craft claimed to have found the still-smouldering remains of a cockpit with three bodies on the beach of Iheyajima Island. One of the three, his head crushed and right arm missing, wore a dark green uniform. A short sword was found nearby. The sailors buried the bodies in the sand. Ironically, the last kamikaze attack of Hirohito's Holy War ended, like the war itself, in failure.

Counterparts of kamikaze included other Special Attack Units, including *kōryū* (two-man midget submarines), *kaiten* (human torpedoes), *shin'yō* (human suicide boats) and *fukuryu* (naval divers, human mines). Although 210 *kōryū* were built in 1945, to be used to defend Tokyo Harbour, because of Japan's surrender they were never used in anger. Several *kaiten* were built and used in combat. However, the advantages of human guidance throughout a torpedo's trajectory proved to be of little use in practice, and they caused minimal damage to enemy vessels. In total, according to the US Navy's statistics, only a few ships were sunk by *kaiten*, resulting in the loss of about 190 men. In return, Japan lost over 100 operators.

A total of 6,197 shinyo boats were produced for the Japanese Imperial Navy and 3,000 for the Imperial Army. Minuro Wada was called up by the navy in December 1943 and killed during a human torpedo exercise at the age of twenty-three.

'I have already been inside the torpedo that crawls at the bottom of the sea at a depth of 105 feet and never surfaces. I piloted another and plunged into the sand at a depth of ninety feet at an angle of forty degrees. I could see my comrade's head under my shoes. When I opened the hatch of a third, a white vapour suddenly escaped from it and I felt as though I had been struck in the face. Now everybody is agreed that I am "a hell of a fellow". And yet at every moment I should like to burst into tears.'

Four hundred Shinyo boats were transported to Okinawa and the rest stored in Japan for the defence of home waters. Between 10 January and 4 May, four US ships were sunk by shinyo, one was crippled and two more damaged.

Fukuryu, or 'kamikaze frogmen', 1,200 of whom had been trained by the time of Japan's surrender, were equipped with 30lb mines and wore diving helmets; they were issued with two bottles of oxygen and were weighed down with 20lb weights. There are only two known attempts to use *fukuryu*, one of which caused minor damage to a US Army landing craft.

The exact number of ships sunk or damaged by kamikaze attacks is a matter of much debate and statistical variance, with several different sets of overall figures. For example, the British carrier HMS *Formidable* suffered structural damage that led to her being scrapped, as being beyond economic repair. There was also a notably ferocious attack on the American carrier USS *Bunker Hill* which, during the invasion of Okinawa, was struck by two kamikazes in quick succession on 11 May 1945, setting her on fire. Casualties exceeded 600, including 396 killed or missing, with 264 wounded. She survived the conflagration, but never saw action again.

According to a wartime Japanese propaganda announcement, the kamikaze missions sank eighty-one ships and damaged 195, and according to its published tally, the attacks accounted for up to 80 per cent of the US losses in the final phase of the war in the

Pacific. However, modern historians have estimated that around seventy US vessels were either 'sunk or damaged beyond repair' by kamikazes.

According to a third analysis, the United States Strategic Bombing Survey (conducted as the war was coming to a close), 2,550 kamikaze missions were flown from October 1944 until the end of the war, with only 475 (or 18.6 per cent) achieving a hit or a damaging near miss. Warships of all types were damaged, including twelve aircraft carriers, fifteen battleships, and sixteen light and escort carriers. However, no ship larger than an escort carrier was sunk. Approximately forty-five ships were sunk in total, the bulk of which were destroyers.

Suicide attacks – especially individual actions in battle – are well known throughout the history of conflict. Even today, as we know only too well from contemporary news reports, suicide bomb attacks still create devastation and suffering on a horrendous scale, where the targets are usually civilians. However, the scale and systematic planning of Japan's kamikaze remains a unique phenomenon.

13

THE PEARL OF THE ORIENT

Despite their huge naval losses, the Japanese were determined to hold Leyte and started sending reinforcements. However, during October 1944, too few Japanese reinforcements arrived to have much effect on operations. The Americans advanced up Leyte Valley to the north coast, pushed inland and sent one division overland to the southwest coast. Bad weather and new Japanese reinforcements – two and a half divisions by late November – slowed the US advances during November and December, but at great cost in men and materiel.

Despite the worsening situation, Hirohito was unrelenting in his demands. He insisted that his military hierarchy continue to drive his people onwards towards a destiny that was looking increasingly bleak: '*Today our imperial state is indeed challenged to reach powerfully for a decisive victory. You who are the leaders of our people must now renew your tenacity and, uniting in your resolve, smash our enemies' evil purposes, thereby furthering forever our imperial destiny.*'

It was only after the war that Hirohito admitted he had made a mistake in attempting to defend Leyte. However, he failed to express any contrition for the 80,000 Japanese dead in the campaign: '*Contrary to the views of the Army and Navy General Staffs, I agreed to the showdown battle of Leyte, thinking that if we attacked at Leyte and America flinched, then we would probably be able to find room to negotiate.*'

However, on a couple of occasions he was seen to offer a traditional acknowledgement of the extraordinary devotion of his men. When his military aide, Kaizō Yoshihashi, was delivering a briefing to Hirohito on the bravery of one of his kamikaze, '*He suddenly stood up and made a deep, silent bow. I was pointing at the map and his majesty's hair touched my head, causing me to feel as though an electric current had run through my body. On another occasion, I informed the emperor about a corporal who had sacrificed himself, the emperor did the same thing: rose and bowed deeply. Both times only the emperor and I were in the room.'*

Despite staggering losses of ships and troops, Japanese soldiers continued to arrive at Ormoc, on the northwest coast of Leyte, and even tried airborne assaults, which accomplished little. The reinforcements were little more than sacrificial offerings on Hirohito's imperial altar. Ormoc fell on 10 December and the Americans declared the island secured on Christmas Day 1944. Japan lost twenty-nine ships and one submarine.

The Americans' second major target was Mindoro, a large island south of Luzon and Manila Bay. Their objective was the construction of airfields for fighter planes that could dominate the sky over the vital island of Luzon, with its major seaport and capital city, Manila. Once again, waves of kamikazes were launched, but Mindoro was quickly overrun in just three days, and a major air base at San Jose was soon completed.

On 9 January 1945, on the south shore of Lingayen Gulf on the western coast of Luzon, almost 175,000 Americans started to establish a twenty-mile beachhead within a few days. With heavy air support they pushed inland, taking Clark Field, forty miles northwest of Manila, in the last week of January. Two more major landings followed: one to cut off the Bataan Peninsula, and another, which included a parachute drop, south of Manila.

On 16 February paratroopers and amphibious units attacked Corregidor simultaneously. The most ferocious battle to take Corregidor, which became christened 'The Rock', happened on the night of 18 February and early the next morning. On a moonless night at 22:30, 500 Japanese marines came out of the Battery Smith Armoury and charged the American and the Philippine positions. The vicious encounter ended in failure, with more than 250 Japanese corpses strewn along a 200-yard length of Cheney Trail. The Americans lost just fourteen dead. The area became known as 'Banzai Point'. Many of the remaining Japanese defenders sought refuge in the maze of tunnels of Malinta Hill. American units moved inland and, using tanks and flame-throwers, devastated pill-boxes and tunnels in the surrounding areas held by the Japanese.

For eight straight days until 23 February, the Japanese launched wave upon wave of banzai charges, mortar attacks and a suicide squad of soldiers with explosives strapped to their bodies. Over 300 Japanese were killed. Subsequently, American engineers poured large quantities of fuel down the tunnels. The explosion that fol-lowed killed everyone in the tunnels. There were no more organised Japanese attacks for the rest of the campaign, only isolated pockets of resistance from handfuls of survivors who continued to fight on until 26 February, when Corregidor was declared secured. Of the Japanese garrison of 6,700, fifty were wounded and only nineteen taken prisoner.

Despite initial indications, the fight for Manila was vicious. It took until the beginning of March to clear the city of all Japanese, who fought on stubbornly and refused to either surrender or to evacuate. Fort Drum, a fortified island in Manila Bay near Cor-regidor, held out until 13 April when a team of US Army engineers went ashore and pumped 3,000 gallons of diesel fuel into the fort, then set off incendiary charges. None of the Japanese in the fort survived the blast.

On 17 April, the Americans made their first landings on Min-danao, the last of the major islands of the Philippines to be taken. Their steady advance was met by yet more stubborn resistance, until, by the end of June, pockets of resistance were compressed into remote areas on both Mindanao and Luzon, where fighting continued until the final Japanese surrender in August. However, some units of the Imperial Japanese Army were out of radio contact with Tokyo, and it was difficult to convince some of them that Japan had surrendered. As on many Pacific Islands, major Japanese officials, including members of the imperial family, had to make personal visits to convince their soldiers that they must surrender by order of the emperor.

By the end of the Philippines Campaign, the death toll was over 334,000, 320,000 of whom were Japanese. In total, 48,000 Americans were wounded. Typically, only 12,500 Japanese soldiers surrendered. There were also several examples of vengeance-fuelled atrocities committed by retreating Japanese troops or those humiliated by the prospect of defeat. One of the most despicable became known as the 'Massacre of Manila'. Bearing a strong resemblance to the Rape of Nanking in its horrific brutality, it was yet another example of how the warped mentality of Japan's military code, supposedly based on honour, duty and loyalty to the emperor, created an awful legacy for Japan to live with for generations to come.

Manila, once the 'Pearl of the Orient', had suffered much deprivation during the Japanese occupation. Its forces looted food supplies, medicines and department stores, stole farm equipment and left fields to rot. The city's economy collapsed and its social fabric fell apart. Just hours after American forces had arrived, Japanese troops rounded up more than 100 suspected guerrillas and their families, herded them into a field less than three miles from the presidential palace, then beheaded the men one after the other. Women and children, including infants, were bayoneted.

Captured battlefield records reveal that the violence was planned.

> When Filipinos are to be killed, they must be gathered into one place and disposed of with the consideration that ammunition and manpower must not be used to excess. Because the disposal of dead bodies is a troublesome task, they should be gathered into houses which are scheduled to be burned or demolished. They should also be thrown into the river.

The 'Tiger of Malaya', Japanese general Tomoyuki Yamashita, the senior military commander in the Philippines, was ordered to make Luzon and its capital a nightmare for American forces in order to buy time for the defence of mainland Japan. Believing that the city, full of hostile civilians, would be too difficult to defend, he divided his army into different groups and prepared to fight a prolonged war of attrition in the mountains and jungles of Luzon's hinterland.

However, Rear Admiral Sanji Iwabuchi, commander of the Manila Naval Defence Force, who had been charged with staying behind to wreck the city's port and waterfront, in order to deny the Americans the use of them, had no intention of abandoning the capital. He was determined to use his marines to conduct an orgy of urban bloodletting similar to the horror of Stalingrad.

To do that, Iwabuchi divided his 17,000 men into several units throughout Manila, with a final redoubt focused on Intramuros, Manila's ancient citadel, which was guarded by towering walls. He had his men barricade the citadel's rooms with desks, chairs and bookcases, and in its corridors build dirt-filled walls four feet thick and seven feet high, with just enough clearance over which to toss grenades. He also ordered dozens of road intersections to be booby-trapped, railroad stakes to be sunk into pavements to act as roadblocks and tank traps, and had depth charges converted into land mines. Iwabuchi then gave the order to begin the total destruction of Manila. Incendiary squads swept through the city, setting fires and dynamiting buildings.

Then the human decimation followed, in waves of mass killings, beginning with the murder of 115 men, women and children at Dy Pac Lumberyard. Over the following days, Iwabuchi's men killed local officials, police officers and several priests suspected of being loyal to the United States.

The Americans crossed the Pasig River on 7 February and began an incredibly bloody urban fight to retake the city. Street by street, the Japanese marines resisted the American advance. However, Iwabuchi soon realised that his defence of the city was a lost cause, and he turned a military encounter into a wanton act of violent revenge against citizens in one of the worst human tragedies of the war. Captured Japanese documents showed that Iwabuchi's policy was unambiguous.

> The Americans who have penetrated into Manila have about 1,000 artillery troops, and there are several thousand Filipino guerrillas. Even women and children have become guerrillas. All people on the battlefield with the exception of Japanese military personnel, Japanese civilians and special construction units will be put to death.

Promising them safety from the battle, hundreds of civilians were herded into the dining hall of Saint Paul's College. Packed with explosives, the room's chandeliers suddenly dropped to the floor and detonated. The explosion was so powerful it blew the roof off the building and punched a hole in the western wall. Those who could stagger through the hole were shot and bayoneted. The following afternoon, Japanese marines stormed the Red Cross headquarters, going from room to room shooting and bayoneting more than fifty civilians, including two infants, one just ten days old. The marines then surrounded a large hall where more than 500 civilians had sheltered in the underfloor crawlspace for protection against the shellfire. The invaders doused the club's furniture with petrol and set it on fire. Others blocked the crawlspace openings and any men who escaped were gunned down, while any women who got out had fuel poured on their heads and their hair set on fire.

There were, if even possible, yet more gruesome crimes. The Japanese converted a house in Singalong Street, where they cut a hole in an upstairs floor, then marched everyone from teenagers to grandfathers to the edge of the hole and forced them to kneel. A marine then decapitated each one, at least two hundred in total, before kicking the bodies into the hole.

According to testimony at the Yamashita war crimes trial, The Bayview Hotel was used as a designated 'rape centre'. Four hundred women and girls were rounded up from Manila's wealthy Ermita district and submitted to a selection board that picked out the twenty-five women who were considered most beautiful. These women and girls, many of them twelve to fourteen years old, were then taken to the hotel, where Japanese enlisted men and officers took turns raping them.

Many Germans sought refuge in a German club, but Japanese soldiers entered and bayoneted infants and children of mothers pleading for mercy, and raped women seeking refuge. At least twenty Japanese soldiers raped a young girl before slicing off her breasts. While the other Japanese soldiers laughed, a Japanese soldier placed her mutilated breasts on his chest to mimic a woman. The soldiers then doused the young girl and two other women with petrol and set them on fire. They then set the entire club on fire, killing many of its inhabitants. Women who were trying to escape from the fire were caught and raped by the Japanese. Twenty-eight-year-old Julia Lopez had her breasts sliced off, was raped by Japanese soldiers and had her hair set on fire. Another woman was partially decapitated after attempting to defend herself from being raped by a Japanese soldier.

Gruesome massacres like these were only a part of scores of smaller and often undocumented atrocities, as marauding troops attacked families in homes and pulled others out of bomb shelters, butchering them in the streets. They went so far as luring victims into an open space on Kansas Street by planting a Red Cross flag. To escape the flames and artillery, refugees often congregated in the large compounds of some of the city's wealthiest citizens. However, they were easy targets for the Japanese, who encircled the homes, set fire to them and shot any escapees. Hundreds of women were rounded up and many of them locked inside the deluxe Bayview Hotel, where Japanese troops assaulted them. Many were raped multiple times for days on end, including Filipino, Russian, Spanish, German and Indian women. Most of the victims were mutilated and killed. Rosa Henson was just one of the victims. She survived and gave evidence at the war crimes trials. When he was unable to answer questions from Japanese soldiers, her father was skinned alive while tied upside down, and her mother was raped. Her sisters were also abused in one of the Japanese Army's 'comfort stations' and one of them had multiple cigarette burns across her body.

The combined death toll for civilians in the Battle of Manila was about 100,000, most of whom were attributed to massacres by Japanese forces, but some historians suggest a higher civilian casualty rate of up to 500,000 dead as a result of the Manila massacre on its own, exclusive of other causes. It should also be stressed that American artillery and bombing were responsible for much of the destruction of Manila's architectural and cultural heritage, which, according to a Japanese estimate, caused 40 per cent of the total Filipino deaths during the battle.

The Allies still had much more of the Japanese empire to liberate, and they still faced the daunting challenge of attacking Japan's mainland islands. Sadly, the death toll from the battles to come would be equally horrendous, and many more atrocities would be committed before the Asia-Pacific Holy War ended.

14

IWO JIMA

1945 had begun with Japan facing the certain prospect of defeat in its Asia-Pacific War, Hirohito's Holy War against the West. It was certainly a war – gruesome and distinctly evil, as they always are – but far from 'holy', in that it was characterised by barbarity and immorality.

It had also become a war which had been transformed from unstoppable conquest in 1942 to a slow and excruciating death by strangulation for Japan from the middle of 1943 onwards. Even so, Japan's leadership saw no reason to change course, or shed its cloak of warrior invincibility. In February 1945, Hirohito consulted his seven senior statesmen concerning the war. They were the six former prime ministers: Hiranuma, Hirota, Wakatsuki, Okada, Konoe, and Tōjō. Plus former Lord Keeper of the Privy Seal, Makino. The meetings produced an overwhelming consensus that the mighty struggle for the emperor and his empire should continue.

The consensus flew in the face of common sense and a grim military situation, both for Japan and its Axis allies in Europe. Germany's Nazi regime was heading inexorably for defeat. Despite Hitler's lunatic obduracy, it was no longer a matter of if, but when. For Japan the situation was equally grim. The army in Burma had been destroyed. The armies in China were exhausted and the tide had turned against them. They were stretched thinly and fighting a costly guerrilla war that in 1944 alone had absorbed 64 per cent of Japan's emergency military expenditure. The high command in Tokyo was also strengthening army air power, stockpiling weapons and organising twenty-nine new divisions, fifty-one infantry regiments and many artillery and tank regiments in preparation, not for attack, or for the defence of its empire, but for a suicidal defence of the homeland.

During 1945, 43 per cent of the army would be stationed in Japan, Korea and Taiwan. Given the emperor's wildly optimistic belief that Japan could somehow stall the inevitable outcome of the war, Baron Reijirō Wakatsuki suggested that the enemy must first be made to see '*the disadvantages of continuing the war*'. Count Nobuaki Makino declared that '*the ultimate priority is to develop an advantageous war situation*'. Keisuke Okada said Japan should wait for '*a moment favourable for us*', then make peace. Hiranuma and Hirota were categorical, advising the emperor to fight on until the bitter end. Hirohito agreed, but with a reservation: '*If we hold out long enough in this war, we may be able to win, but what worries me is whether the nation will be able to endure it until then.*'

Perhaps Japan's biggest fear was that Soviet leader Josef Stalin would renege on his Neutrality Pact with Japan. Even after the Yalta Conference of early February, when Britain, the US and the Soviet Union appeared to act in unity and Tōjō said that he thought it no better than fifty-fifty that Stalin would honour his pact, Hirohito still ignored the warnings. Hirohito's position was clearly naïve at best, given that Stalin was highly likely to grasp the opportunity afforded by Japan's increasing weakness to improve the Soviet Union's position in East Asia.

One of the insightful accounts of the tragic events in Japan in 1945 comes from a selection of letters between a young boy, Ichirō Hatano, who had just started high school, and his mother, Isoko, when they lived as refugees from Tokyo. Isoko read child psychology at university and was married to a professor of psychology. The first letter from Ichiro to his mother is dated 1 January 1945.

'*This is a very quiet New Year. Can it be a wartime New Year? What a happy time we have had. And yet I cannot stop myself worrying about the soldiers at the front. We are all Japanese. It is a hard life they are having. Not all of those who are there went because they wanted to. It does not seem fair to me that, because some of us are a bit younger, we are allowed to have such an easy time of it. Couldn't we make ourselves useful in some way suitable for our age? They talk about local defence, but the old people can manage that. It is horrible to have nothing to do but wait, with your hands in your pockets, for the war to end. All the more so since, as Father says, things are going from bad to worse.'*

The reply from his mother, Isoko, dated 18 January, illustrates the ominous nature of Japan's domestic regime.

'At about midday a member of the secret police came to the house. The secret police is the branch which deals with the repression of subversive ideas. This man has been to the house twice before and I was not terribly surprised to see him come, but yesterday he questioned us particularly closely. Your father had done nothing wrong, but the police probably have their eye on him because they consider him a "liberal". I don't know where they have got this idea from, but they maintain that the professors' teaching is detrimental and that, for that reason, the morale of soldiers who come from the University is poor.'

On the same day, army pilot Shin Hasegawa described his despondency, not just about the war, but about human nature.

US air raids on Japan from China and India, sporadic and with few tangible results, had been going on for some time. Septuagenarian Tsunejirō Tamura's diary chronicled the bombing of Japan from as early as 8 December 1944, with the resulting destruction causing shortages of food and fuel. His entry for 9 December records:

'It's clear and cold, very cold, but there's no charcoal. With no fuel to burn, nothing's quite as hard on old bodies as the cold. Although New Year's is coming, we haven't had a single rice cake [. . .] Even if we ate rice cakes, it wouldn't be a typical New Year's when you're being attacked by the enemy. It was Tokyo's fourth attack, and now there are completely burned-out areas in that city. The fires continued from noon until 5:30 p.m. They say six thousand people died and their bodies filled the underground passages of Mitsukoshi Department Store, but they still couldn't handle them all. It occurred to me that we haven't known anything this tragic. Oh, how I'd like to forget the world! Mine is the utter humiliation. I'm just unlucky! Enemy planes, come! Kill me! Then I'd forget the world!'

As more and more Pacific islands came under American control, their proximity to Japan meant that high-intensity bombing, and the resulting mass destruction of both Japan's infrastructure and its population, became an important strategic option. Given the level of hostility, and indeed hatred, at that point in the war, the Americans targeted the civilian population and its urban centres with impunity. Although, as in Europe, the logic of the onslaught was to break the Japanese people's will to resist, it had little or no effect.

Initially, at the beginning of 1945, high-altitude (above 20,000 feet) bombing was imprecise and ineffective because of cloud over the Japanese mainland and the power of the jet stream in the area. Even so, the Japanese people knew that their vulnerability was all too obvious. Ichirō Hatano, writing to his mother on 16 February, expressed his fears.

'So now Suwa has been bombed for the first time since we have been here. I don't know whether you saw the aeroplanes, but since we had taken shelter in the mountains, we could easily make out the B29s as they flew by, leaving long wakes of white behind them. As it was the first time I had seen them, they struck me as a beautiful sight rather than something terrifying. But when I remember that our country is being devastated by these machines [. . .] when I think that Tokyo may be destroyed, I can hardly contain myself.'

Ichiro was right to be concerned about the fate of Japan's cities and their populations. Massive B-29 Superfortress combat operations against Japan, including relentless incendiary attacks on sixty-seven Japanese cities, known as Operation Meetinghouse, would begin in March. However, before the horror of the bombings intensified, the country had to face a huge American attack on a strategically important island just 750 miles south of Tokyo.

Operation Detachment, the amphibious invasion of the volcanic island of Iwo Jima, began on 19 February 1945. Iwo Jima is part of the Bonin Islands, which run due south of Tokyo, located 750 miles to the north. A US force of 60,000 took part in the assault, confronted by approximately 21,000 Japanese troops. As Japanese commanders had demonstrated on Peleliu in September 1944, attempts to fight Allied forces on the landing beaches were abandoned, replaced by yard-by-yard battles of attrition from one well-defended killing zone to the next. General Tadamichi Kuribayashi ordered the construction of heavily fortified strongpoints, bunkers and artillery positions, often connected by extensive tunnel systems with stockpiles of ammunition and food.

Kuribayashi was a fascinating character whose reputation has put him on a par with Admiral Isoroku Yamamoto in Japanese military history. Born in Nagano in 1891, in 1923 he graduated second from the 35th class of the Army War College with excellent marks and received a military sabre from the emperor himself. Apparently, senior officers approached him with offers of their daughter's hand in marriage, but he turned them all down.

Like Yamamoto, Kuribayashi was designated as deputy military attaché to Washington in 1928. For two years, he travelled across the United States, conducting extensive military and industrial research, and studied at Harvard. According to Vice Admiral Shigegi Kaneko, who attended Nagano High School with Kuribayashi, '*He once organised a strike against the school authorities. He just escaped expulsion by a whisker. He was already good at poetry, composition and speech writing, and was a young literary enthusiast.*' Kuribayashi knew America well and, just before the attack on Pearl Harbor, told his family that America was the last country in the world Japan should fight.

On 25 June 1944, Kuribayashi wrote to his wife, Yoshii, describing the conditions his men faced.

'*There is no spring water here, so we must do with rainwater. I long for a glass of cold water, but nothing can be done. The number of flies and mosquitoes is appalling. There are no newspapers, no radios, and no shops. There are a few local farms, but no shelters suitable for anything other than livestock. Our soldiers pitch tents or crawl into caves. The caves are stuffy, and the heat and humidity are intolerable. I, of course, endure similar living conditions [. . .] It is a living hell and I have never experienced anything remotely like it in my entire life.*'

He wrote to Yoshii again, on 2 August: '*There are so many flies that they get into your eyes and your mouth. There are ants everywhere – like the pilgrims all moving en masse to Zenkóji Temple – and they come crawling up all over your body, lots of them at once. There are cockroaches, too – filthy, grotesque insects – all over the place. The only good news is that there aren't any poisonous insects or snakes. For food, there were a few wild papayas and bananas, but so many soldiers picked them that there are none left now. As it's a piping hot volcanic island, vegetables don't really grow here.'*

Long before the Americans landed, Kuribayashi knew that he was likely to die on Iwo Jima. On 5 September 1944, he wrote to Yoshii: *'It must be destiny that we as a family must face this. Please accept this and stand tall with the children at your side. I will be with you always.'*

In order to prepare his soldiers for an unconventional style of fighting, Kuribayashi composed six 'Courageous Battle Vows' which were widely distributed among his men.

We shall defend this island with all our strength to the end.

1. We shall fling ourselves against the enemy tanks, clutching explosives to destroy them.
2. We shall slaughter the enemy, dashing in among them to kill them.
3. Every one of our shots shall be on target and kill the enemy.
4. We shall not die until we have killed ten of the enemy.
5. We shall continue to harass the enemy with guerrilla tactics even if only one of us remains alive.

Kuribayashi also composed a set of instructions to the soldiers of his 'Courage Division'.

Preparations for battle

1. Use every moment you have, whether during air raids or during battle, to build strong positions that enable you to smash the enemy at a ratio of ten to one.
2. Build fortifications that enable you to shoot and attack in any direction, without pausing, even if your comrades should fall.
3. Be resolute and make rapid preparations to store food and water in your position so that your supplies will last even through intense barrages.

Fighting defensively

1. Destroy the American devils with heavy fire. Improve your aim and try to hit your target the first time.
2. As we practised, refrain from reckless charges, but take advantage of the moment when you've smashed the enemy. Watch out for bullets from others of the enemy.
3. When one man dies a hole opens up in your defence. Exploit manmade structures and natural features for your own protection. Take care with camouflage and cover.
4. Destroy enemy tanks with explosives, and several enemy soldiers along with the tank. This is your best chance for meritorious deeds.
5. Do not be alarmed should tanks come toward you with a thunderous rumble. Shoot at them with anti-tank fire and use tanks.
6. Do not be afraid if the enemy penetrates inside your position. Resist stubbornly and shoot them dead.
7. Control is difficult to exercise if you are sparsely dispersed over a wide area. Always tell the officers in charge when you move forward.
8. Even if your commanding officer falls, continue defending your position, by yourself if necessary. Your most important duty is to perform brave deeds.
9. Do not think about eating and drinking but focus on exterminating the enemy. Be brave, O warriors, even if rest and sleep are impossible.
10. The strength of each of you is the cause of our victory. Soldiers of the Courage Division, do not crack at the harshness of the battle and try to hasten your death.
11. We will finally prevail if you make the effort to kill just one man more. Die after killing ten men and yours is a glorious death on the battlefield.
12. Keep on fighting even if you are wounded in the battle. Do not get taken prisoner. At the end, stab the enemy as he stabs you.

Kuribayashi's response to overwhelming American firepower was simple: dig in and dig deep. He discouraged his subordinates from viewing banzai charges as viable tactics, impressing on them that effectively delaying and then killing the enemy were the priorities. By the time the Americans began bombarding Iwo Jima, all Japanese civilians had been evacuated from the island and Kuribayashi had done everything within his limited means to make the US assault as costly as possible.

The underground installations were extremely successful even before the battle began. They protected the soldiers from the massive bombardments inflicted on the island as a softening-up before the ground assault. On 8 December 1944, almost three years to the day after Japan's attack on Pearl Harbor, Iwo Jima was hit by the biggest combined aerial assault and naval bombardment since the start of the Pacific War. Kuribayashi wrote a letter to his wife that same afternoon.

'Just as I expected, we were attacked by large planes that came in thirteen waves from around 8:30 in the morning until about 2:00 in the afternoon. They were followed by a naval bombardment lasting one and a half hours, and I only just came out of the shelter now (3:00 p.m.). Bombs landed quite close to us, but luckily, they didn't do any damage. The overall number of casualties is tiny.'

On that single day, a combined total of 192 fighters and bombers flew over Iwo Jima and dropped more than 800 tons of bombs. Three heavy cruisers and six destroyers delivered a sustained naval barrage. Above ground, the Japanese lost ten planes, but the underground tunnels were untouched, and casualties were almost non-existent. Up to that point, the island had been bombarded sporadically. But from 8 December until the landing, the bombardment continued for seventy-four days without pause.

The Japanese soldiers would dive underground when air raids and naval bombardments started, but when they were over, they were soon above ground to resume their work. The massive bombardment had destroyed every single tree and blade of grass, but their underground world was unharmed. According to the official

1. A Yokohama Samurai Warrior, Edo Period (Pre Meiji-Restoration) circa 1865.

2. Imperial Japanese Army opening fire with their Japanese-made Type 22 repeating carbines. 1st Sino-Japanese War 1894–1895.

3. The 1904–1905 Russo-Japanese War. 500lb shells to be used in the Japanese attack on Port Arthur, January 1905. The massive weapons were central to Japan's success.

4. The Japanese Invasion of Manchuria 1931. Imperial Japanese Army Cavalry entering Mukden (Shenyang), September 1931.

5. Following the capture of Nanking on 13 December 1937, a Japanese officer prepares to execute a Chinese prisoner of war during the Nanking Massacre.

6. USS *Cassin* (right), a Mahan-class destroyer, was in drydock in Pearl Harbor on 7 December 1941 when her neighbour, USS *Downes* (left), was hit by a 500lb bomb dropped by the Imperial Japanese Navy. *Downes'* fuel tanks were ruptured, causing huge fires on both *Downes* and *Cassin*. Both ships were lost and decommissioned.

7. With fixed bayonets, soldiers of the Imperial Japanese Army guard men of Britain's Suffolk Regiment, some of the 120,000 British, Australian, Indian and Chinese forces who surrendered at the fall of Singapore on 15 February 1942. British prime minister, Winston Churchill, said the defeat was, 'The scene of the greatest disaster to British Arms which our history records'.

8. Japanese prisoners of war aboard USS *Ballard* after being rescued from a lifeboat fourteen days after the Battle of Midway. They were from the Engineering Corps of the Imperial Japanese Navy aircraft-carrier *Huryū*. *Huryū* was scuttled the day after she was attacked from the air and set on fire on 5 June 1942. Thirty-nine men had been aboard the lifeboat. Thirty-four survived to be picked up by *Ballard*.

9. The USS *Missouri* about to be hit by a A6M Zero Kamikaze off Okinawa on 11 April 1945. The plane hit *Missouri* below her main deck, causing minor damage and no casualties. It is likely that the Zero's bomb load did not detonate. The name of the Kamikaze pilot who died on impact is not known.

10. Some of the survivors (military and civilian) of the Battle of Okinawa, one of the bloodiest of the Asia-Pacific War. The battle lasted from 1 April to 22 June 1945.

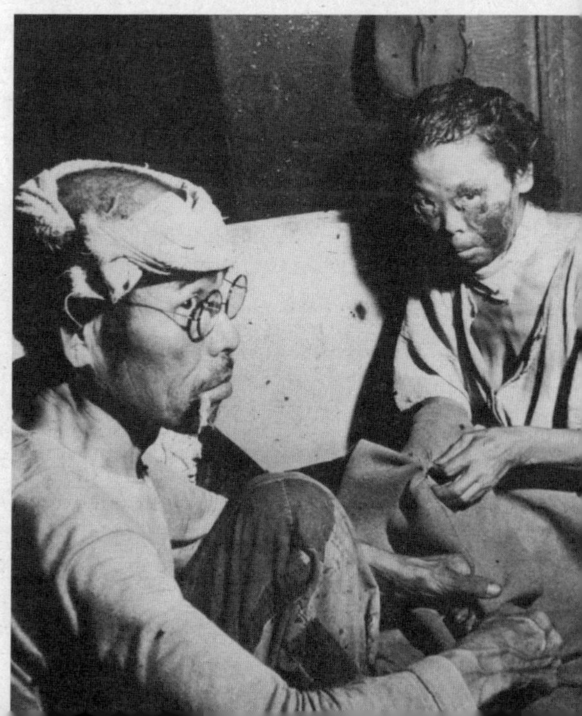

11. The charred remains of Japanese civilians after the 10 March 1945 firebombing of Tokyo. As many as 100,000 people died. One million were made homeless.

12. Taken on 5 October 1945, two of the victims of the atomic bomb detonated above Hiroshima on 6 August 1945. They are in a damaged bank building in the centre of Hiroshima. Many, well over 100,000 people, died in the blast, but thousands more died from injuries, disease and radiation sickness.

13. General Yoshijirō Umezu signs the Instrument of Surrender on behalf of Japan aboard USS *Missouri* moored in Tokyo Bay on 2 September 1945.

14. His rehabilitation complete, Hirohito is given a rapturous welcome as he visits Hiroshima in 1947.

history of the US Marine Corps, a total of 6,800 tons of bombs were dropped on the island over the seventy-four-day period. In the five naval bombardments conducted in December and January, 2,031 6-inch shells, 6,472 8-inch shells and 15,251 5-inch shells were fired. As far as the Americans were concerned, so intense was the bombardment that they wouldn't have been surprised if the island had ceased to exist. But the aerial photographs taken by reconnaissance planes told a different story. The 450 defence positions that had been in place when the bombardment started had increased to 750 just before the landing.

Toshiharu Takahashi was a survivor of Iwo Jima. He served as a corporal in the 1st Mixed Brigade of Engineers. Of the 278 people in his unit, only thirteen survived.

'The guns that were trained on the island all spurted fire at the same time. On the island there was a huge earthquake. There were pillars of fire that looked as if they would touch the sky. Black smoke covered the island, and shrapnel was flying all over the place with a shrieking sound. Trees with trunks one metre across were blown out of the ground, roots uppermost. The sound was deafening, as terrible as a couple of hundred thunderclaps coming down at once. Even in a cave thirty metres underground, my body was jerked up off the ground. It was hell on earth. Next, large planes – many tens of them – came all together. They made a deep rumbling sound as they came. They were silver. Once over the island they dropped one-ton bombs – terrifying things. [. . .] A timid man would go insane. [. . .] They made craters ten metres wide and five metres deep in the earth. No one could survive in these conditions. Any Japanese soldiers, like the runners who went outside, were all killed.'

Takatsugi Kojima was a survivor from the same battalion.

'As we waited for the Grummans [US fighter planes] to pull out, we used to gather in the entrance to the bunker and talk endlessly about the good old days back home. Our main topics were eating and water. [. . .] One soldier suddenly shouted out for us all to come and see. We were thrilled to see that there was dew glistening on the tips of the Japanese pampas grass that was still in the shade. We pressed it to our lips as if in a silent kiss.'

A post-war Japanese Monograph, written by former officers of the Japanese Imperial Army and Navy shortly after the end of the war, summarised the thinking.

> In the light of the above situation, seeing that it was impossible to conduct our air, sea, and ground operations on Iwo Island [Jima] toward ultimate victory, it was decided that to gain time necessary for the preparation of the Homeland defence, our forces should rely solely upon the established defensive equipment in that area, checking the enemy by delaying tactics. Even the suicidal attacks by small groups of our Army and Navy airplanes, the surprise attacks by our submarines and the actions of parachute units, although effective, could be regarded only as a strategical ruse on our part. It was a most depressing thought that we had no available means left for the exploitation of the strategical opportunities which might from time to time occur in the course of these operations.

When the Americans landed on 19 February, Kuribayashi held his fire for an hour. The sudden, unexpected scale of the defenders' artillery and mortar assault made it obvious that the pre-attack American bombardment had had little effect on the Japanese defences. Japanese firepower had a devastating effect on the build-up of American men and equipment on the beaches, and caused many casualties. The unstable black sand and volcanic cinders of the beaches' stepped terraces bogged down wheeled and even tracked vehicles, causing congestion at the waterline, where the US marines and infantry came under constant fire. Despite the setbacks, the landings were successful, and the marines began to move inland, but momentum was slow with progress measured only in yards.

During the night of 21/22 February, US ships were subjected to the only kamikaze attack of the invasion. The escort carrier *Bismark Sea* was lost, and fleet carrier *Saratoga* was so badly damaged that she had to return to the States for repair and never returned to combat. While the marines reached the summit of Mount Suribachi on the morning of 23 February – when Joe Rosenthal's famous photograph of five marines raising the Stars and Stripes was taken – the battle for the entire island would take another five weeks. As the marines advanced, rather than banzai charges, they encountered well-coordinated counter-attacks by the Japanese. US tanks were put out of action by mines, suicide squads or well-camouflaged anti-tank guns, and the Americans were subjected to constant artillery, mortar and small-arms fire. Many Japanese positions had to be taken by direct ground assault or by sealing off entrances. After nine days, the US drive to the north had progressed only 4,000 yards at a cost of 7,000 US casualties.

Among Kuribayashi's men was Private Takeo Abe, who survived the battle and spent the remainder of his life repatriating the remains of his comrades. He never forgot the conditions they endured.

'*We were forced to spare rations for battle, and we foraged around for edible weeds. Suffering from chronic diarrhoea, empty stomachs, and lack of water, we dug bunkers in the sand under a merciless sun and constructed underground shelters that were steamy with heat. We used lukewarm salt water from a well on the beach for cooking, and saved what little rainwater we could for drinking. But one water-bottle a day was the most we ever had to drink.*'

As the battle intensified, for once, Hirohito acknowledged the bravery and sacrifice of his forces: '*I am fully satisfied that naval units have taken charge of defence and are cooperating very well with the army. Even after the enemy landed, they fought ferociously against much greater forces and contributed to the entire operation.*'

On 17 March 1945, Kuribayashi sent his farewell message to Imperial Headquarters, accompanied by three traditional death poems that were, in effect, a subtle protest against the military command that so readily sent men to their deaths.

The battle is entering its final chapter. Since the enemy's landing, the gallant fighting of the men under my command has been such that even the gods would weep. In particular, I humbly rejoice in the fact that they have continued to fight bravely though utterly empty-handed and ill-equipped against a land, sea, and air attack of a material superiority such as surpasses the imagination. One after another they are falling in the ceaseless and ferocious attacks of the enemy. For this reason, the situation has arisen whereby I must disappoint your expectations and yield this important place to the hands of the enemy. With humility and sincerity, I offer my repeated apologies. Our ammunition is gone and our water dried up. Now is the time for us to make the final counter-attack and fight gallantly, conscious of the emperor's favour, not begrudging our efforts though they turn our bones to powder and pulverise our bodies. I believe that until the island is recaptured, the emperor's domain will be eternally insecure. I therefore swear that even when I have become a ghost, I shall look forward to turning the defeat of the Imperial Army to victory. I stand now at the beginning of the end. At the same time as revealing my inmost feelings, I pray earnestly for the unfailing victory and security of the Empire. Farewell for all eternity.

As the battle began to run its course, Kuribayashi radioed his colleague, Major Horie.

I have just 400 men under my command. The enemy besieged us by fire and flame from their tanks. In particular, they are trying to approach the entrance of our cave with explosives. My men and officers are still fighting. The enemy's front lines are 300 metres from us, and they are attacking by tank firing. They advised us to surrender by loudspeaker, but we only laughed at this childish trick, and we did not set ourselves against them.

Major Yoshitake Horie commanded the Iwo Jima radio station and later wrote: '*General Kuribayashi commanded his battle under candlelight without a single rest or sleep, day after day. Radio broadcasts, newspapers, and magazines from Japan encouraged him thoroughly, especially when the old and young men, boys and girls of his native place prayed to God for his victory.*'

A memoir by First Lieutenant Takeshi Tamada, quoted in the official history, includes the following description of what happened in the Command Bunker on the night of the 17th, before the move to the bunker of the Kita Engineering Corps.

'On the evening of March 17, we burned our insignia of rank, any important documents, and our private possessions. Everyone in the head-quarters cave was presented with one cup of sake and two cigarettes from the emperor. Lieutenant General Kuribayashi grasped the pommel of his sword with his left hand and made a speech to the following effect, "Even if you have to eat grass, bite the earth, or throw yourselves on the ground, I believe that you will fight and, in so doing, find a way out of this fatal situation. With things as they are, each one of you must kill one hundred – there is nothing else for it. I believe in your devotion. Please do as I do."'

Then on the evening of 23 March 1945, Kuribayashi radioed a last message to Horie.

All officers and men of Chichi Jima – goodbye from Iwo.

Major Horie later wrote, *'I tried to communicate with them for three days after that but received no answer.'*

Only 216 survived the battle, to be taken prisoner, and an esti-mated 3,000 went into hiding. By August, most had been killed, captured or had surrendered, except for one group that carried on fighting until 1949. After the war, the General's son, Taro Kuribayashi, interviewed several survivors of the Japanese garrison. As a result, he believes that his father was killed in an artillery barrage during the final assault.

'My father had believed it shameful to have his body discovered by the enemy even after death, so he had previously asked his two soldiers to come along with him, one in front and the other behind, with a shovel in hand. In case of his death, he had wanted them to bury his body there and then. It seems that my father and the soldiers were killed by shells, and he was buried at the foot of a tree in Chidori village, along the beach near Osaka Mountain. Afterwards, General Smith spent a whole day looking for his body to pay respect accordingly and to perform a burial, but in vain.'

There were several Japanese commanders during the Asia-Pacific War who behaved atrociously, especially towards civilians and prisoners of war. There were also many who led their men bravely and resourcefully, but none with more integrity and courage than General Tadamichi Kuribayashi – a real soldier's soldier.

The importance of the outcome of the Battle of Iwo Jima is the subject of much debate among historians. Ostensibly, the island's landing strips and its proximity to the Japanese mainland were important to America's bombing strategy and invasion plans. However, neither the US Army nor the Navy were able to use Iwo Jima as a staging area. Navy Seabees did rebuild the airfields for Air Force pilots, but only for emergency landings. This somewhat stark fact has led many to suggest that the human sacrifice on both sides was too great a price, and that the fall of the island had only a psychological value rather than a strategic one.

15

TYPHOON OF STEEL

As the Asia-Pacific War's battles got closer and closer to Japan, the country's civilians were drawn into the conflict en masse, including teenagers. On the mainland, high school students were drafted to work in munitions factories and a range of civil defence duties, but on Okinawa they were conscripted into the army, and many young women were trained as student nurses to augment the Okinawa Army Hospital.

Militarism had entered Japan's school curriculum in the 1930s during the war in China. Girl students played the role of 'special war correspondent' to inform their classmates of Japan's victories. Marksmanship was added to the curriculum until ammunition could no longer be spared. The students trained like soldiers, conducted air-raid drills, practised with bamboo spears, and marching became part of life. To test their stamina, they had to undertake gruelling forty-five-mile marches. They were being moulded and indoctrinated into ideal *gunkoku shojo* – 'patriotic girls' who would be as loyal to the Empire as any soldier.

Okinawa is an irregular-shaped island in the centre of the Ryukyu Islands, a long 790-mile chain of mountainous islands southwest of Japan proper, northeast of Taiwan and the Philippines, and west of the Bonins (which include Iwo Jima). Okinawa itself is a large island, sixty-six miles long and about seven miles wide. A sub-tropical coral and limestone island, lush with vegetation, it is ideal as a holiday destination but a nightmare for soldiers in battle. Also, its many subterranean caves offered the Japanese perfect locations for defensive redoubts and created many battlefield horror stories as the Americans used grenades, flame-throwers and napalm to flush out those, both military and civilian, sheltering in them.

Like England in 1944, preparing for the D-Day assault on Europe, Okinawa had the harbours and airfields needed to stage a huge amphibious invasion of mainland Japan. The island had been invaded by Japan's Satsuma Domain in 1609 and became formally incorporated into Japan in 1879. However, the Okinawan people remained ethnically and linguistically distinct from the mainland Japanese people. An influx of Malay, Chinese, Mongol and other races had created a noticeably different culture in Okinawa from their northern Japanese neighbours. Unlike the military traditions of the northerners, the Okinawans had no history of warfare and neither made nor wore weapons. In plain terms, on Japan's northern islands, Okinawans were seen as simple peasants, useful as 'hewers of wood and drawers of water'.

The numbers involved in the Battle for Okinawa were colossal, the greatest amphibious assault of the entire Asia-Pacific War, and military historians still argue about which was bigger: D-Day or Okinawa. The Americans committed 541,000 men, 3,000 aircraft and an armada of epic proportions: thirty-nine aircraft carriers, eighteen battleships, twenty-seven cruisers, 177 destroyers, and numerous support ships. They were supported by Task Force 57, a British and Commonwealth fleet. By comparison, Japan had only 76,000 Japanese troops, 40,000 Okinawan conscripts and a small fleet: Operation Ten-Go, comprising nine escorts, a light cruiser, eight destroyers and the mighty *Yamato*, the most powerful battleship afloat. However, the Imperial Japanese Navy was short of fuel and could supply only enough for a one-way ticket for its fleet. Its objective was to cause as much mayhem and damage as possible, then to beach its vessels and for its sailors to join the land battle. In the end, Okinawa brought about the final destruction of Japan's navy as a fighting force.

Yamato's suicide mission ended long before she reached Okinawa. Early in the morning of 7 April 1945, American scout planes located *Yamato*, still only halfway to Okinawa. A massive strike force of 280 fighters, bombers and torpedo planes was launched. For two hours, *Yamato* suffered a merciless attack from the planes of no fewer than eleven fleet carriers. Like a swarm of killer bees attacking their prey, a feeding frenzy followed. *Yamato* took two hits during this attack, and two escorting destroyers went down. A second aerial onslaught of over a hundred aircraft pressed the attack and, listing badly, she started to go down. In an attempt to trim her, Admiral Seichi Itō made the ruthless decision to flood the starboard outer engine room, drowning three hundred men at their stations. She had taken ten torpedo and seven bomb hits, and was finished.

Despite the counterflooding, *Yamato* continued to list, and once she reached thirty-five degrees the order was given to abandon ship. The captain and many of the bridge crew tied themselves to their stations and went down with her, while the rest attempted to escape. They could only watch helplessly from the water as American planes circled overhead, ready to deliver the coup de grâce.

At 14:23, *Yamato*'s forward magazines detonated in a spectacular fireball. It was like a tactical nuclear weapon going off. Her ninety-degree list had caused the shells for her main batteries to slide in their magazine, hitting their fuses and exploding. The eruption sent thousands of pieces of shrapnel into the air, which killed most of the sailors swimming on the surface of the water. The underwater concussion killed those near the submerged main deck, while those unfortunate enough to be near her smokestack were caught in the massive suction created by the huge open funnel as the ship went under.

Of the ten warships that had set out with the task force, six were still afloat, but barely. The destroyers *Isokaze* and *Kasumi* were shattered hulks, adrift in the East China Sea. Over 4,000 men who had sailed aboard *Yamato* and its escorts were dead. Of *Yamato*'s 3,000-man crew, only 269 were saved.

Later, a navigation officer on one of Japan's surviving destroyers reported that a pillar of fire reached a height of 6,500 feet and its mushroom cloud rose to 20,000 feet. The flash from the explosion was seen as far away as Kagoshima on the Japanese mainland and was said to have destroyed several American planes observing the sinking.

The Battle for Okinawa began on 1 April and lasted for almost three months. Such was the scale and ferocious intensity of the battle that it became known in Japanese as *tetsu no bōfū* – the 'typhoon of steel' in English. The Americans created an entire army, the 10th, a cross-branch force of infantry and marines with both air and naval elements, which consisted of over a quarter of a million personnel. The Japanese defence force was the 32nd Army, less than 120,000 strong, made up of 76,000 regulars, plus 40,000 conscripts, supported by the remnants of the Combined Fleet, a force that was so depleted, especially after the loss of the *Yamato*, that it was of little consequence. Mitsuri Ushijima was the commanding general of the Japanese defenders. A man who had opposed the attack on the United States, he tried to transport many Okinawans to other islands and to mainland Japan. He had prepared a solid defence structure on the island. It included trenches, bunkers and a command headquarters in a network of tunnels under Shuri Castle in Naha, the island's capital city.

Ushijima's chief of staff was Isamu Chō, an ultranationalist who favoured aggressive attack rather than tactical defence in meeting the American threat, while Senior Staff Officer Hiromichi Yahara was an advocate of attritional tactics, to hold and diminish the invaders for as long as possible. Not only would that tactic delay the inevitable fall of Okinawa, but also give the mainland more time to prepare for the day when the might of America's military machine would be unleashed on the homeland. Indeed, many in Japan's hierarchy still hoped that, if Japan could show the Americans what it would cost them, especially in terms of personnel, they might consider a peace deal.

However, Chō soon objected to the tactic of attrition, and recommended banzai charges at the Americans. Yahara disagreed but went along with it. When it became obvious that Chō's suicide attacks were not working – instead causing massive Japanese casualties and loss of ground – Chō allowed Yahara to continue to make tactical and operational decisions. Knowing that he did not have the firepower to fight the Americans head-to-head in battle – and indeed could not possibly win – Yahara decided to fight from caves as long as possible and then, once the caves were lost, to retreat and regroup, continuing to defend, until there was nowhere left on the island to offer space for further retreat.

Northern Okinawa fell relatively quickly, with US marines making rapid inroads in the first two weeks of April. The ground was mountainous and wooded, with the Japanese dug in on Mount Yaedake, a heavily ridged area cut by deep ravines. There was heavy fighting before the US marines finally took Yaedake on 18 April. However, it was not the end of the fighting in the north. On 24 May, the Japanese mounted Operation Gi-Gou when a company of Giretsu Kuteitai commandos was airlifted for a suicide attack on Yontan Airfield. Four aircraft aborted the mission with engine problems and three more were shot down. However, five managed to crash-land on the airfield. About ten surviving commandos then wreaked havoc on the supplies and nearby aircraft. They killed two US servicemen, destroyed 70,000 gallons of fuel, nine aircraft, and damaged twenty-nine more, before being almost annihilated. One member of the raiding party survived and was able to make his way across the battlefield, reaching the headquarters of the 32nd Army on 12 June.

Following the disastrous banzai charges of 4 May, initiated by Chō in the south, Ushijima had turned to Yahara and summoned him to a meeting on the evening of 5 May. He spoke plainly to his senior staff officer.

'He looked at me pensively and then spoke softly. "Colonel Yahara, as you predicted, this offensive has been a total failure. Your judgement was correct. You must have been frustrated from the start of this battle because I did not use your talents and skill wisely. Now I am determined to stop this offensive. Meaningless suicide is not what I want. When I left Tokyo, both War Minister Umezu and Army Chief of Staff Anami urged me not to be hasty ordering a last suicidal charge. Now our main force is largely spent, but some of our fighting strength is left, and we are getting strong support from the islanders. With these we will fight to the southernmost hill, to the last square inch of land, and to the last man. I am ready to fight, but from now on I leave everything up to you. My instructions to you are to do whatever you feel is necessary." [. . .] Now that our forces

were exhausted, he finally recognised what I had been advocating from the start of the Okinawa battle.'

Yahara was frustrated and furious at his commander's words: he realised it was now far too late to accomplish anything. He knew Okinawa was being sacrificed for the sake of the nation, and he was far from happy about it.

'In mid-May came news of Germany's capitulation. We now realised that we were doomed. It was nonsense to continue the war in this corner of the Pacific after our only real ally had collapsed. A man may ruin himself as a matter of pride, to save face. He should not, however, jeopardise his nation for such a reason. A nation should never be sacrificed for the sake of its leaders.'

Despite Yahara's disdain for Tokyo's leadership, he persevered, even though he knew that it was only a matter of time before the battle was lost – and that the price on both sides would be dreadful.

'The beautiful, peaceful countryside [. . .] was now steeped in the blood of thousands of soldiers, Japanese and American. Enemy tanks fired at our headquarters, and direct hits echoed ominously throughout the limestone caves. Machine-gun fire day and night was punctuated by the rumble of artillery. The Inoue Battalion was almost totally annihilated, including its leader.'

Like a good and loyal soldier, Yahara still put on a brave face.

'The battle was at fever pitch, but we were losing. Like the last flare of a dying candle, we sent a message asking Imperial Headquarters for more air support [. . .] "We have lost many elite troops, but still believe in the immortality of the Empire. We are surrounded by the enemy, but our fighting spirit remains strong."'

By the end of May, the Americans had entered Naha, which was largely deserted, and the Japanese had conducted a skilful night-time retreat aided by the monsoon storms. The 32nd Army was able to move nearly 30,000 personnel into its last defence line on the Kiyan Peninsula, which, in the latter stages of the battle, led to the greatest slaughter on Okinawa, including the deaths of thousands of civilians. Hill 89 became the 32nd's final headquarters, sited in an underground cave with three openings.

'*We climbed down the ladder of the central shaft to a level passageway. After walking sixty or seventy metres, we turned right and were at the western cave opening. In some places it was difficult to squeeze past the rock formations of this natural cave. Low-hanging stalactites dripped water, and it was dangerous to walk without a helmet. It was an awful place.*'

The Kiyan Peninsula measures eight kilometres from east to west, and four kilometres from north to south. It was to be the place of the 32nd Army's final showdown. Following their swift retreat, and anticipating the Americans' inevitable advance, Yahara's men enjoyed a brief respite in surroundings that would soon become a violent battlefield.

'*We sat there on rugs and chairs to enjoy the fresh air. Seventy days of cave dwelling had taken a toll on my health. After sitting in the sun for a while, I felt so lethargic that I had to return to the darkness of the cave to regain energy. I said that I felt like a mole. General Chō chuckled, "Hey, we are not moles," he said. "We are geisha girls. By day we are lifeless, but in the darkness, we come to life," and he laughed loudly.*'

When Allied forces began moving closer to Okinawa in November 1944, girls aged from fifteen to nineteen began their nursing training with the army. They became known as the Himeyuri Students, sometimes called the 'Princess Lily Corps', a group of 222 students and eighteen teachers from local schools. They were mobilised by the Japanese Army on 23 March 1945.

The nurses were deployed to a front-line cave hospital, under constant gunfire and bombings, where they performed crude surgery and amputations, buried the dead, and transported materiel to front-line troops. They operated while under continuous fire throughout the all-but-three-month battle. They had assumed the field hospital would be a proper building, with sterile wards and modern facilities. Instead, they found themselves in a series of muddy tunnels and caves, with little more than pallets for beds. Rows of patients lined the raw cavern walls. From the outside, it was just another Japanese fighting hole, full of soldiers and weapons.

Sixteen-year-old Kikuko Miyagi was one of the Princess Lily girls. She was working in the caves when they received a visit from

General Mitsuri Ushijima: *'I had the American book "Gone with the Wind" with me. The commander noticed it, and I thought he was going to yell at me. But he asked what I was reading, and then left. It stuck in my mind. I thought he was very kind.'*

Students and staff from all twenty-one of Okinawa's schools had been conscripted to support the military. While girls nursed, the boys were split between two units. The younger ones were sent to the signal corps and the older ones joined the *Tekketsu Kinnotai* – 'Blood and Iron for the Emperor Corps' – which did labouring jobs like digging tunnels and moving supplies. However, later in the battle many boys would be issued with explosives to make suicide attacks against American tanks. By the end of the battle, at least 2,000 young students had been killed, some as young as thirteen.

For Miyagi, the experience was incredibly harrowing from the beginning: *'Wounded soldiers were being carried in, in large numbers. Some didn't have limbs. Some didn't have faces. There were young men in their twenties and thirties, screaming like babies. Thousands of them.'* Terrifyingly, for the young woman, it was only the start of her trauma.

The teenagers were just a few thousand among the tens of thousands of Okinawans who served the military. Some volunteered willingly to prove to the mainland Japanese that, contrary to what many of their northern neighbours believed, they were loyal Japanese. However, many were coerced in varying degrees and became part of an Imperial Headquarters mission that was not designed to defend Okinawa or its people, but to make its conquest as costly as possible and to delay the invasion of mainland Japan for as long as possible. The Okinawans were simply cannon fodder.

On 4 June, US marines launched an amphibious assault on the peninsula. Ten days later, 4,000 Japanese sailors of the Naval Base Force, including its commander Admiral Ōta, committed suicide within the tunnels of the underground naval headquarters at Oroku. Ota had written to Ushijima before he died, informing him that they would remain in post and fight to the death: *'May our fortunes in war last forever. Though I die on the desolate battlefield of Okinawa I will continue to protect the great spirit of Japan.'*

Ushijima had replied, urging him to withdraw his remaining units. Admiral Ōta, however, was determined to remain at Oroku. When he showed no intention of withdrawing, Ushijima sent a personal letter urging him to retreat. But for all his efforts, he was unable to change the admiral's mind.

By 17 June, the remnants of Ushijima's 32nd Army were pushed into a small pocket in the far south of the island. The end was nigh. On 18 June, General Ushijima issued his final order.

My Beloved Soldiers,

You have all fought courageously for nearly three months. You have discharged your duty. Your bravery and loyalty brighten the future.

The battlefield is now in such chaos that all communications have ceased. It is impossible for me to command you. Every man in these fortifications will follow his superior officer's order and fight to the end for the sake of the motherland.

This is my final order.

Farewell.

Nurse Miyagi and the other girls were as much in the firing line as the Japanese army. Her work had been unrelentingly grim. They had run out of anaesthetic for amputations. At night, she had scrounged for water and food to keep the patients alive. Helping the doctors was not like in films and documentaries, where theatre nurses hand surgeons the tools of their trade. One of the student nurses, Hisa Kishimoto, had to hold down a patient's limb while the doctor amputated it. On one occasion, when holding a soldier's hand as it was detached, she realised the still-warm fingers were gripping her after it was no longer part of his body.

As the Americans advanced, she retreated with the Japanese Army every night. With the American shelling at its worst, Miyagi's group of eighteen nurses decided to commit suicide rather than submit to the rape, mutilation and killing that Japanese soldiers had told them they would face if captured. The girls asked for hand grenades and memorised how to use them: pull the pin, bang the grenade on a rock, hold it to your stomach and wait until you are blown to pieces. Then, suddenly, American troops appeared and opened fire: *'There was a rain of bullets. The Americans must have thought we were with the soldiers. Aosa, Ueki and Nakamoto were killed instantly. Their bodies fell on top of me. Then the firing stopped. The Americans must have noticed they were shooting girls. On the other side of a boulder, ten nurses used their grenades to kill themselves. My class-mates were all dead. I will never forget'.*

Miyagi wriggled out from beneath the bodies of her friends, still clutching her hand grenade, but she was too numb to use it. An American soldier grabbed it from her, a courageous action, since she could have blown him up as well as herself. Then, to her immense relief, Miyagi found that the Americans, instead of cutting off her nose and ears, were treating her injuries. Although she survived, she was an exception. Of her corps of 320 student nurses, 217 died.

In the final days, their position hopeless, Yahara had time to reflect. When his troops had first reached Mabuni, they had encountered little evidence of war damage: just a few large craters where random bombs had fallen.

'The fields had still glistened with beautiful shades of green. Two weeks of fierce battle changed the scenery completely. [. . .] It was now a wasteland, the darkened terrain exposing a gateway to hell. Early one morning I left the cave and saw dark clouds rolling turbulently across the sky, with gun smoke creeping across the land. [. . .] I was overwhelmed by the ghostly sight of the battlefield that had sucked the blood from thousands of soldiers. As a wise old man once said, "Even the demons of the world would mourn at this sight."'

Yahara received a message on Sunday 17 June from General Simon Buckner, the US commanding general, with a proposal for surrender.

To General Ushijima,

    The forces under your command have fought bravely and well. Your infantry tactics have merited the respect of your opponents in the battle for Okinawa. Like myself you are an infantry general, long schooled and experienced in infantry warfare. You must surely realise the pitiful plight of your defence forces. You know that no reinforcements can reach you. I believe, therefore, that you understand as clearly as I, that the destruction of all Japanese resistance on the island is merely a matter of days. It will entail the necessity of my destroying the vast majority of your remaining troops.

General Buckner's proposal was regarded by Ushijima as an affront to Japanese tradition.

As the end approached on 19 June, the girls of the Lily Corps were trapped in the caves with the last remnants of the 32nd Army. One of the nurses, Ruri Morishita, was in the Third Surgical Cave, trying to decide how and when to best make her move. Then someone said they heard footsteps outside and everyone fell silent. There were about a hundred people in the cave. Students huddled around the sick to muffle the sound of their coughing. A Signal Corps soldier set up a machine gun in the cave, ready to open fire as soon as the enemy approached. Then a voice called down in Japanese, '*Are there any civilians in this cave? Any soldiers? If you are in the cave, come out! Otherwise, we'll blast the cave!*'

Realising that the machine gunner would get them all killed, Morishita grabbed a friend and went deeper into the cave. The machine gunner never got a chance to fight back as white phosphorous grenades were hurled into the cave. When they exploded, the space filled with white smoke and people began choking to death. A soldier yelled, saying to urinate into a rag and cover their mouths with it, which Morishita believes saved her life. She crawled along the ground, listening to classmates cry and scream, calling out for their mothers, their friends, for water.

One of them begged for a grenade to kill herself but their teacher had confiscated them all, saying he'd give them back when the time was right to die together. Another teacher began to sing a patriotic song before setting off a grenade and killing himself. Morishita passed out after that and was discovered alive three days later. Of the hundred or so nurses and soldiers in the cave, about eighty had died, including forty-two Lily Corps students and a teacher.

When the end came, with the Americans on the verge of taking the cave that had become their final redoubt, Generals Ushijima and Chō insisted that Yahara must escape to Tokyo to report on the heroics of the 32nd Army. He was required to bear the shame of survival, rather than suicide. Inevitably, the two generals then prepared for their own suicides. When they were ready, each thrust a traditional hara-kiri dagger into his bared abdomen. At the same time, a master swordsman from their unit quickly and skilfully beheaded them with a razor-edged sword.

Disguised as a civilian, Yahara escaped from the cave until he was eventually captured by the Americans and interrogated. He was repatriated to Japan in 1946.

The Americans had fired 7.5 million shells and almost 30 million bullets on Okinawa in three months; 12,000 Americans died taking the island and at least 110,000 Japanese defending it. In addition, it is thought that at least 100,000 Okinawan civilians died – approximately a third of the island's population.

Both strategically and psychologically, the capture of Okinawa by the Americans was of huge significance, as were the costs, in terms of men and materiel, involved in the battle. There were no more battles to fight, other than for the Japanese Motherland – a daunting prospect for both adversaries in the Asia-Pacific War.

16
ARMAGEDDON

'Armageddon' is perhaps an overused word for catastrophic events. After all, there is only one battle that ends the world. Even so, what Japan endured from the beginning of 1945 for the next eight months came very close to a national Armageddon.

1945 brought not only the horrors of the final collapse of Hirohito's Holy War, the humiliations and tragedies of Burma, the Marianas, Iwo Jima, Okinawa and troop withdrawals from China, but also the terrors of an ungodly war reaching into almost every home and community on the Japanese mainland.

Japan had to face not only fearsome attacks on its land, infrastructure and people, but also the devastation of a cultural heritage and beliefs. The divine emperor would become mortal, its warrior tradition would be destroyed, its invincibility made myth. In short, two millennia of history came to an end, leaving the nation with an uncertain future during which they would have to live with the conflicting traumas of guilt, humiliation and anger. For an extraordinary period of three and a half years, Japan had conducted a merciless war of aggression and brutality, then, as 1945 dawned, its enemies were about to respond in kind: 'As you sow, so shall you reap.' Hirohito's Holy War had become a war of hatred and vengeance on both sides.

1945 became not only a year of death and destruction, but also a year of privation, hard labour and misery. In a society which had traditionally subjugated women to a life of domesticity, by 1944 women made up 40 per cent of workers in coal mines and 60 per cent in other vital wartime industries. Young people were mobilised en masse. The 'Students Wartime Mobilisation Law' of June 1944 made all children aged eleven to thirteen and all university students liable for war work. They worked on farms, in factories and construction, in preparing defences, or they joined the armed forces.

Dance halls, clubs, theatres, brothels and geisha houses, as well as public baths were all closed. Rationing was wholesale and severe. Women were encouraged to wear *monpo* (peasant clothes). Soap production fell by 96 per cent and toilet paper was rationed to three pieces per person per day. Food shortages were severe, which had a noticeable impact on health and well-being. Daily calorie intake went down from 2,265 in 1937 to 2,000 in 1941, then 1,900 in 1944 and 1,650 in 1945. One way around rationing was to fail to report deaths, so that the rations of the deceased could be used. Another was to resort to eating wild roots, pumpkins, grasshoppers and other insects.

When large numbers of civilians were evacuated from the cities, they found conditions in the villages they reached to be just as bad. The appalling lack of hygiene in overcrowded villages led to outbreaks of various diseases associated with inadequate sewers. In many districts, household rubbish was burned by members of the neighbourhood association. Human waste had traditionally been taken away by truck into the countryside to use as fertiliser. As both trucks and drivers were scarce, there was a build-up of sewage, which led to a sharp decline in public health.

For Japanese civilians like Tsunejirō Tamura, their physical well-being was challenged but so was their state of mind. He wrote in his diary on New Year's Day, 1945: '*Wartime conditions have come to prevail with extraordinary speed. How will we survive in this harried world? The new year promises to be one filled with problems.*'

Civilians quickly became accustomed to frequent air raids, which took place day after day. Tamura noted on 16 January: '*Enemy American aircraft have been bombing day and night, dozens of times – Tokyo, Nagoya, Shizuoka, and especially the munitions factories outside Nagoya, which produce more than 60% of our munitions and are number one in our imperial country. The bombings have cut Japan's productive capacity, and the indiscriminate bombing is intolerable.*'

Although the torments of Japan's citizens at home were not as grim as the deprivations being endured by its forces overseas, the war was biting hard on the home front. By the end of the month Tamura was lamenting: *'I've been holed up in my house and haven't gone out for some time. With the cold and the frequent attacks of enemy aircraft, I haven't bathed or washed my face. I sleep in my clothes and eat quickly in bed. A truly human existence has been impossible for some time: because I have only one bowl of rice and a watery miso soup with greens floating in it and live like a pig. I've become quite thin and lack the energy to go out.'*

While Japan's citizens braced themselves for a future even more bleak than 1944, the high command in Tokyo was assembling the men and materiel to ensure that the future would be even more bloody and harrowing than Iwo Jima and Okinawa – and it would happen in Japan's heartland. Also, given Hirohito's wildly optimistic belief that they could still influence the outcome of the war, any talk of negotiating peace had to happen beyond the emperor's earshot.

When the US Army Air Force started planning for its attacks on the Japanese mainland in 1943, it estimated that incendiary bomb attacks on Japan's six largest cities could cause physical damage to almost 40 per cent of industrial facilities and result in the loss of 7.6 million man-months of labour. Somewhat horrifyingly, it also estimated that the attacks would kill over 500,000 people, render about 7.75 million homeless and force almost 3.5 million to be evacuated. In preparation, napalm production was increased from 500,000 lbs in 1943 to 8 million lbs in 1944. The napalm went from nine US factories to bomb-assembly plants which made the M-69 incendiary weapons and packed them into E-46 cluster bombs, which were shipped across the Pacific and stored for future use.

Fortunately, Japan's cities were emptying. Bombing raids that had begun in 1944 were becoming more intense, and people hurried to Japan's interior. More than 10 million Japanese, one-seventh of the national population, moved to the mountains and remote rural areas to find refuge. The cities lost 58 per cent of their 1940 populations, and the ones with more than a million residents lost two-thirds. More than 4.2 million people left Tokyo during the last year of the war, and the government ran special refugee trains from Tokyo and other major cities to the mountains.

By January 1945 the alerts were so frequent, and the unheated houses so cold, that most people slept in their street clothes. The first daytime incendiary raids by America's 21st Bomber Command took place on 27 January in Tokyo and 4 February in Kobe. Two days later, Tadayoshi Obata, a statesman with close connections to the cabinet, declared, '*the often-repeated expression "sure victory" is misleading because it is identical with "sure death" [. . .] Our leaders should frankly reveal the real state of affairs, while our people for their part must be ready for any emergency.*'

The US aerial assault on mainland Japan had been developed in stages, based on the distances from accessible airfields and the range of bomber aircraft available. At first, carrier-based attacks were launched. Airfields in China were used, but when the Mariana Islands were taken (Saipan, Tinian and Guam) the Americans had Japan at their mercy. Also, the appearance of the Boeing B-29 Superfortress bomber in 1944 gave the Americans the fearful weapon that they would use to pulverise Japan's major industrial and urban areas. Manned by a crew of twelve, it was a leviathan of the skies with the ability to load ten tons of bombs. Almost 4,000 of them were built from 1942 until the end of the war. Initially, bombing raids took place in daylight, and were aimed at industrial and military targets. However, their success was limited because of mechanical failures, Japanese air defences, strong jet-stream winds and frequent poor weather over Honshu, Japan's major island.

Consequently, American tactics changed in January 1945. The new campaign became much more accurate and brutally deadly. It was decided to attack by night, at low altitude. The B-29s were stripped of guns and armour, to accommodate a larger bomb load and to use pathfinder aircraft to mark the target area with napalm bombs. The first attack of what became known as 'firebombing' – codenamed Operation Meetinghouse – was launched against Tokyo on the night of 9/10 March. Coinciding with Japan's Armed Forces Day, it was the most destructive air raid of the war.

On the afternoon of the 9th, 346 B-29s left the Marianas bound for Tokyo. They began to arrive over the city at 2:00 am on the 10th, where 279 of them dropped 1,665 tons of bombs. The main target of the bombardment was the densely populated, largely working-class area along the Sumida River in eastern Tokyo, including Asakusa, Honjo and Fukagawa. The raid caused a massive inferno that destroyed sixteen square miles, 7 per cent of the city's urban area. The Tokyo fire department reported that 83,793 people were killed during the raid, another 40,918 were injured and just over a million lost their homes. Post-war estimates escalated the death toll to as high as 100,000.

The suffering on the ground was almost incalculable. The narrow lanes, canals and rivers of the area trapped thousands, who suffocated because the firestorm stole so much oxygen. Katsuko Yamamoto, a fifty-nine-year-old foster mother to eight children, kept her family together in the midst of the disaster by tying them together, literally: *'We could hardly breathe, we couldn't see at all. I thought that if we all fled right there in the midst of the fire, scattering in every direction, we'd all burn up and die. I felt a rope at my foot and used it to tie the whole family together. The eldest son led the way, and I carried the newborn baby.'* Yamamoto and the children reached safety in front of a local cinema, but at another, the *Meijiza*, the bodies of suffocated victims were said to be piled more than two metres high. Many thousands escaped the flames by jumping into the rivers, only to drown in the confusion.

Dr Shigenori Kubota, head of a military rescue unit, drove up to the Ryōgoku bridge before dawn: *'Countless bodies were floating, clothed bodies, naked bodies, all as black as charcoal. It was unreal. These were dead people, but you couldn't tell whether they were men or women. You couldn't even tell if the objects floating by were arms and legs or pieces of burnt wood.'*

In a desperate attempt to survive, Hidezo Tsuchikura took his two children to nearby Futaba School. At first they hid in the basement fire shelter, then in the gym, and finally managed to make it to the roof. They found a water tower and Tsuchikura was able to cover his daughter when she caught fire. Their clothes were steaming from the heat. The Tsuchikura family survived. When they came down from the roof, they found every floor packed with people who had been boiled or baked to death: *'But the swimming pool was the most horrible sight of all. It was hideous. More than a thousand people had jammed into the pool, which had been filled to the top. Now there wasn't a drop of water, only the bodies of the adults and children who had died.'*

According to nine-year-old Haruyo Nihei, *'I had spent the day playing with friends before my mother called me in for a simple meal and then we went to bed. It was just another ordinary day for us children.'* That evening, her father woke her. *'He came dashing in and told us to get up because tonight's raid was different.'* Initially, the family took refuge in a shelter, but when the flames approached, her father realised that the heat was so intense, they would be consumed by the heat. *'There was a strong wind that night and as I came out of the shelter, all I could see around us was fire; burning clothing, tatami mats, and debris were blowing down the road and it looked like a flowing river of fire. I remember seeing other families, like us, holding hands and running through the fires. I saw a baby on fire on a mother's back. I saw children on fire, but they were still running. I saw people catch fire when they fell onto the road because it was so hot.'*

Fourteen-year-old Shizuo Takeuchi remembered: *'There were small raids virtually every night so we always went to bed fully dressed so we would be able to get to the shelter faster. I was frightened all the time because of the air raids. We could hear the roar of the engines of the planes above us and there were these black shadows coming and going in the night sky. The following morning there was utter silence across the city. There were lines of people going back to where their homes had once been and everyone was just speechless. There was smoke and ash and I saw people with terrible burns. There were bodies everywhere but burned so badly that no one could ever recognise them. It was like being in a silent movie. I saw an old lady crawling along the road. I saw a black mass on the pavement and realised that it had been a person.'*

Tsunejirō Tamura was shocked, a feeling that soon turned to anger and despair: *'I was shocked when I heard that the dead and wounded numbered thousands. Corpses, arms, and legs were hanging from the electric wires, household goods were strewn on railroad tracks, the interiors of houses were burned out, and only their unburnable foundation stones remained. There's just emptiness. For a day and a night, the survivors were surrounded by madly raging fires, fires that couldn't be put out, and there was no helping them. Children cried out for their parents; parents searched for their children. It was a living hell. How could there be a living heart in all this? [. . .] I hate it! I hate it! The black market prospers, morality has declined, and demons feast on the flesh of the poor. Living this tragic short life we've been given is hateful. Who started this? I resent what they have done.'*

Kazuo Watanabe, a professor at Tokyo University, began to keep a diary on 11 March, the day after the catastrophic air attack on Tokyo: *'The bombardment destroyed my beloved old Hongō neighbourhood. All my memories and all my dreams are forever destroyed. I must endure trial after trial.'*

He had no doubt who was to blame: *'I curse those who have swelled our people's pride. This is the source of all our unhappiness. [. . . I am] ashamed of the way in which the country has behaved itself. What point is there in preaching love for humanity and goodwill, for urging intellectual cooperation among the nations? What point is there in preaching repentance and redemption to people about to commit suicide?'*

In his mind, there was only one solution: *'Our country must die. And then it must be reborn. The siege of Tokyo is beginning. This is the time when all Japanese must become truly aware of what war is, what militarism is, and what politics are when led by fanaticism. [. . .] Sooner or later, we will be defeated. The militarists with the sacrosanct imperial power that they have arrogated are pushing us into murder and suicide. I have been against the war from the start. This war is neither holy nor just.'*

In ten days the Americans flew 1,595 sorties, unloaded 2 million bombs and burned down vast areas of Tokyo, Nagoya, Osaka and Kobe. Officials in Kobe estimated that the raid of 17 March left many thousands homeless. By mid-April, the government announced that 3 million people had been forced to take refuge because fire raids had burned down their homes during the previous six weeks.

Former foreign minister Shigenori Tōgō was a witness to the aftermath of 10 March, when he took a train from Ueno Station to Karuizawa. His words were full of admiration for the survivors of the aerial bombing, but also tinged with resignation and sadness.

'It was the morning after the indiscriminate bombing of Tokyo, and the train was filled to overflowing with victims, carrying suitcases or cloth-wrapped bundles. It was a pitiful sight. I heard many say that even though they had been burned out, having managed to escape Tokyo with their lives they would not complain if only Japan could win the war. The gallant spirit was touching, and I could not keep the tears from my eyes at the thought of this pathetic nurturing of confidence in a victory which the inexorable march of events had already put beyond the pale of hope [. . .] and our soldiers were obliged to continue unendingly, step by step, their bitter retreat before the advancing enemy.'

During the last nine months of the war, 14,054 tons of bombs were dropped on the urban areas of Nagoya. No Japanese city other than Tokyo received as many attacks. In fact, the city was attacked twenty-one times between 13 December 1944 and 24 July 1945, during which 113,460 buildings were destroyed, 3,866 people were killed and 471,701 driven from their homes. Nagoya's biggest attack came on 11 March, the night after the huge attack on Tokyo, and there was another firebombing raid on 19 March. Nagoya Castle, which was being used as a military command post, was largely destroyed on 14 May 1945. On 26 July, the *Enola Gay* dropped a conventional 'pumpkin bomb' (a conventional bomb replica of the 'Fat Man' plutonium bomb) on to Nagoya as part of the training for the atomic attacks on Hiroshima and Nagasaki.

Osaka was hit on 13 March, three days after Tokyo, in a raid that began just before midnight and lasted for over three and a half hours. A total of 274 B-29s attacked in three waves. The first wave from Guam dropped incendiary bombs which started a firestorm. The second wave flew from Tinian and the third from Saipan. By the end, over 1,700 tons of bombs had been dropped, killing 3,987 people, with a further 678 missing. Over eight square miles of the city had been totally destroyed, leaving thousands homeless.

Kobe was the next target in the firebombing campaign and was attacked by 331 B-29s on the night of 16 March. The resulting firestorm destroyed seven square miles of the city, about 50 per cent of its area, killed 8,000 people and rendered 650,000 homeless.

Tsunejirō Tamura described the aftermath of the raid on Osaka: '*The city of Osaka was almost completely wiped out by a night-time air raid. Horrible-to-look-at corpses were piled here and there. The living look for relatives and they do so without having had a grain of rice or a drop of water, searching with bloodshot eyes. It was a scene of incredible carnage and was overwhelming.*'

Nine days after the devastating attack on Tokyo, on 18 March, accompanied by his doctor and a chamberlain, Hirohito toured the city by car. His aide Kaizō Yoshihashi described the scene that greeted the emperor.

'*Digging through the rubble with empty expressions on their faces they became reproachful as the imperial motorcade went by. [. . .] Were they resentful of the emperor because they had lost their relatives, their houses and belongings? Or were they in a state of utter exhaustion and bewilderment (kyodatsu jōtai)? I sympathised with how his majesty must have felt upon approaching these unfortunate victims.*'

There was a pause in the heavy bombing of the cities during the Battle for Okinawa, when the B-29s were directed to attack military targets. However, the firebombing raids resumed on 13 April, when 327 B-29s attacked Tokyo and destroyed over eleven square miles of the city. Two days later, the Superfortresses attacked again, destroying another six square miles of Tokyo, over three square miles of Kawasaki, and one and a half square miles of Yokohama. The raids were relentless. More major attacks against Tokyo took place on the nights of 23 and 25 May. In the first, 520 B-29s destroyed 5.3 square miles of southern Tokyo. The second, carried out by 502 B-29s, destroyed 16.8 square miles of the city's central area, including the headquarters of several key government ministries and much of the Imperial Palace. By then, 50.8 per cent of the city had been obliterated and Tokyo was taken off the target list. The firebombing campaign ended in June, but not before raids in May had destroyed ninety-four square miles of buildings – one-seventh of Japan's urban area.

Although there was no international treaty at the time protecting civilians from air attacks, Japan's cabinet proclaimed that indiscriminate bombing was a war crime. Captured Allied airmen were subject to trial and possible execution. Many were killed after a brief trial or were summarily executed by the Kempeitai (the infamous Japanese secret military police).

Thirty-three airmen were killed by army personnel at Fukuoka, including fifteen who were beheaded shortly after the Japanese surrender was announced on 15 August. Mobs of civilians also killed several Allied airmen before the Japanese military arrived to take the men into custody. In addition to the killings, most captured B-29 crewmen were brutally interrogated by the Kempeitai. Of the 545 Allied airmen who were captured in the Japanese home islands, 132 were executed and twenty-nine were killed by civilians. Another ninety-four airmen died from other causes while in custody, including fifty two who were killed on 25 May when they were deliberately left in a prison in Tokyo during the raid on the city. Between six and eight US airmen, shot down on 5 May, were subjected to vivisection at the Kyushu Imperial University. Many of the Japanese personnel responsible for the deaths of Allied airmen were later prosecuted in the Yokohama War Trials. Several of those found guilty were executed and the remainder were imprisoned.

Author Fūtarō Yamada's thoughts dwelt on vengeance: *'Probably they do not recognise that the creatures living in the world below them are also members of the human race. No doubt they think of us as swarms of little yellow monkeys [. . .] That being the case, it is of course more than proper for us to wish to slaughter hundreds of thousands of Americans]. . .] It won't be enough to drag down to hell an American for each Japanese who dies. We will kill three of them for each one of us.'*

In contrast, schoolboy Ichirō Hatano was becoming more aware of Japan's growing crisis. After the death of Adolf Hitler became public knowledge, he wrote to his mother on 8 May, expressing his fears.

'In the end Germany has lost [. . .] This means that Japan will have to fight the whole world singlehanded [. . .] People are saying: "Now we shall show what we are made of," but they still can't quite hide their fears [. . .] But when will the war end, and how? Is it really a case of "kill or be killed", and if we lose, shall we all be slaughtered? When I thought

that there was something splendid about our fighting, the idea of death did not frighten me much. But now it just seems silly to die. They say our soldiers have done some horrible things in China and elsewhere.'

Ichirō wrote again to his mother on 23 May.

'Those soldiers are glad to go, Mother. They are going for their country's sake. If they are killed, nothing can be done about it. Later on, I shall go away like that. I'm not specially interested in dying for His Majesty the Emperor, perhaps because I have never seen him close to, but if it is for my country I am ready to die at any time. Don't you think that is fine?'

By the middle of May 1945, the Philippines, Iwo Jima, Okinawa and Burma had gone. The Empire was in its death throes and Hirohito's Holy War had become a shibboleth of death. On the mainland, with almost all their resources exhausted, the militarists now turned to children to save their regime.

Aiko Takahashi was married to a doctor and living in Tokyo. She observed what was happening.

'Children in grade schools (five to eleven) or younger, and older people are practically all evacuated to other parts of the country from Tokyo. Young people are drafted into the army, and technicians and scholars are also drafted to serve in various capacities or sent to the front. [. . .] A truck was sent from the Metropolitan government to take away those patients who were temporarily under my husband's care. From the second-floor window fretfully I looked down. The truck had no side panels, and all the patients were put down in a manner not too different from piling up firewood. To me they could not look like living creatures. It was much worse than an imaginary picture of hell. Yet that was exactly what was taking place right in front of my eyes. No gas, no electricity, and our taps are without water. Life in the city is miserable.'

Although Japanese soldiers were still fighting all over an ever-diminishing empire, the final battle of the Asia-Pacific War had come right up to the edge of Japan's ancient shores. Its outcome was still unknown, but its beginning was frighteningly ominous for the months to come. The firebombings continued for several weeks, with an estimated 300,000–330,000 Japanese civilians killed, at least 8 million left homeless, and with an estimated 40 per cent of Japan's urban areas destroyed, including 60 per cent of Tokyo lost in the flames.

The agony would go on for another three months, during which time the government in Tokyo, the military in its imperial bunkers, and Hirohito in his palace all refused to accept the inevitability of defeat. While they continued to do so, tens of thousands more would die.

17

THE RADIANCE OF A THOUSAND SUNS

As the weeks passed, the Japanese military prepared for the last great battle, the ultimate fight to the death, Operation Ketsugō. It was nothing if not ambitious – to the point of being absurd. The Japanese planned to commit the entire population to resisting the invasion. The simple objective was to spill as much American blood as possible to make them give up. Also, there was just the unlikely possibility that the sheer scale and cost of Japan's Ketsugō might evoke in the enemy's thinking either admiration for the Japanese defenders or sympathy for their endless sacrifice, and thus create an empathy that would lead to honourable talks. On Okinawa, civilians unable to fight had been ordered to commit suicide rather than fall into American hands, and there is little doubt that the same order would have been given in the home islands.

Aircraft would be vital to the success of Ketsugō. In addition to Japan's few remaining fighters and bombers, more than 10,000 kamikaze aircraft were ready for use in July (with more by October) to attack Allied ships offshore. Japan's remaining major warships numbered only four battleships (all damaged), five damaged aircraft carriers, two cruisers, twenty-three destroyers and forty-six submarines. However, without sufficient fuel to put them to sea, the navy planned to use its anti-aircraft firepower to defend naval installations while docked in port.

The navy had thousands of warplanes and nearly 2 million personnel in the home islands. In addition, it had 400 *kōryū* (midget submarines), 120 *kaiten* (manned torpedoes) and 2,412 *shin'yō* (suicide motorboats). It had trained a unit of *fukuryu* (divers) to serve as suicide bombers. They were to be armed with contact-fused mines and would dive under landing craft and blow up both the landing craft and the men in them. Mines were to be anchored to the sea bottom off each potential invasion beach for their use by the suicide divers. Up to 10,000 mines were planned and 1,200 suicide divers had been trained by the time of the Japanese surrender.

On land, as of March 1945, the Imperial Japanese Army had only one combat division in Kyushu, the first objective for the Allies. Four veteran divisions were withdrawn from the Kwantung Army in Manchuria to strengthen the forces in Japan, and forty-five new divisions were activated between February and May 1945, sixteen of which were high-quality mobile divisions. By August, the formations, which included three tank brigades, had a total of 900,000 men. Although the Japanese were able to muster new men, equipping them was more difficult. The army had sixty-five divisions in the homeland but only enough equipment for forty and ammunition for thirty.

Amidst great secrecy, an underground bunker in Matsushiro, Nagano Prefecture, was being prepared to shelter the emperor and the imperial general staff during an invasion. With the emperor safe, his subjects – all of them – would fight for him. New units of the Volunteer Fighting Corps were organised. They were not really 'volunteer'; Japanese social mores rendered them compulsory, while the police called them the 'Final People's Movement'. They were expected to fight with the Imperial Japanese Army's soldiers. Then, if all else failed, they should revert to urban guerrilla warfare, before forming final redoubts in the mountains. The units included all healthy men aged fifteen to sixty, and women aged seventeen to forty, a total of 28 million people, primed to provide 'combat' and, later, 'combat roles'.

Strategic absurdity began when it came to weapons, training and uniforms, which, on the whole, were non-existent. Civilian clothing had to suffice, training had to be done by old men, and weapons had to be improvised. Many were armed with nothing better than antiquated firearms, Molotov cocktails, bows and arrows, swords, knives, bamboo or wooden spears, and even clubs and truncheons. Schoolgirls in remote Shimane Prefecture prac-tised with awls (sharp woodworking marking tools). One of them,

Yukiko Kasai, was told to draw on the tradition of the samurai: *'You must be ready to settle the war by drawing on our Japanese spirit and killing them. Even killing just one American soldier will do. You must prepare to use the awls for self-defence. You must aim at the enemy's abdomen. Understand? The abdomen! If you don't kill at least one enemy soldier, you don't deserve to die!'* She knew that it was ridiculous to face American flame-throwers and machine guns with woodworking tools, but did her duty and did the drills anyway.

For almost all Japanese, disillusionment or opposition could only be expressed in secret. Tsuneko Ezaki, an eighteen-year-old girl, wrote on 21 July in her diary: *'Everything considered, I wish I had ended up dying during the bombings. If only there weren't a war, we wouldn't have to pretend we're happy.'*

In June, a propaganda campaign called for 'The Glorious Death of One Hundred Million'. The bizarre suggestion was that it was *'glorious to die for the holy emperor of Japan, and every Japanese man, woman, and child should die for the emperor when the Allies arrive'*.

When the fateful month of August arrived, the situation for the homeland civilians was dire. In addition to acute food shortages, which forced many to resort to the black market, they were forced to work for the war effort, to the point of exhaustion, and all while enduring constant air attacks. Historian Saburō Ienaga described the horror of what they faced.

Bombs dropped from 20,000 feet did not distinguish between soldier and civilian. The August 7th 1945 attack on the Toyokawa Naval Arsenal was a hideous example of total war. Labour service workers and student workers were employed at the arsenal under military supervision. Between 2,000 and 3,000 civilians were killed in the air raid. Among the dead were women's volunteer corps members, female students, and more than fifty elementary school students. An eyewitness described the carnage, 'An arm lay on the ground. There was a skull split in half, a headless torso, a girl's head hung from a tree by the road, the hair caught in the branches. A young worker with no legs, face burned black, crawled around on her hands.' Several hundred young women and girls were blown to bits, burned, and mutilated.

If the humiliations of the dismantling of its empire and the horrors of the firebombing of its cities were not enough, there were two even more awful abominations to come.

The steps that led to what became known as the 'Manhattan Project' were first taken in 1939 by US President Roosevelt after his intelligence agencies told him that Hitler's German scientists were already working on a nuclear weapon. The president launched the Advisory Committee on Uranium to research uranium's potential role as a weapon. Based on the committee's subsequent findings, funding was found for Columbia University, where physicists Enrico Fermi and Leo Szilard focused on uranium enrichment and nuclear chain reactions. By 1941, the committee's name had changed to the Office of Scientific Research and Development (OSRD).

On 28 December 1942, Roosevelt sanctioned the formation of the Manhattan Project with the objective of weaponising nuclear energy. Along with Edward Teller and others, theoretical physicist Robert Oppenheimer, who was already working on nuclear fission, was made director of the Los Alamos Laboratory in New Mexico, in 1943. The Los Alamos Laboratory was established on 1 January to begin research and testing, and on 16 July, at a remote site near Alamogordo, New Mexico, the first atomic bomb was successfully detonated. Called the 'Trinity Test', it produced an enormous mushroom cloud 40,000 feet high. The Atomic Age had dawned.

Oppenheimer's team had developed two distinct types of bomb: a uranium-based design called 'Little Boy' and a plutonium-based weapon called 'Fat Man'. Just a month later, with another catastrophic loss of life, in Hiroshima and Nagasaki, the two weapons would finally bring an end to the Asia-Pacific War. The devastation and suffering they brought led to two questions that have been debated ever since: from a strategic perspective, was their use necessary? From a moral perspective, was their use justified?

There are many factors to consider in answering those questions. The consensus among US military leaders in 1945 was that the Japanese would fight to the death in resisting the Allies' Operation Downfall, a planned full-scale invasion of the island nation, resulting in extraordinary casualty levels on both sides. The death tolls predicted were 1 million Allied lives and 10 million Japanese. There was also the very real fear that the resulting chaos and anger would render Japan ungovernable. From the Allied perspective, Downfall envisaged an amphibious attack on the southern island of Kyushu (Operation Olympic) on 1 November 1945, which would be an even bigger onslaught than D-Day in Europe, including sixteen divisions (almost 240,000 men) and almost 500 warships.

Olympic would be followed by Operation Coronet, an attack on the main island of Honshu, on 1 March 1946. Even larger than Olympic, it would have involved forty-five divisions (675,000 troops) and an armada of over 620 ships. Both Olympic and Coronet would have been supported from the air by fourteen bomber groups, ten fighter groups, 1,000 Superfortresses, 500 Lancasters and 250,000 airmen.

Another important factor was the Allies' Potsdam Conference, which took place on 26 July in occupied Germany. An ultimatum was issued to Japan, calling for unconditional surrender and for the Japanese to form a new, democratic and peaceful government, or face 'prompt and utter destruction'. Significantly, the Potsdam Declaration offered no role for Hirohito in Japan's future – something that guaranteed that Japan would not submit to the Allies' demands.

Finally, the Soviet Union was an unknown quantity in the scenario. It had a neutrality pact with Japan: but would the Kremlin honour it? Or would Stalin unleash on Japan his formidable and newly victorious Red Army in eastern Asia? Needless to say, Stalin had already promised his Allied partners that he would invade Japan's Asian conquests, and had begun planning an attack.

Thanks to the iron grip of fanaticism and Hirohito's equivocations, Japan had missed several opportunities to find a route to peace through Moscow. The belief in the supreme god-emperor made it impossible for Japan's leaders to accept the humiliation of defeat, let alone the ignominy of 'unconditional surrender' and the unbearable torture of the 'absolute victory' of the enemy. Japan's leaders were blinded by ideology, when they first had an opportunity to seek peace and save millions of lives in February 1945. Both former prime minister Prince Fumimaro Konoe and foreign minister Mamoru Shigemitsu had warned Hirohito that the Soviet Union was unlikely to honour its neutrality pact. It was obvious by then what the fate of Japan's cities would be, but Hirohito was unmoved. Another opportunity came in June, when the Holy War was clearly a lost cause. Germany had been defeated, Japan was alone and its cities were being systematically destroyed. Instead of grasping the nettle, the Supreme War Council took the fateful decision to plan for the die-hard defence of the homeland. The third opportunity came after Potsdam. Instead of accepting a defeat that was inevitable, even with a suicidal defence of the mainland, Japan's leaders rejected Potsdam outright.

So, what of the questions of strategic necessity and moral culpability? Well, the projected cost of Operation Downfall in human terms, even if significantly exaggerated, makes an overwhelming case for the strategic justification of the two atomic bombs. As for the morality of it, while it is true that it was the Americans who created the bombs and used them – with little thought about the suffering they would cause – it was surely Hirohito's extraordinary vacillations that condemn him, and result in him bearing the greater part of the guilt for allowing his people to suffer as they did. Had he not wanted to preserve himself as emperor, and the *Kokutai* (body politic) who served him, he would have seen the obvious, acted like a true leader of his nation, and striven for peace.

Like most people she knew, Hiroko Nakamoto – just fifteen years old at the time – was shocked when it became clear that the war had come to the door of her homeland.

'Time went on and we knew the war was getting more intense. We could bear it because we were sure Japan was winning. Soon it would be over. Our radio broadcasts told us of the glorious victories of our armies and the defeats suffered by the Americans. We read in the newspapers of the number of islands taken over by the Japanese, the number of American warships sunk by our planes. We heard only good news of Japan. And

we believed it. Thus it was a great shock to us when the newspapers and radios informed us that the war was moving closer to us and we Japanese must be prepared for a last fight on our own territory, on our own mainland. We young girls could not believe what we heard. The history of our country went back more than two thousand years. In all that time Japan had never been invaded. We had been taught that it never could be. Our country was protected by the gods. We were confident we would win this war as we had all others, because we were the country of the gods.'

Schoolboy Ichirō Hatano wrote to his mother on 24 July, expressing his doubts about the prospects of victory.

'I wonder what truth there is in the story about Chiba. According to somebody who comes from there, the Chiba regiment have run out of munitions; if the enemy landed on the beach at Kujukuri they would have to fight them off with bamboo spears. Apparently, they have already made the territorial regiment, made up of old men and young soldiers who have been invalided out, drill with bamboo spears. The enemy will attack with bombs and guns; it is absurd to meet them with such weapons. Father says that Japan will lose the war; I don't want to believe him, but I am becoming less and less confident every day.'

There are many memorable days in the history of the world: the beginning of wars, or the end of them; victories or defeats; the births and deaths of famous people; occasions of great celebration, or moments of tragedy. For Japan, 6 August 1945 is a date written indelibly in its collective consciousness.

At 8:14 a.m. Hiroshima time, a heavily adapted B-29 Superfortress, the *Enola Gay*, arrived over the city, a major port and capital of Hiroshima Prefecture in the south of Honshu. In 1945, it had a population of 345,000. Just after 8:15 a.m., the bomb 'Little Boy' fell away from its carrier. The plane jumped nearly ten feet at the sudden loss in weight. Having less than forty-five seconds to get clear of the subsequent explosion, *Enola Gay* banked sharply on a 155-degree turn. Not even the scientists who designed the bomb were sure that she would survive the shock waves from the blast.

'Little Boy' fell almost six miles in forty-three seconds, before detonating at an altitude of 2,000 feet. The bomb exploded with the force of more than 15,000 tons of TNT. Less than 2 per cent of the bomb's uranium achieved fission, but the resulting reaction engulfed the city in a blinding flash of heat and light. In less than a second, the temperature at ground level reached 7,000 degrees Fahrenheit. The bomb vaporised people half a mile away from ground zero. Bronze statues melted, roof tiles fused together, and the exposed skin of people miles away burned from the intense infrared energy unleashed. At least 80,000 people died instantly. More than 100,000 more died later as a consequence of the bomb – about 50 per cent of the population.

Dr Michihiko Hachiya was a physician who worked as the Director of the Hiroshima Communications Hospital. As an eyewitness who lived about a mile from the epicentre of the explosion, he kept a diary of what happened over the following weeks. His first entry, on 6 August, is compelling.

'The hour was early, the morning still, warm, and beautiful. Shimmering leaves, reflecting sunlight from a cloudless sky, made a pleasant contrast with shadows in my garden as I gazed absently through wide-flung doors opening to the south. Suddenly, a strong flash of light startled me, and then another. Through swirling dust, I could barely discern a wooden column that had supported one corner of my house. It was leaning crazily, and the roof sagged dangerously. Moving instinctively, I tried to escape, but rubble and fallen debris had blocked my way. Moving cautiously, I managed to reach my garden. To my surprise I discovered that I was completely naked. How odd! All over the right side of my body I was cut and bleeding. A large splinter was protruding from a mangled wound in my thigh and something warm trickled into my mouth. My cheek was torn. I discovered as I felt it gingerly, my lower lip laid wide open. Embedded in my neck was a sizeable fragment of glass which I matter-of-factly dislodged, and with the detachment of one stunned and shocked I studied it and my blood-stained hand.'

Like so many others that day, Dr Hachiya's life had, in an instant, been changed for ever. His immediate thoughts were for the safety of loved ones.

'Where was my wife? Suddenly thoroughly alarmed, I began to yell for her: "Yaeko san! Yaeko-san! Where are you?" Frightened and irrational, I called out again, "It's a five-hundred-ton bomb! Yaeko-san, where are

you?" Yaeko-san, pale and frightened, her clothes torn and bloodstained, emerged from the ruins of our house holding her elbow. Seeing her, I was reassured. My own panic assuaged, I tried to reassure her, "We'll be all right, only let's get out of here as fast as we can."'

Hiroko Nakamoto was on her way to work when disaster struck.

'Suddenly, from nowhere, came a blinding flash. It was as if someone had taken a flashbulb picture a few inches from my eyes. There was no pain then. Only a stinging sensation, as if I had been slapped hard in the face [. . .] I tried to open my eyes. But I could not. Then I lost consciousness [. . .] I do not know how I got there or how long it was before I awoke. The air was heavy with a sickening odour. It was a smell different from anything I had ever known before. Now I saw dead bodies all about me. I passed a streetcar that was stalled. It was filled with dead people. I stumbled on. But now a great fire came rolling toward us, and I knew it was impossible to get home.[. . .] There was a river nearby, and the people who could walk began walking toward the river – burned people with clothes in shreds or no clothes at all, men and women covered with blood, crying children.'

Nakamoto would survive her ordeal and her terrible injuries. Although she would have to live through excruciating pain, and be scarred for life, she was one of the lucky ones.

'I followed them. When I reached the river [. . .] for the first time I looked at my body. My arms, my legs and ankles were burned. And I realised that the left side of my face must be burned, too. These were strange burns. Not pink, but yellow. The flesh was hanging loose. I went down to the water's edge and tried to pat the skin back with salt water from the river, as I saw others doing. But we could not stay by the river. The fire was coming closer, and the heat was more intense. Everyone started moving again, away from the fire, moving silently, painfully. There were no streets left, only the wreckage of buildings. It hurt to walk on my burned feet. It was impossible to move anywhere without stepping on nails, splintered wood, broken glass.'

Michiko Yamaoka lived just 1,400 yards from the bomb's ground zero. She was walking to her work in the local telephone exchange, which was just 550 yards from the epicentre.

'I could still hear the very faint sound of planes. I thought, how

strange, so I put my right hand above my eyes and looked up to see if I could spot them. The sun was dazzling. That was the moment. There was no sound. I felt something strong. It was terribly intense. I remember my body floating in the air. I don't know how far I was blown. When I came to my senses, my surroundings were silent. There was no wind. I was under stones. I couldn't move my body. I heard voices crying, "Help! Water!" It was then I realised 1 wasn't the only one.'

Nothing could have prepared her for the unprecedented scenes she would witness as she tried to make sense of what had just happened. This was a life-changing day – a truly unimaginable catastrophe.

'I couldn't really see around me. I tried to say something, but my voice wouldn't come out. Nobody there looked like human beings. Until that moment, I thought incendiary bombs had fallen. Everyone was stupefied. Humans had lost the ability to speak. People couldn't scream, "It hurts!" even when they were on fire. People didn't say, "It's hot!" They just sat catching fire. My clothes were burnt and so was my skin. I was in rags. I had braided my hair, but now it was like a lion's mane. There were people barely breathing, trying to push their intestines back in. People with the legs wrenched off. Without heads. Or with faces burned and swollen out of shape. It was a living hell.'

Schoolboy Ichirō Hatano, now sixteen, wrote to his mother on 7 August.

'They say that Hiroshima has been bombed and that there has been a lot of damage [. . .] Atom bombs are a new and extraordinarily powerful weapon; they kill every living thing in the area. Is it possible for such things to exist, and if they exist is it possible for people to use them? There are international agreements prohibiting the use of poison gas because it is inhuman; how can people be allowed to use a bomb so much more terrible than gas? Was the army completely unaware the enemy had a weapon like this? It was stupid to hope that we could possibly win this war with bamboo spears. Our will to fight is melting away.'

On 9 August, three days after Hiroshima, a second atom bomb was dropped on Nagasaki, another busy port city on the island of Kyushu, southwest of Honshu. The Superfortress *Boxcar* released the plutonium bomb 'Fat Man' at 11:02 a.m. It detonated fifty-three seconds later. The north of the city was destroyed and more than 10 per cent of the city's population was killed. Among the 35,000 deaths were 150 Japanese soldiers, 6,200 out of the 7,500 employees of the Mitsubishi Munitions plant, and 2,000 Koreans. The industrial damage to Nagasaki was significant, leaving as much as 80 per cent of industrial production destroyed. 'Fat Man' was more powerful than the bomb dropped over Hiroshima, but because of Nagasaki's more uneven terrain, there was less damage.

Ten-year-old Makoto Nagai was the daughter of local doctor, Takashi Nagai. Her words contain a childish sense of awe and wonder: '*There was a terrific rush of wind and a noise like thunder. The biggest thing that ever was. Ugly and beautiful. It was like a pillar of fire. I thought an airplane had crashed into the sun.*'

On the day before the bomb, Dr Takashi Nagai had said goodbye to his wife and gone to work as usual: '*Three days later, I managed to return home. I found her at once, a black lump in the remains of the kitchen, just her pelvis and other bones scorched by the fire. She was still warm. I picked her up, put her in a bucket, and took her to the cemetery.*'

To make matters even worse, the day before the second bomb, the Soviet Union reneged on its neutrality pact – as many among Japan's elite had predicted – and declared war on Japan.

Popular novelist Jun Takami recalled: '*We were taken completely by surprise by the Soviet declaration of war. Perhaps people on the inside foresaw it, but we knew nothing. We had instead been secretly hoping that the Soviet Union would mediate. Everybody had the same thought. The attitude displayed toward the Soviet Union in newspaper articles was adulatory. And then, all of a sudden, came the Soviet declaration of war.*'

Ichirō Hatano's words of 13 August reflect both the moral dilemma of the atomic bomb, but also a growing angry defiance among Japanese civilians.

'*The effects of the bombs are terrible. Asahi has reprinted an article from a European newspaper, which protests in the name of humanity. I agree. The Swede is right when he points out that, if the Americans wanted to test the atom bomb, they should have given the population time to evacuate the town [. . .] The official communiqués are asking the people to unite in holy wrath against the cruelty of our enemies. I don't know whether unity is possible; but there is no doubt that young people like me are convinced of the wickedness of an enemy which acts contrary to all the laws of humanity. This being so, we shall never surrender to these torturers; we would rather die. It is obvious that we are going to lose the war, but we must not weaken.'*

The next day – without any regard for the naked aggression of his country, or its countless acts of cruelty – Kafu Nagai also wrote angrily about the circumstances in which Japan found itself.

'Japan is standing at the last line of defence. It is being driven over a precipice where pitch-black storm winds howl. One step farther, and we'll drop into a hell of destruction. The American forces that grabbed Iwo Jima and massacred Okinawa send thousands of planes night and day without let-up, and a huge fleet is cruising in nearby waters, ready to bombard, strafe, and shell, again and again. Most of our cities have been reduced to ruins. Innumerable people have fled to the countryside, and on top of everything else, the enemy has invented a terrifying atomic bomb that in one instant wiped out Hiroshima. The phoenix-like Soviet Union, which annihilated Germany, our only ally, on August 8th finally declared war on Japan. And we have spent eight years in hard fighting with that monster, the Chinese people. Can Japan, hacked all over with wounds, still confront America and Britain and do battle against the entire world?'

However, twenty-four hours later, despite the protestations of Hatano and Kafu, their anger would have to be assuaged and their defiance would become futile. The atom bomb had finally done what conventional weapons had failed to do.

Sadly, it was not logic or common sense which had prevailed, but sheer expediency on the part of Hirohito. He knew that he had no choice but to surrender, no matter how ignominious. He knew he had to throw himself and his people on the mercy of his enemies, and hope that his nation could survive.

18
ENDURING THE UNENDURABLE

When, at noon on 15 August 1945, Hirohito uttered the memorable words 'enduring the unendurable' no one in Japan could believe that their god-emperor had lowered himself to say them. He had never spoken in public before, and for most people his surrender speech was a far bigger national disaster than Japan's many defeats in battle, the firebombing of its cities and the annihilation of Hiroshima and Nagasaki. His thin, shaky voice and his use of classical Japanese only added to the incredulity of it all. People listened on their knees, weeping openly; most were bewildered, many were angered and some did not believe it was actually happening.

Hisako Yoshizawa, a personal secretary to a Tokyo businessman, listened to the broadcast in the street, like most Japanese.

'A siren went off, and we heard the emperor's voice. People silently bowed their heads, and in an instant the streets were dead quiet. Word by word, the emperor's voice reached us, and tears ran down our cheeks. People's faces had no particular expression. Perhaps they were exhausted.'

Yoshizawa wrote again the next day: 'The expressions on people's faces haven't changed much at all. When one meets people, instead of uttering the usual greetings, they blurt out, "What's happened is terrible!" The military is calling for complete resistance and appealing to all citizens. This is a very difficult problem. The true nature of a people is apparent when they lose a war, rather than when they win, and the day has arrived when we should reveal Japan's greatness. Now that we've been defeated in war, I'm eager that our national identity as a people is not completely ruined.'

The shock of the broadcast was profound, but it soon dawned on the population that the Japan they thought they knew was over.

Hiroko Nakamoto was still recovering from the terrible injuries she sustained when the atom bomb was dropped on Hiroshima.

'For the first time in history, on this day our emperor's voice was heard on the radio. We had lost the war. Never before had Japan been defeated. It was the country of the gods. And always before, the gods had protected us. But this time, there was no miracle. It was a terrible shock to know that we were a conquered nation. We had made enormous sacrifices for the war. Not only soldiers, but thousands and thousands of civilians, men, women and children, had been killed. Our homes were destroyed. Great areas throughout our country were bombed out. My own city, Hiroshima, lay in ruins. Nagasaki was still burning. We young people had even sacrificed our education. All for defeat!'

Tokyo housewife Aiko Takashi was overcome with emotion as she listened to the emperor's words: *'Noon came. With a dispassionate, heavy and even trembling voice, His Majesty read his declaration of Japan's defeat. Each word, each phrase penetrated through my heart. I could feel my eyes water, and finally could not restrain myself and had to hold a handkerchief against my eyes.'*

The diary of Musei Tokugawa, a popular radio commentator, details his feelings on hearing the 'jade voice' of the emperor.

'The sound of a gong announced it was noon. At the command, we stood at attention on the tatami. [. . .] The jade voice began to be audible. The physical sensation when I heard his voice for the first time, made every cell in my body shake. What a pure voice it was! A feeling of gratitude soaked through to the tips of my hair. [. . .] No doubt every household, every school, every company, every factory, every government office, every army barracks in Japan heard the broadcast, all in equal stillness. I wonder if there will ever again be in the world a monarch like this one, a people like this one. So lovely a country will never perish!'

Shintarō Uno was an officer serving with the 41st Infantry Regiment in China: *'I never dreamt the Emperor would give up so easily. Officers like me didn't believe Japan could lose. I was ordered to burn the regimental flags and did it with tears streaming down my face. I only hope the victors will deal with us in a gentlemanly manner.'*

The greatest worry for Yokohama housewife Yu Aihara was her husband, who was serving in China: *'At the news of the surrender, all the energy drained out of my body. Then the radio news continued and I heard that soldiers abroad would be disarmed and repatriated to Japan. I felt so relieved, and I prayed all night through. God, please stop my husband committing suicide.'*

Although it had indeed happened, the surrender had been very nearly thwarted. Six days before the broadcast, even after the use of two atomic bombs, the news that the Soviet Red Army had crossed the border in Northeast Asia, and with America massing its formidable forces offshore, Hirohito was still hesitating. Only he could make the decision to surrender, but he waited for a day and a half before telling his chief adviser, Lord Keeper of the Privy Seal Marquis Kōchi Kido, at 10 a.m. on 9 August, to *'quickly control the situation'* because *'the Soviet Union has declared war and today began hostilities against us.'* Kido, who was a strong supporter of accepting the Allies' Potsdam demands, communicated with Prime Minister Kantarō Suzuki immediately to ask him to arrange a conference of the Imperial War Council for later that day.

The conference took place in an air-raid shelter in the Imperial Palace, late in the evening of 9 August. According to Shigenori Tōgō, *'The Emperor then spoke. "Unless the war be brought to an end at this moment, I fear that the national polity [Kokutai] will be destroyed, and the nation annihilated. It is therefore my wish that we bear the unbearable and accept the Allied reply, thus to preserve the state as a state and spare my subjects further suffering. I wish you all to act in that intention." All the attendees wept. It was an inexpressibly solemn and moving scene.'*

By the end of the meeting, the following text had been agreed.

The Japanese Government is ready to accept the terms enumerated in the tripartite joint declaration which was issued on the 26th of last month, with the understanding that the said declaration does not compromise any demand which prejudices the prerogatives of His Majesty as a sovereign ruler.

Chief cabinet secretary Hisatsune Sakomizu then ordered the drafting of the 'Imperial Rescript Ending the War'. Despite the dire circumstances, with the help of two scholars of the Chinese classics, it then took over three days before a version of the rescript was given to the Suzuki cabinet. Six hours of contentious argument ensued until a modified version was approved and, on the night of 14 August, Hirohito signed it. Sadamu Shimomura, Head of the Military Information Division, together with Kido then persuaded the emperor to record the suitably opaque final version for broadcast to the nation. At the same time, the Suzuki government notified all the Allied nations that it had accepted the terms of the Potsdam Declaration.

Hirohito's words were cleverly constructed. They described his new image as a pacifist, anti-militarist and passive observer of the war, and emphasised both his 'benevolence' and his claim of imperial sovereignty. Hirohito did not use the word 'surrender', nor did he speak about regret, or offer any words of comfort to those who had suffered at the hands of his warriors. There was also a significant omission: he failed to mention his reluctance to use his power to end the war much earlier.

To ensure the correct understanding of the obscure court-style language, radio announcer Nobutaka Wada reread the entire rescript in ordinary language. A cabinet announcement followed, condemning the United States for use of the atomic bombs in violation of international law, and the Soviet Union for declaring war against Japan.

Wada later commented: '*We ourselves invited a situation in which we had no choice but to lay down our arms. We could not live up to the great benevolence of the emperor, but he did not even scold us. On the contrary, he said that whatever might happen to himself, "I can no longer bear to see my people die in war." Before such great benevolence and love, who among us can escape reflecting on his own disloyalty.*'

The Asia-Pacific War was now over – but not entirely. There were many arch-militarists who refused to accept Hirohito's surrender. In several military barracks individuals strived to deny the surrender order. Seventeen-year-old kamikaze pilot Yasuo Kuwahara witnessed the extraordinary events in his barracks. He recalled the stricken faces of his comrades.

'*A score of men sprang up and would have rushed to their planes had not the commander intervened. After we had returned to our barracks, motors groaned overhead, there was the screech of diving planes, followed by two sharp explosions. We rushed forth to see flames crackling on the airstrip. Sergeants Kashiwabara and Kinoshita had quietly sneaked to their planes and become some of the first Japanese to suffer death rather than the humiliation of surrender. [. . .] A wave of suicides followed. Several officers placed a pistol in their mouths as Yoshida had done and squeezed the trigger. Men committed hara-kiri, bit off their own tongues, cut their throats, or hanged themselves.*'

A much more co-ordinated threat to the surrender was brewing within the army in Tokyo. It is known as the 'Kyūjō Incident'. Its leaders were Major Kenji Hatanaka and Colonel Jirō Shiizaki, officers at the army ministry. They led a battalion of rebels into the Imperial Palace on the evening of 14 August, just hours before the surrender announcement was to be broadcast to the nation. Using open deceit, Hatanaka and Shiizaki told the commander of the Second Imperial Guards Regiment that the army's leaders had ordered the palace closed and secured against any intruders. The palace guards, believing the ruse, agreed to comply with their instructions. But General Takeshi Mori, commander of the guards, was suspicious and refused to comply and was shot dead in cold blood. The rebels then forged an order in General Mori's name and sealed it with his official imperial seal. The order instructed the Imperial Guards to occupy the palace, prevent any communication with anyone outside the palace moats, and protect the emperor.

Shortly before midnight, Hirohito walked into a soundproof bunker under the palace, where a team of NHK technicians had set up recording equipment. The emperor read the surrender rescript into a microphone. Only one take was needed. The technicians transferred the recording on to two vinyl records, which were pressed on the spot and deposited in a safe under the palace.

With the Imperial Guards supporting them, the coup leaders cut the phone lines, closed the gates and cut off all traffic into and out of the palace. They then searched the labyrinthine catacombs

under the palace, interrogating members of staff at the points of
bayonets. They searched for Marquis Kido, but never found him.
In fact, as Lord Privy Seal, only he knew where the vinyl recordings were stored – in a panic-room bunker, in a secret part of the
catacombs. The rebels found it difficult to interpret the archaic
signs marking the locations of various rooms, and went around in
frantic circles. At one point, they threatened the palace chamberlain, Yoshihiro Tokugawa, who refused to yield, and lied about the
whereabouts of Kido and the recordings.

The aged Prime Minister Suzuki, who had survived an assassination attempt nine years earlier, was warned moments before his
would-be killers arrived. Other rebel detachments occupied the
major radio stations, intending to intercept the emperor's surrender
recording before it could be broadcast to the nation. With dawn
close, Hatanaka and Shiizaki knew that their plan was failing. No
senior officers had supported the revolt. Even Admiral Onishi, who
had been an ardent advocate of fighting to the end, had given up
the cause and was preparing to commit suicide.

General Shizuichi Tanaka, commander of the Eastern Army,
was determined to end the rebellion. An entire division of troops
surrounded the Imperial compound. The rebel leaders knew that
the game was up and at 8:00 a.m. they did the very thing they
wanted to stop, and surrendered. Hatanaka pleaded to be allowed
to broadcast a ten-minute appeal over the radio but was refused. He
and Shiizaki were not arrested – probably because it was accepted
that they would take their own lives. For several hours, the two men
wandered around Tokyo, giving out leaflets, detailing what they had
done and why. When the emperor's broadcast was transmitted, they
joined dozens of civilians on the public plaza opposite the palace.
Everyone was kneeling in floods of tears, some were committing
suicide; Shiizaki and Hatanaka joined them by shooting themselves.

The recordings were delivered to NHK and prepared for the
lunchtime broadcast. Apart from the fact that his people had never
heard the emperor speak before, the audio quality of the broadcast
was poor. And because Hirohito used the traditional court language
of the palace, many of his audience were not sure what he said, and

were left bemused. Also, because he avoided the word 'surrender' – referring instead to the 'Joint Declaration of the Powers', about which the Japanese people knew very little – the confusion was significant. The war was officially over, but the people of Japan faced uncertainty, anxiety and fear.

There were, in addition, the thousands who faced certain death from radiation sickness in Hiroshima and Nagasaki and those who would survive but with pain, multiple operations and terrible scars.

Dr Michihiko Hachiya, working at a hospital in Hiroshima, noticed: '*People who appeared to be recovering have developed new symptoms. So many patients are now dying without our understanding why. We are all in despair.*'

Fourteen-year-old Senji Yamaguchi was a survivor. He described his symptoms: '*A fierce pain jolted my body as one of the nurses peeled off the gauze patches. I cried out, "Please kill me!" There was also a young girl in the hospital who like me had burns on her face. She would have been beautiful but for the terrible scars. The night before her discharge, she hanged herself. I refused to let her death dishearten me. I vowed to go back to school no matter how many people laughed at my scars.*'

Over the next fifty years, more than 100,000 people would die from the after-effects of the two bombs.

One of the biggest concerns for the people of Japan was the future of their beloved emperor. What would the Allies do with him? As most people thought he was the embodiment of the nation, his fate was also Japan's destiny and that of all his people. As his role in the war was known to only a few in the highest echelons of the government, he was thought to be blameless for any of Japan's actions and for its losses and its defeat. Many blamed the militarists and ultranationalists, most blamed themselves for the nation's failings, hardly anybody blamed Hirohito. Even liberals and anti-war activists believed that the emperor had been a passive, and largely helpless, victim of the warmongers around him.

The Americans were conscious that they needed Hirohito's presence to help them govern the country. They also knew that Japan's strategic location was vital to America's security in the new post-war world order that was emerging: an empowered Kremlin, and the likelihood of victory for Mao Tse Tung's communists in China. For those very real pragmatic reasons, the US did little to explode the myth of Hirohito's innocence. Indeed, despite the compelling evidence proving the emperor's active participation from the outset of the war, there was never any question of Hirohito being indicted for war crimes. Even so, the Japanese, unaware of the realpolitik behind the scenes, were anxious about His Majesty's future.

Author Fūtarō Yamada expressed the nation's shared concern.

'What will happen to the emperor? Surely, he will abdicate, but something more drastic may occur. According to the newspapers, at the final meeting in his presence the emperor said, "When We think of Our country being reduced to ashes, whatever may happen to Our person does not merit consideration." At this, they say, members of the cabinet all sobbed aloud. Someone said, "Having heard these words of His Majesty, even if the unthinkable should afflict His Majesty, we shall fulfil our duty to erect a shrine to his memory, however small, regardless of the wishes of the Allied forces."'

Within days, countless letters began to arrive for the occupying forces, most of them anonymous. At least one of them – a rarity – blamed Hirohito.

To the honourable General MacArthur

 In our country the emperor is above God. If something should happen to His Majesty we would lose our purpose in life.

The Emperor made the country go to war with more power and authority than Hitler. If this man is allowed to escape punishment, there will be no justice.

If it ever happens that His Majesty is brought to trial, many Japanese would hold a tremendous hatred toward all Americans. I beg you with this petition written in my blood.

There was also anger directed at prime warmonger, Hideki Tōjō. The prevailing sentiment was captured by Fūtarō Yamada.

'Why didn't General Tōjō kill himself the night of the broadcast, like a man, the way Army Minister Anami Korechika did? Why didn't

General Tōjō use a Japanese sword like Army Minister Anami? It was obvious that an arrest warrant would be issued, but he went on living, reluctant to die. Then, like a foreigner, he used a pistol. He aimed at himself and missed. A Japanese can't help but give a bitter smile. If he had something to look forward to, something that had kept him from committing suicide up to this point, why didn't he bear the unbearable and allow himself to be taken by the police? If death was what he wanted, he should have killed himself on the day of the Imperial Rescript. If he wanted to stay alive, he should have stood in a court of law and reiterated his beliefs. There could be no greater disgrace.'

When the looming presence of US General Douglas MacArthur arrived in Japan – playing the role, as only he could, of the conquering hero – the reality of defeat became even more stark for the Japanese. Atsugi Air Base, eighteen miles outside Tokyo, had been the base of one of the Imperial Navy's kamikaze squadrons. The pilots had fled, leaving a corps of boys to prepare the base for the arrival of the American invaders. For the first time in their history, the Japanese were faced with the reality of a foreign occupation.

Journalist Masuo Kato summed up the general air of uncertainty: *'There were rumours that armed members of the Kamikaze corps were hiding in the nearby hills, ready to strike. The people had been suddenly told to withdraw from a fight to the death and their reaction was still impossible to predict.'*

With Kato waiting on the tarmac to report on his arrival, at 2 p.m. on 30 August, a plane arrived carrying MacArthur, Japan's new ruler, replete with his grandiose new title.

'The Supreme Commander paused on the sunlit airfield as he savoured the moment, very much like a great actor making a carefully planned entrance. Now that the Westerners have arrived, how long will they stay?'

When, earlier in the day, MacArthur had left Manila for Tokyo, 30,000 Japanese soldiers were ordered to line the route. They were told to turn their backs in deference to their new overlord. In Japan, Ichirō Hatano, who had just heard the new police instructions, was anxious about what they implied.

'The police are giving orders about the Americans. "Avoid personal

contact as much as possible. If an American starts a conversation, answer him calmly. Women should dress modestly and go out alone as little as possible." Being occupied is more frightening than being bombed.'

Three days later, on 2 September, on the USS *Missouri* in Tokyo Bay, the official surrender was signed. The responsibility for signing was given to Japan's Foreign Minister, Mamoru Shigemitsu.

'Japan's leaders have tried to avoid taking responsibility for the surrender. So, it is my duty to carry through this last decisive act. I was surrounded by enemy onlookers. Then General MacArthur entered. MacArthur declared the war was over and requested us to sign the surrender. It comes hard to us Japanese to use the word "surrender". Military circles contend it should be referred to as a ceasefire. But, whatever you call it, Japan's rebirth will depend on accepting that she has surrendered as a result of defeat.'

With the ceremonial final signature, the ordinary Japanese had to come to terms with the reality of conquest by invaders who had been described as murdering beasts.

Schoolboy Naokata Sasaki feared the worst: *'The word came, "they are on their way". What would they be like? They came down the road towards us. We had images of glaring demons with horns sprouting from their heads. We peeped out to try and catch a glimpse of them. We were disappointed, no horns at all. Friends who had bumped into them on the streets brought back chocolates. They're good people, they said. I told them it couldn't be true. They must be lying.'*

A particular shock for the public happened when the news emerged that on 25 September, Hirohito had met MacArthur. That they had met was not unusual, but the fact that MacArthur had not been given an Imperial audience – but instead, the emperor had gone to the US embassy to meet his conqueror – was seen as offensive to a living god.

Jun Takami expressed the widespread sense of dismay: *'I was astonished to read in the newspaper that the emperor had called on General MacArthur. Nothing like His Majesty the Emperor personally going to a foreigner's residence had happened before. It has certainly come as a great shock to the Japanese people. [. . .] We have been taught that His Majesty the Emperor is a sacred being whom we cannot approach.*

When I think back to the fact that freedom, which naturally should have been given by the people's own government, could not be given, and instead has been bestowed for the first time by the military forces of a foreign country, I cannot escape feelings of shame. I am ashamed as someone who loves Japan, ashamed for Japan's sake. It would be understandable if an occupation army, coming in after a war in which we were defeated, had restricted our freedom, but the opposite has occurred, our freedom has been guaranteed. What a shameful thing! [. . .] What a humiliation!'

With the end of the war, over 6.6 million Japanese had to be repatriated. The total was made up of roughly equal numbers of military personnel and civilians. The repatriation of soldiers and other members of the armed forces began in early September.

Sergeant Kunimitsu Iida arrived from Okinawa: *'It took three days for us all to get ashore. It was the first time in eight years I'd been home. They sprayed us all over, on our heads and up our sleeves. We were so hungry that the clothes that we had carried were soon exchanged for food. All of us were worn out and had no strength to even talk to each other.'*

The repatriation of civilians was different. There were no legal provisions in place and, in the days immediately after the surrender, Japanese nationals overseas were told to stay where they were. That was a serious problem for many, especially those trapped in China or in those areas controlled by the Soviet Red Army. As most men and boys had been drafted into the armed forces, most of the stranded civilians were women, young children and the elderly. Needless to say, in many places, abuse and worse were commonplace, and tens of thousands died.

Yoshie Fukushima, a kindergarten teacher, married a military vendor and settled with him in Tungning, near the Soviet border at Vladivostok. Her husband was called up in 1945, leaving her at home with their infant son. When the Red Army appeared, like all her neighbours, she was stranded. Despite the fact that she possessed only what she could carry, and that Japan was hundreds of miles away, she decided to walk with her child on her back. It took her eighteen months to get home to her mother in Kanazawa on

Japan's west coast. She ate frogs, snakes and rats; both she and her child almost died from disease; she witnessed the Soviets massacring Japanese soldiers; she was nearly raped, saved only by her disease-ridden body, and spent months begging for small change.

'I finally got enough money to go into the business of selling tobacco, one cigarette at a time. I took up a place where lots of Japanese passed by. I would describe my husband and then ask them if they'd seen him. But I didn't even know the name of his unit. Eventually, my son and I were able to return to Japan. It was February 1947. I remember how green the wheat seemed as we approached the port of Sasebo. When we finally got to Kanazawa, I knew my husband hadn't made it back. For years I lived thinking alternately that he might be alive or that he was already dead. One day in 1955, I received a letter from a man in the Tochigi Prefecture. He wrote, "Fukushima Masaichi, who died in my prison camp four hundred miles from Moscow, might be your husband." He had been dead since 18th May 1946.'

With the Allied liberation of territories conquered by Japan came countless stories describing the appalling treatment meted out to Allied prisoners of war. Of the 132,134 Allied servicemen held in captivity during the war, 35,756 died, an appalling death rate of 27 per cent.

Yoshikichi Kasayama was one of several native Koreans who worked as guards in prisoner of war camps. His camp was in Java, where he worked under a Japanese corporal.

'We beat and kicked prisoners in order to make them work. There wasn't much to eat, and army regulations specified that we were to feed ourselves first. What was left went to the prisoners. So they got really thin. Every day they died and there was no time to dig graves and when you put several hundred corpses in one place, everything reeks with the smell of rotting bodies, the stink of death.'

1st Lieutenant Hiroshi Abe was a construction supervisor on the Burma Railway – the notorious 'Death Railway' – at Song-kurai, in Thailand. Over 1,100 Australian and 670 British prisoners worked under Abe's supervision: *'I really didn't do anything wrong. I just worked there. We had to have human labour because we didn't have machines. If a prisoner looked lazy or seemed to be loafing, he'd be beaten up. I didn't really know anything about the Geneva Convention. In my camp 3,100 died.'*

Another consequence of the end of the Asia-Pacific War was the inevitable war crimes trials, in which over 5,000 Japanese were convicted and more than 900 executed. Hirohito, the 'powerless figurehead' who liked to parade in full uniform on his grey horse to mark Japan's victories, escaped any punishment and lived quietly in his Imperial Palace until he died in 1989, at the age of eighty-seven. The only mild inconvenience he had to endure was, under pressure from the Allies, the renouncement of his divinity on New Year's Day 1946. The rest of the royal family, including Hirohito's brother, Prince Chichibu, whose wartime track record was dubious, also escaped any condemnation, let alone punishment. To facilitate the deception, MacArthur made sure that any incriminating evidence implicating Hirohito and the Imperial family was withheld from the war crimes lawyers.

On 3 May 1946, the major Tokyo war crimes trials began, where Japan's leaders were accused of waging aggressive war and committing countless atrocities. Student Takashi Asai was in no doubt about the significance of the trials: *'The period of feudal darkness is passing. Those of us who believe in liberalism can hardly find a way to express our joy. The most important thing for our country at present is to completely uproot the fanatical militarists. The punishment for war criminals should be death.'*

There were further consequences of the arrival of tens of thousands of conquering American GIs and marines. They were all young men, far from home. They had achieved a great victory and were soldiers, not peacekeepers. The diary entry of Jun Takami for 24 October recorded an increasingly common sight.

'A young Japanese woman was walking along the platform with an American soldier. She boarded the train, the soldier remained behind. The woman stuck her head out of the window to chat with him. Presently, the train began to move, and she called out, "Baibai". All the passengers in the carriage turned towards the woman, their expressions showing contempt and even hatred. I was one of them. She continued to lean from the window and looked as if she intended never to leave it. Her stance

showed she was fully aware of the gaze of the other passengers and the emotions in their eyes. She had come to look like a woman at a so-called "Special Comfort Facility".

Despite the opprobrium expressed by the Allies on the contentious issue of 'comfort women' throughout Japan's empire, within a week of Hirohito's surrender, the decision was taken in Tokyo to launch a 'Recreation and Amusement Association'.

The Japanese authorities decided to set up the RAA expressly for the benefit of Allied occupation troops, on 21 August. In fact, the Home Ministry had already sent a directive to prefectural governors and police chiefs three days earlier, ordering them to make preparations for 'comfort facilities' in areas where Allied occupation troops would be stationed. It is distinctly paradoxical that the Americans rushed to use them so readily.

The 'facilities', which operated with government funds, included dance halls, restaurants and bars, as well as brothels. They were intended to be staffed by women already involved in prostitution. However, because there were not enough women in the sex trade, more women were needed. As there was an abundance of single and widowed women, and those facing poverty and shortages of food, recruitment was broadened. Newspaper ads appeared that obscured the nature of the work, while promising food, clothing and shelter. Government officials used patriotic language in describing the comfort facility system, praising women who would sacrifice themselves to be 'patriotic barricades' preventing sexual violence against Japanese women and girls.

Indeed, sexual violence became a growing problem. The bars were packed every night and the 'Yanks' had money to burn. On Okinawa, Allied troops were estimated by one Okinawan historian to have raped 10,000 Okinawan women during the war.

The Official History of the Ibaraki Prefecture Police, northeast of Tokyo, outlined local concerns:

> Sadly, we police had to set up sexual comfort stations for the occupation troops. The strategy was, through the special work of experienced women, to create a breakwater to protect

regular women and girls. As expected, after it opened it was elbow to elbow. The comfort women [. . .] had some resistance to selling themselves to men who just yesterday were the enemy, and because of differences in language and race, there was a great deal of apprehension at first. But they were paid highly, and they gradually came to accept their work peacefully.

On 28 August, an advance wave of occupation troops arrived in Atsugi, just south of Tokyo. By nightfall, the troops had found the RAA's first brothel. Seiichi Kaburagi, the chief of public relations for the RAA, later recalled the scene.

I rushed there with two or three RAA executives and was surprised to see 500 or 600 soldiers standing in line on the street. The American Military Police were barely able to keep the troops under control. The GIs paid up front and were given tickets and condoms.

Kaburagi also told the story of Natsue Takita, a nineteen-year-old whose relatives were killed in the war. She had responded to an advertisement seeking an office worker but was told the only positions available were for comfort women, and was persuaded to accept the offer. She jumped in front of a train a few days after the brothel started operating.

The first RAA brothel, called *Komachien* ('Babe Garden'), opened on 20 September. It had thirty-eight women, but because of high demand more than 100 were soon employed, each of whom serviced from fifteen to sixty clients a day. The charge for a quick session with a prostitute was fifteen yen – about a dollar.

From the beginning of the Occupation, several Allied military officials cooperated with the Japanese government's RRA system. The governors of Chiba and Kanagawa Prefectures requested the establishment of brothels for the troops, and the US military police offered their help if necessary. American medical officers established prophylactic stations in red-light districts and inside the larger brothels, distributing tens of thousands of condoms every week. By early 1946 military chaplains were condemning the brothels, citing violations of war department policies and lamenting the moral degradation of US troops they caused. The complaints led to an order, issued on 21 January, ending licensed brothels. The ending of official RAA operations did not affect 'voluntary prostitution' by individuals, and brothel owners were easily able to circumvent the order by renting space in their former brothels to 'voluntary' prostitutes. Ultimately, in an attempt to stop the spread of sexually transmitted diseases, which had become rampant, all brothels and other facilities offering prostitution were made 'off-limits' to Allied personnel, on 25 March 1946. Astonishingly, during its seven months of operation, at least 50,000 women had worked for the RAA.

And so, Hirohito's Holy War had turned out to be far from 'holy'. As a god, he might have had the right to declare one – but, of course, he was not a god, merely a mortal with all the weaknesses of humankind. As a consequence of his actions – or lack of action, dragged along by a coterie of warmongers – his people and the people of many other countries (as many as 32 million dead) paid an awful price.

Japan would never again be the place it had been for millennia – although many resisted the inevitability of change and, to this day, a few still do. We will never know if Hirohito came to the same conclusion. Perhaps he did. But it must have been clear to him – and if it was not, it is highly likely that MacArthur told him – that his future status would be no more than that of a ceremonial figurehead.

The future required the emperor to retreat behind his Chrysanthemum Throne with dignity and allow his people to govern themselves and pursue their own destiny.

EPILOGUE

As the dust of war began to settle, what were the Japanese left to ponder as they looked to the future?

For some, their reflections were tinged with bitterness, where thoughts of 'revenge' and 'vengeance' were prominent. Author Fūtarō Yamada's words encapsulated the sentiments of many of his fellow citizens.

'At the appropriate time, we must make plans to take revenge on America. This may be forever impossible, but it is even more impossible to permit America to consider Japan eternally as a fourth-rate nation. We prefer to struggle in a perpetual sea of blood rather than be looked upon as inferiors, to be slaves [. . .] The Americans say that the Japanese have no sense of humour. But what's so funny about flying over cities you've bombed indiscriminately and intimidating them? The Japanese will not smile again until the day of vengeance [. . .] No matter how much the newspapers praise America, there lies dormant in ninety per cent of the youth of Japan the resolve to take up bravely the sword of vengeance as soon as a spark is struck.'

In contrast, others had a very different response to Japan's defeat and surrender, believing Japan had no choice other than to change. To survive, it had to bury its past. While it could retain its memories of the past – and, indeed, innocent nostalgia for days gone by – what it could never allow again was for its past to determine its future.

One such advocate was Konokichi Sumiyoshi, a student who was a witness to Japan's terrible journey, but who nevertheless gave determined voice to a more hopeful vision for his country's future.

'We cannot deny that we had high hopes for the old Japan. But the fact is that the militarists totally ignored reality. Japan had closed itself

off and been fearful of the outside world. We must create a new nation from the ashes of the old.'

As of the time of writing in 2025 – eighty years after the war – Japan has indeed found a new identity and destiny. It has been a rocky ride at times and its giant neighbour on the mainland is suddenly a more challenging proposition. However, Japan's modern democracy is strong, and the country has a stable welfare system, enjoys modest prosperity and has the fourth largest economy in the world: truly 'a new nation'.

After completing the manuscript for this book, I decided to take a short break to reflect on what had been a very difficult exercise. The witness research had been harrowing. It is one thing to read about the horrors of war and the anguish of those swept up by the events, but quite another to read first-hand accounts from those who had committed atrocities and those who had suffered and died during the terrible events of the Asia Pacific War. The task of then trying to keep a clear head to avoid writing a polemic or a distorted account, was also a significant challenge.

I am not a professional historian with an academic reputation to maintain, I am an impassioned writer of history who tries to focus on stories that tell us about ourselves. I use the words of witnesses to describe the deeds of fellow human beings, people who are just like everybody else. I concentrate on times of war, simply because it is in those circumstances that human nature, its propensity for both good and evil, becomes most visible. There is what may be a vain hope hidden in my ambition: that accounts like the one outlined in these pages, will lead us to think about how fragile stability, normality and peace can be and how blurred our sense of right and wrong can become.

So, what of the Asia Pacific War as a lesson from history? Do we need to apportion blame or assign guilt? Victors usually blame the vanquished and conventional wisdom has cast Japan as the aggressor in the war and the perpetrator of wicked deeds during the conflict. In simple terms both views are accurate, but it presumes innocence on the part of the Allies who fought Japan. However, 'innocence' is a misleading word because it conceals the acts of vengeance inflicted on Japan at the end of the war and ignores the complex set of circumstances that created modern Japan and the economic and strategically vulnerable position it was in during the 1930s.

After 1945, it was far too easy to conclude that, like the Germans, the Japanese were horribly flawed people because they committed such evil deeds. We demanded that they purge themselves of their sins through official apologies and ritual reflections on their sinful nature, a demand made not only of the original sinners, but also of the children and grandchildren who inherited their abhorrent nature. However, the blame game by the victors and the intimidation of the vanquished is too easy, because it simply allows us to put evil in a coffin, bury it in the past and move on to the next dreadful conflict. Although it is important to identify human weakness, cowardice and wickedness, it is vital to explain that behaviour of that sort has reasons and is created by a process of cause and effect that is hugely complex.

For example, when greedy Western powers began to assail Japan's shores, they found a feudal society with a culture and traditions that were distinctly mediaeval. Japan was vulnerable and frightened by the sudden appearance of foreigners with ill intent and awesome weapons. The alien visitors were bent on conquest, if not by force of arms, then by coercion, manipulation or intimidation. As they did with all the peoples around the world who were not part of European culture, they regarded the Japanese as inferior human beings and thought that they would be far better off if they were subjugated, educated and civilised.

However, Japan's traditions and system of values made them a far tougher nut to crack than many other lands that the West had brought under its control. Japanese discipline, social orderliness, propensity for hard work and its warrior pedigree allowed them to resist Western attempts to control them. Indeed, to meet the challenge it faced, it chose to systematically borrow the West's institutions and methodologies, especially in technology, political systems and in its military. In particular, the chivalrous warrior tradition of the samurai was on the one hand discarded, but at the same time incorporated into the new Imperial army and navy. Although this made Japan's armed forces a formidable weapon, it created a dangerous paradoxical heritage in the minds of many Japanese, both the low-born and the elite. It was a psychological conflict between the values of an honourable and noble past and the dishonourable and base values of new mindless bureaucrats, greedy merchants and exploitative entrepreneurs.

The potential tensions became starkly clear with the 1889 Meiji Restoration (sometimes called the 'Honourable Restoration') when the old order of the shoguns was swept away and the power of the emperor was restored. A journey began in which subsequent emperors and their governments struggled to control a social and political brew that was in a constant state of flux. Democracy had been borrowed from the West and became the anvil on which competing forces struck repeated blows: left and right; past and present, passive and aggressive.

As the world around Japan developed and indeed became smaller, Japan's vulnerability became clear again. How could it compete and become the thing it desired most: to be a 'first-class' nation? Imperial Russia encroached and was beaten back. Korea, Manchuria and China offered a solution to Japan's greatest problem, its lack of resources and living space, and were slowly swallowed by a beast that became ever more ravenous. These successes tipped the balance of power in the turbulence of its domestic politics. Militarists and nationalists were emboldened and flexed their muscles. Democracy came under threat, repression increased, and dissidents were silenced. Crucially, the emperor, to protect the Kokutai, the 'body politic', in effect the ruling elite, gave in to the pressure, chose pragmatism over morality and allowed the military free rein.

The die was cast. When, during the global turmoil of the 1930s, Japan felt isolated and cornered, it believed it was strong enough to act decisively and chose to strike out into the Pacific and Southeast Asia to secure the resources it needed and build the empire it craved. It climbed an escalation ladder that became terrifying in its consequences. As we have read, the legacy of Japan's medieval military psychology brought horror across its conquered lands and created a thirst for vengeance among the peoples it conquered and challenged. Japan's Holy War was doomed to ignominious failure.

Its hope that, through its show of military prowess, indefatigable willingness to fight and vast territorial conquests, it would bring the United States to the negotiating table was lost on the morning of 7 December 1941 at Pearl Harbor. At that moment, the horrors of the next four years, especially the unimaginable awfulness of 1945, were all but inevitable.

And so, one of history's darkest stories ended catastrophically, leaving a legacy of hurt and pain that still resonates to this day and will continue for many generations to come.

ACKNOWLEDGEMENTS

I am indebted to several people who have helped me get this book to the point where it is vaguely readable. Anything short of that is entirely my fault, not theirs.

As with all my books, Alex Clarke, a friend, mentor and great publisher has – alongside his excellent team – guided me through the increasingly complex world of getting a book in front of its audience.

Equally crucial to this process was my editor, Shan Morley Jones. Like a literary wizard, Shan managed to transform my jumbled text into logical sequences and a coherent narrative.

My eternal gratitude goes to my good friend and colleague of many years, Gill Blake, who took on the onerous and often distressing task of helping me source powerful and compelling witness material. The book would have been far less valuable without her contribution.

I would also like to thank Michie Smart for helping with the nuances of Japanese names and places.

Finally, to my wife Lucy and my boys, Charlie and Jack, a huge thank you for allowing me to ignore and abuse you throughout the many months of heartache it took to get this book done.

EMPEROR HIROHITO'S SURRENDER SPEECH, 1945

To our good and loyal subjects:

After pondering deeply the general trends of the world and the actual conditions obtaining to our empire today, we have decided to effect a settlement of the present situation by resorting to an extraordinary measure.

We have ordered our government to communicate to the governments of the United States, Great Britain, China, and the Soviet Union that our empire accepts the provisions of their Joint Declaration.

To strive for the common prosperity and happiness of all nations as well as the security and well-being of our subjects is the solemn obligation which has been handed down by our imperial ancestors, and which we lay close to heart. Indeed, we declared war on America and Britain out of our sincere desire to ensure Japan's self-preservation and the stabilization of East Asia, it being far from our thought either to infringe upon the sovereignty of other nations or to embark upon territorial aggrandizement.

But now the war has lasted for nearly four years. Despite the best that has been done by everyone – the gallant fighting of the military and naval forces, the diligence and assiduity of our servants of the state, and the devoted service of our 100 million people – the war situation has developed not necessarily to Japan's advantage, while the general trends of the world have all turned against her interest.

Moreover, the enemy has begun to employ a new and most cruel bomb, the power of which to damage is indeed incalculable, taking the toll of many innocent lives.

Should we continue to fight, it would not only result in an

ultimate collapse and obliteration of the Japanese nation, but also it would lead to the total extinction of human civilization.

Such being the case, how are we to save the millions of our subjects or to atone ourselves before the hallowed spirits of our imperial ancestors? This is the reason why we have ordered the acceptance of the provisions of the Joint Declaration of the Powers.

We cannot but express the deepest sense of regret to our allied nations of East Asia, who have consistently co-operated with the empire towards the emancipation of East Asia. The thought of those officers and men as well as others who have fallen in the fields of battle, those who died at their posts of duty, or those who met with untimely death and all their bereaved families, pains our heart day and night.

The welfare of the wounded and the war sufferers, and of those who have lost their homes and livelihood, are the objects of our profound solicitude.

The hardships and sufferings to which our nation is to be subjected hereafter will certainly be great. We are keenly aware of the inmost feelings of all you, our subjects.

However, it is according to the dictate of time and fate that we have resolved to pave the way for a grand peace for all the generations to come by enduring the unendurable and suffering what is insufferable.

Having been able to safeguard and maintain the structure of the imperial state, we are always with you, our good and loyal subjects, relying upon your sincerity and integrity. Beware most strictly of any outbursts of emotion which may engender needless complications, or any fraternal contention and strife which may create confusion, lead you astray, and cause you to lose the confidence of the world.

Let the entire nation continue as one family from generation to generation, ever firm in its faith of the imperishableness of its divine land, and mindful of its heavy responsibilities, and the long road before it.

Unite your total strength to be devoted to the construction for the future. Cultivate the ways of rectitude; foster nobility of spirit;

and work with resolution so that you may enhance the innate glory
of the imperial state and keep pace with the progress of the world.

14th day of the 8th month of the 20th year of Shōwa

WITNESSES

For many witnesses, particularly those quoted second-hand from other sources, little or no biographical material exists.

The witnesses are listed in order of first appearance in the text.

Epigraphs

Hiroko Nakamoto. She was born and educated in Hiroshima City, Japan. When she was a child, a fortune teller read her palm and told her that one day she would go to faraway lands. Those 'faraway lands' sounded like something from a dream, a dream that would never exist. Japan was under the shadow of war and her people lived from one air raid to the next. Then came the morning of 6 August 1945. It was a morning full of sunshine and terrible destruction. Dreams became nightmares, real ones, and out of these nightmares came the realisation of that 'faraway lands' prophesy. In 1951, Hiroko went to the United States to attend Bowling Green State University, where four years later she graduated with a BA in Fine Arts. From there she went to the Pratt Institute to study Interior Design. She continued her studies in France and Italy. Finally, she went to Tokyo, Japan, where she set up her own interior design studio.

Preface: The 'Enigma' that is Japan

Tarō Asō. A right-wing politician who served as prime minister of Japan from 24 September 2008 to 16 September 2009. In 2012 Asō became deputy prime minister and finance minister. The son of a business tycoon, he is part of the political and imperial hierarchy of Japan. He is a grandson of a prime minister and his father-in-law was also a prime minister, while his sister is married to a cousin of the Emperor Akihito.

Ruth Benedict. The American anthropologist's work during the war included a major study, largely completed in 1944, aimed at understanding Japanese culture. She played a major role in explaining the status of the Japanese Emperor in his country's society and culture, and helped make the recommendation to US President Roosevelt that it was wise to allow Emperor Hirohito to continue his reign after Japan's surrender.

Yoshisaburō Okakura. He was appointed professor at the Seventh Higher School in 1894 and was professor at the Tokyo Higher Normal School for twenty-five years from 1896. In the interim, he visited Britain and the United States. The doyen of teachers of English in Japan, he was famous as a radio teacher of the language after resigning from the Tokyo Higher Normal School. He compiled a large English–Japanese dictionary and became professor at St Paul's (Rikkyo) University in Tokyo.

Komakichi Nohara. He was the son of a Japanese father and a German mother. In the 1920s, he was a member of the League of Proletarian Revolutionary Writers and worked at the Japanese embassy in Berlin. He worked as a speechwriter for Ambassador Oshima and interpreter for military talks between the Wehrmacht leadership and the Japanese military leadership in Berlin. He wrote in German and his work *The True Face of Japan* was translated into several languages.

1. The Way of the Warrior

Razan Hayashi. A Japanese scholar who, with his son and grandson, established the thought of the great Chinese Neo-Confucian philosopher Chu Hsi as the official doctrine of the Tokugawa Shogunate from 1603 to 1867. Hayashi also reinterpreted Shinto, the Japanese national religion, from the point of view of Chu Hsi's philosophy, creating the basis for the Confucian version of Shinto that evolved in later centuries.

Sokō Yamaga. An Edo Period military strategist and Confucian philosopher who created the first description of the role and obligations of the samurai (warrior) class of Japan. Yamaga's outline became the catechism of what came to be known as *bushidō*, the warrior's code of philosophy of Japan's military throughout the Tokugawa Period (1603–1867) and through to the end of the Second World War.

Ieyasu Tokugawa. The founder and first shogun of the Tokugawa Shogunate of Japan, which ruled from 1603 until the Meiji Restoration in 1868. He was one of 'The Three Great Unifiers' of Japan. He once lived as a hostage on behalf of his father. He later succeeded as daimyo after his father's death and seized power in 1600, after the Battle of Sekigahara, and was made shogun in 1603. He implemented a set of careful rules known as the *bakuhan* (military) system, designed to keep the daimyo and samurai in check under the Tokugawa Shogunate.

Kaishū Katsu. A Japanese statesman and naval engineer during the late Tokugawa Shogunate and early Meiji Period. He was made Vice Minister of the Imperial Japanese Navy in 1872, then First Minister of the Navy from 1873 until 1878. Although his influence within the navy was minimal, he served in a senior advisory capacity on national policy. During the next two decades, Katsu served on the Privy Council and wrote extensively on naval issues.

Nariakira Shimazu. A Japanese feudal daimyo of the Edo Period, the 28th in the line of Shimazu clan lords of the Satsuma Domain. He was said to be an intelligent and wise lord and was greatly interested in Western learning and technology. Nariakira's views became the foundation of the new Meiji government and included centralising the government around the emperor and westernising the Japanese military.

Prince Hirobumi Itō. The first prime minister of Japan and a leading member of the group of senior statesmen who dictated Japanese policy during the Meiji Era. He chaired the bureau which drafted the constitution for the newly formed Empire of Japan. He modelled it on British and German models, particularly the Prussian Constitution of 1850.

Saburō Ienaga. Born in 1913, Ienaga was a historian and lecturer at the Tokyo University of Education from 1949 to 1977. In 1953, the Japanese Ministry of Education published a textbook by Ienaga, but censored what it said were factual errors and matters of opinion in his descriptions of war crimes. Ienaga challenged the ministry for violating his freedom of speech, a case which he won. However, the book was withdrawn. He was nominated for the Nobel Peace Prize in 1999 and 2001.

2. A Nation Galvanised

Shūsui Kōtoku. A prominent figure in radical politics in Japan and vehemently opposed to the Russo-Japanese War. He served five months in 1905 before leaving for the United States. When he returned, he resumed his activism until execution for high treason in 1911.

Inazō Nitobe. A Japanese educator, diplomat, agronomist and politician who travelled to the United States to study agricultural policy. After returning to Japan, he served as a professor at Sapporo Agricultural College, part of Kyoto Imperial University, and Tokyo Imperial University. He died in 1933.

Etsu Inagaki Sugimoto. She was born in 1874. Her father had once been a high-ranking samurai official but with the breakdown of the feudal system shortly before her birth, the economic situation of her family took a turn for the worse. Although originally destined to be a priestess, she became engaged through an arranged marriage to a Japanese merchant living in Ohio. In 1898, she journeyed to the United States, where she married her fiancé and became the mother of two daughters. After her husband's death, she returned to Japan, but later returned to the US for her daughters to complete their education. Later, she lived in New York where she turned to literature and taught Japanese language, culture and history at Columbia University. She also wrote for newspapers and magazines. She died in 1950.

Baron Ghiichi Tanaka. Born in 1863 in Yamaguchi Prefecture. He made his name in the Russo-Japanese War. He was appointed minister of war in 1918, and had dreams of a Japanese empire in Siberia. He became prime minister in 1927. His efforts to deal with the 1927 economic crisis in Japan led to an inflationary spiral and caused social unrest. When he moved to punish army officers involved in the assassination of the Manchurian leader Chang Tso-lin, the army refused to back him, and his cabinet fell. Tanaka died a short time afterwards.

3. Hirohito

Michinomiya Hirohito. Born in April 1901. As Emperor Shōwa, he was the 124th emperor of Japan and reigned for sixty-two years, the longest reign in Japan's history. In line with ancient custom, imperial family members were not raised by their parents. Hirohito spent his formative years in the care of courtiers, then attended schools for the nobility where religious and military education dominated his curriculum. Importantly for Japan's future, Hirohito's visits abroad, particularly to Europe in 1921, gave him the opportunity to assess his nation's status in world affairs and helped him understand its options for the future. Because of his father's illness, he became regent in 1921 and was soon confronted with the trauma of the 1923 Great Kantō Earthquake and was also subject to an assassination attempt amidst much political violence.

Hirohito's role in the politics of Japan – especially its increasing militarisation, its imperial expansion into the Asian mainland, and its actions in the Second World War – is still the subject of much debate, as is the decision that he was spared from prosecution for war crimes. The Americans took the view that Japan would be all but impossible to govern if the emperor and his family were held to account for the actions that took place in his name. So, at the small price of renouncing his divine status, he became Japan's constitutional democratic monarch and oversaw his country's recovery and subsequent growth. Upon his death, he was succeeded by his son, Akihito, who, citing old age, abdicated in 2019, to be succeeded by his son, Naruhito, beginning the Reiwa era. Aged ninety at the time of writing, Akihito is still alive with the title Emperor Emeritus.

Daisuke Nanba. A Japanese student and member of the Japanese Communist Party who tried to assassinate the Crown Prince Hirohito on 27 December 1923.

Nobuaki Makino. A Japanese politician and Lord Keeper of the Privy Seal of Japan. He served as Hirohito's chief adviser on policy and was a major factor in the increasing militarisation of Japan by encouraging support for ultranationalists. He consistently attempted to restrain the emperor from acting against the Imperial Army's expansionism. After his retirement in 1935, he did attempt to avoid war with China and the United States and remained close to Hirohito.

Ikki Kita. Drawing on a vast range of influences, Kita described himself as a socialist, but was more akin to a German national socialist. He has also been called the 'ideological father of Japanese fascism'. His publications were heavily censored, and he ceased writing after 1923. Even so, Kita was an inspiration for right-wing Japanese politics into the 1930s, particularly his advocacy for territorial expansion and a military coup. In 1936 he was arrested for allegedly joining the 'February 26 Incident'– a failed coup – and was executed in 1937.

Kōzaburō Tachibana. From a samurai family, he was a Japanese political activist and ultranationalist. He called for the formation of a 'patriotic brotherhood' to unselfishly lay down their lives to save the people in accordance with the emperor's wishes. He died in 1974.

Korekiyo Takahashi. A Japanese politician, and prime minister from 1921 to 1922. As minister of finance, following the onset of the Great Depression, he introduced controversial policies which lowered interest rates and introduced deficit spending by the central government. His decision to cut spending in 1935 led to unrest within the Japanese military, which led to his assassination in February 1936.

4. China

Kiichirō Hiranuma. The son of a low-ranking samurai, he was a leading right-wing politician and prime minister in 1939. He was convicted of war crimes in 1945 and sentenced to life imprisonment. He was paroled in 1952 and died shortly afterwards.

Kanji Ishiwara. A general who, with fellow general Itagaki Seishirō, was responsible for the 'Mukden Incident' in Manchuria in 1931. After the war, Seishirō was convicted of war crimes and executed but Ishiwara escaped punishment because he had spoken out against Hideki Tōjō, when he became minister of war in 1940.

Shirō Azuma. A Japanese soldier who admitted his participation in war crimes against the Chinese during World War II and participated in the Nanking Massacre. He visited China several times to apologise and help Chinese historians find evidence of brutality. In 1987, he published his diary, *My Nanking Platoon*, which was translated into Chinese and English.

Yukio Omata. A war correspondent for the *Yomiuri* newspaper.

Prince Fumimaro Konoe. A Japanese politician who served as prime minister of Japan from 1937 to 1939 and from 1940 to 1941. He presided over the invasion of China in 1937 and played a central role in transforming his country into a totalitarian state by dissolving all other political parties. The 'Marco Polo Bridge Incident' took place a month after his appointment, and he was central to all Japan's actions during the war. At the end of the war, after coming under suspicion of war crimes, Konoe committed suicide in December 1945 by taking cyanide.

Shōzō Tominaga. After graduating he went to Manchuria, to work for a company in charge of grain distribution all over Manchukuo, before being enlisted in 1941.

Shin Hasegawa. Born in 1922 in Fukushima Prefecture. He became an army special pilot. On 12 April 1945, he was killed in action on Okinawa as a member of the Special Attack Unit. He was twenty-three years old.

5. The Mighty Escalation

Sōkichi Takagi. A career sailor, in 1937 Akagi became Chief of the Navy Ministry's Research Section. He acted as a political contact for the navy through government officials and politicians, and developed contacts with liberal intellectuals. An opponent of Japan's war on the United States, he was removed from his position in 1942 and reassigned to a naval district.

Yōichi Yanagida. Born on 5 March 1919, he was conscripted in February 1942, and entered Chiba Army Air Defence School in May. He was killed in an accident on 1 October 1942 in Kisarazu, Chiba Prefecture. He was twenty-three years old.

Eiichiro Jō. A naval officer aide-de-camp to Hirohito who, in 1937, helped plan and direct the first air offensive against China's cities from the aircraft carrier *Kaga*. He was also an amateur scientist with an interest in meteorology. On returning to Japan, he served on the Navy General Staff and taught at the Navy and Army War Colleges. He then went back to China as vice commander of the Thirteenth Naval Air Force, charged with bombing operations deep within China. After a year in China, Jō was assigned to the Imperial Palace. His duties required him to make daily war situation reports and convey top-secret navy materials and orders to the emperor. Jō was descended from the Kyushu warrior Takefusa Kikuchi who had participated in saving Japan from the Mongol fleet in the thirteenth century, when fortuitous 'divine winds' (kamikaze) destroyed the invaders. His ancestry was part of Jō's determination to save Japan from the American fleet by drawing up the first detailed plan for a 'kamikaze' Special Attack Corps in June 1943. Jō's idea to recruit young pilots to fly their Zero fighters into the decks of American ships was later adopted and put into practice in the Philippines by his friend, Vice Admiral Takijirō Ōhnishi.

6. Pacific Expansion

Shigenori Tōjō. He was Minister for Foreign Affairs at both the start and the end of the war. He also served as Minister of Colonial Affairs in 1941, and assumed the same position, renamed the Minister for East Asia, in 1945. He was arrested on war crimes charges, held at Sugamo Prison and later sentenced to twenty years' imprisonment. He died in prison in 1950.

Shigeru Nambara. A Japanese political scientist who served as the President of the University of Tokyo and the Japan Academy and was a member of the House of Peers (*Kizoku-in*), the upper chamber of the Imperial Diet.

Isoroku Yamamoto. The son of a middle-rank samurai, he was a Marshal Admiral of the Imperial Japanese Navy and the Commander-in-Chief of the Combined Fleet during the Asia-Pacific War. He oversaw both the attack on Pearl Harbor and the Battle of Midway. A veteran of the Russo-Japanese War and a Harvard graduate (1919–1921), he was fluent in English. While at Harvard, he learned to play poker and was good enough to win sufficient money to be able to hitchhike across America, and later became a naval attaché in Washington. Yamamoto was killed in April 1943 after US code breakers identified his flight plans so that the US Army Air Force was able to shoot down his aircraft over the jungles of Bougainville, in Papua New Guinea.

Osami Nagano. He was a Marshal Admiral of the Imperial Japanese Navy and, in April 1941, became Chief of the Imperial Japanese Navy General Staff and Commander-in-Chief in the Asia-Pacific War until he was removed in February 1944. He was arrested by the International Military Tribunal as a war criminal but died of a heart attack in prison during the trial.

7. The Turning Point

Marquess Kōichi Kido. He served as Lord Privy Seal of Japan from 1940 to 1945 and was the closest adviser to Emperor Hirohito throughout the Asia-Pacific War. He was convicted of war crimes and sentenced to life imprisonment in Sugamo Prison in Tokyo. He served six years before being released in 1953. In 1951, as the Occupation of Japan was ending, Kido sent a message to the emperor, advising him (as he had advised three years earlier) to accept responsibility for the defeat, and abdicate at the end of the American Occupation. In addition, Kido opposed the idea of continuing to punish war criminals under Japanese law after the end of the American Occupation. Kido died in 1977, at the age of eighty-seven.

Saburō Sakai. One of the top Japanese pilots during the Asia-Pacific War; he claimed to have shot down over sixty Allied aircraft. He joined the Japanese Navy at the age of sixteen and was one of only seventy students accepted into flight training out of 1,500 applicants. He went to the US several times, and met his former adversaries. He died in 2000, at the age of eighty-four.

Matome Ugaki. An admiral in the Imperial Japanese Navy during the Asia-Pacific War, he is remembered for his extensive and revealing war diary. On 15 August 1945 – when Hirohito announced defeat and called for the military to lay down its arms – Ugaki made a last entry in his diary, noting that he had not yet received an official cease-fire order, and that as he was to blame for the failure of his valiant kamikaze pilots to stop the enemy, he would fly one last mission himself to show the true spirit of *bushidō*. Prior to boarding his aircraft, Ugaki posed for pictures and removed his rank insignia from his dark green uniform, taking only a *wakizashi* (ceremonial short sword) given to him by Admiral Yamamoto. What happened thereafter is not clear, except that the next morning, the crew of a US LST-926 tank landing craft claimed to have found the still-smouldering remains of a cockpit with its pilot inside on the beach of Iheyajima Island in the Okinawa Group. The sailors buried the remains in the sand.

Harukichi Hyakutake. A general in the Asia-Pacific War, he was in command of the Imperial Army's Seventeenth Army in the Solomons. He led its survivors off Guadalcanal in January 1943. He suffered a stroke and was relieved of his duties in 1945, but could not be repatriated until the surrender of Japan later that year. He died in 1947, in Tokyo, at the age of fifty-eight.

Kiyoshi Kiyosawa. A Japanese journalist and writer who is most well known for his wartime diary that was written between 1942 and 1945, and published in 1948, when it caused a sensation. It was first published in English under the title *A Diary of Darkness*. He died from acute pneumonia just before the end of the war, at the age of fifty-five.

Sei Ito. A Japanese modernist writer of poetry, prose and essays, and a translator. He died in 1969, at the age of sixty-four.

Tokuro Nakamura. He was mobilised in October 1942, at the age of twenty-three, and left for the Philippines in June 1944. There is no record of what became of him.

Hajime Sugiyama. A Japanese field marshal and one of Japan's military leaders for most of the Asia-Pacific War. As army minister in 1937, he was behind the launch of hostilities against China in retaliation for the 'Marco Polo Bridge Incident' and was a major supporter of war against the US. He served as the army's de facto commander-in-chief. Ten days after Japan's surrender, on 2 September 1945, he committed suicide by shooting himself four times in the chest in his office. While he did so, his wife also committed suicide at home.

Ken Yuasa. A surgeon who was drafted into the army and became a member of the infamous Unit 731. Along with at least 1,000 other doctors and nurses, during his service in occupied China, he conducted vivisections on Chinese prisoners and civilians, which produced typhoid and dysentery bacilli for use in biological warfare. After the war, Yuasa was imprisoned, having admitted his guilt to the atrocities. He returned to Japan after his release, in 1956, and toured the nation advocating peace and reconciliation.

8. A 'Truly Grave' Situation

Toshihiro Ōura. A probational officer posted near the Munda Point airfield on the southwest tip of New Georgia. His diary, found on the battlefield, was translated in 1943 by Dye Ogata and Frank Sanwo, Military Intelligence Nisei interpreters. Ōura served with the Japanese Army's 15th Anti-aircraft Field Defence Unit, which was commanded by Colonel Shunichi Shiroto.

Toshiro Kuroki. A first lieutenant who commanded the 3rd Company of the 20th Engineer Regiment attached to the Army's 20th Division, stationed in New Guinea.

Atsushi Tsutsui. Born in August 1918 in Chiba Prefecture. He joined the army in February 1942 and was twenty-five-years old when he was declared missing in action in New Guinea, in February 1944.

9. Burma, A Portent of Things to Come

Tokuhei Miura. Born in 1918 in Ashiya Township, Fukuoka Prefecture, Miura graduated from Iizuka City Vocational School. At his conscription examination in 1938 he was given a B grade and exempted from military service. When, despite his lowly status, his call-up notice eventually came, he closed his accessory shop and joined a cohort that included a dry goods store clerk, a tailor, and a watch salesman. Miura would return from the front as a sergeant.

Renya Mutaguchi. A lieutenant general in the Imperial Japanese Army and commander of its forces during the Battle of Imphal. Historians have variously described him as 'eccentric', 'reckless' and a 'fanatic'. Notoriously, he provided his soldiers with only twenty days of food for the nearly four-month-long Battle of Imphal, which led to a catastrophic death toll before the battle had even begun, losing 55,000 out of his 90,000 men to starvation. In the end only 12,000 of his soldiers returned to Japan, a staggering 87 per cent casualty rate. After the end of the war, he was arrested and extradited to Singapore, where he was convicted of war crimes. He was released from prison in March 1948 and returned to Japan, where died in August 1966.

Kinpei Matsuoka. A sub-lieutenant, born on 10 August 1923 and killed in action outside Moulmein, Burma on 27 May 1945. He was twenty-one years old.

Hideko Nagai. Graduated from the Nursing Training Course at the Wakayama Red Cross Hospital in October 1943. She was just eighteen when drafted as a member of 490th Relief Squad (Nursing Team) with a chief nurse, twenty nurses and a male assistant. After working in Singapore and Thailand, she arrived in Burma in February 1944. After an Allied attack, she and several other nurses were captured by Burmese guerrillas. She then worked with British and Indian nurses, mainly treating Japanese POWs in India, before eventually being repatriated to Japan. Most of her colleagues were not so fortunate and died from disease or being caught in crossfire. Two of them committed suicide by poisoning.

Yasumasa Nishiji. Fought in Hong Kong, Singapore and Java before being deployed to Burma in 1944. He survived the war and committed his memories to a private account of his experiences, many of which were illustrated by simple but poignant drawings.

Takashi Sakimoto. Joined the 13th Telegraph Regiment of the Central China Expeditionary Army in March 1941. In May 1943, he was deployed to Burma. Despite a traumatic retreat, during which most of his colleagues died, he survived the war. In August 1945, he went to work at the Japan Transport Izumi Branch, automatically becoming a union member. In 1954, at the urging of the All-Japan Transport Union, he was elected to the Izumi City (Osaka Prefecture) Parliament.

11. Gyokusai

Yoshitsugu Saitō. A lieutenant general in the Imperial Japanese Army. A native of Miyagi Prefecture, he graduated from the 24th class of the IJA Academy in 1912 and rose steadily through the ranks with various cavalry regiments. He commanded Japanese forces during the Battle of Saipan and committed suicide during the battle.

Aiko Takahashi. Born in Tokyo in 1894. She attended schools in the Tokyo area and graduated from Utsunomiya Girls High School. Her family emigrated to the United States in 1916 or 1917, and she spent her twenties and early thirties there before returning to Japan.

Masatake Okumiya. After his service in the Imperial Japanese Navy, he became a historian. He later joined the Japan Air Defence Force and wrote extensively about Japan's role in the Asia-Pacific War.

Kiyoshi Takeda. A graduate of the Anti-submarine Defence School at Kurihama, he was killed at sea off the island of Saichu (near Korea) in April 1945, at the age of twenty-two.

Naruhiko Higashikuni. A Japanese imperial prince, a career officer in the Imperial Japanese Army, and the 30th prime minister of Japan from 17 August 1945 to 9 October 1945, a period of just fifty-four days.

An uncle-in-law of Hirohito, he was the only member of the imperial family to head a cabinet department and was the last general officer of the Imperial Japanese military to become prime minister. He was the founder of the Chiba Institute of Technology, and lived to the age of 102.

12. Kamikaze

Yasuo Itabashi. Born in Fukushima Prefecture in 1923. An experienced combat pilot, when he discovered that most of his comrades in the 503rd Air Group had been killed, he made clear his wish to fly on a special-attack mission as soon as possible. Instead, he was reassigned to the 601st Air Group, based at Katori Air Base in Ibaraki Prefecture, where he trained navy pilots to fly dive-bombers. On 9 August 1945, Itabashi finally got his wish. At 2:14 p.m. that afternoon he flew from a naval air base on Kyushu as a member of the No.4 Great Shield Special-Attack Squadron and was killed in action in Kingazan Bay off the island of Okinawa. At the time of his death, he was twenty-one years old and a superior flight petty officer. He was also the second of his siblings to die in a special attack; his older brother, Origasa, was killed in an attack on an American carrier in the seas off the Philippines in November 1944.

Daisetsu Suzuki. A Japanese essayist, philosopher, religious scholar, translator and writer, especially of books and essays on Buddhism, Zen and Shinto that were instrumental in spreading interest in both Zen and Shinto to the West. Suzuki was also a prolific translator of Chinese, Korean, Japanese, Vietnamese and Sanskrit literature. Suzuki taught at Western universities and was a professor at Ōtano University. He was nominated for the Nobel Peace Prize in 1963.

13. The Pearl of the Orient

Kaizō Yoshihashi. An army aide-de-camp to the emperor Hirohito from 21 December 1944 to 30 November 1945. His duties were to report on military affairs to the emperor and act as a close attendant.

14. Iwo Jima

Tsunejirō Tamura. Kept a diary from 1910 and chronicled domestic life in Japan from his home in northern Kyoto. He was in his seventies during the war and owned and ran several billiard halls. Billiards in Japan is called 'fourball', an Asian form of carom, played on a pocketless table with two white and two red balls.

Tadamichi Kuribayashi. A general in the Imperial Japanese Army, part-time writer, poet, diplomat, and best known for having been the commander of the Japanese garrison at the Battle of Iwo Jima.

Horie Yoshitake. A field-grade army officer who was a liaison officer on Iwo Jima for the Imperial Japanese Navy. He specialised in logistics.

15. Typhoon of Steel

Mitsuri Yoshido. Born in Tokyo in 1923. In 1943, as an undergraduate student of law at Tokyo Imperial University, he was drafted into the Japanese Navy. He became a radar officer aboard battleship *Yamato* with the rank of ensign, serving on the ship's bridge. His survival of *Yamato*'s final mission made him among the most important primary sources for the demise of the battleship. He completed his wartime memoir in 1946, but the text remained unpublished as he carefully revised the draft over and over again; it was finally published in 1952. In December 1945, he began working for the Bank of Japan and remained there for his entire career, becoming an executive officer in the 1970s. In the 1960s and 1970s, Yoshida published several works on various topics, including several on the Pacific War and the Vietnam War. In most of his writings, he stressed the fact that war was hell, and it was not enough merely to hate war.

Mitsuri Ushijima. Born in 1887 in Kagoshima, where his father had been a samurai in the service of the Satsuma Domain. He graduated from school with honours and decided to follow in his father's footsteps. In 1908, Ushijima graduated from the 20th class of the Imperial Japanese Army Academy with honours, and was noted for his mastery of the *Jigen-ryū* school of Japanese swordsmanship. He was the commanding general of the 32nd Army, which fought in the Battle of Okinawa. At the end of the battle Ushijima committed suicide.

Hiromichi Yahara. The senior staff officer in charge of operations of the 32nd Japanese Army on Okinawa. When his superiors, Lieutenant General Cho and Lieutenant General Mitsuro Ushijima, decided to commit gyokusai in the Mabuni caves, Yahara requested permission to do the same, but Ushijima refused, telling him that he must be a witness to what happened during the battle for Okinawa. Disguising himself as a civilian, Yahara joined a large group of civilians sheltering in a cave. The group was discovered by the Americans, who convinced the group to surrender. Yahara led them out and was thought to be a Japanese teacher of English. Three weeks after his escape, his true identity was discovered; he became a prisoner of war and was interrogated. After the end of the war, Yahara was repatriated to Japan in January 1946 and later wrote his account of the battle, *Decisive Battle for Okinawa*, first published in Japanese in 1973. He died in 1981, at the age of seventy-eight.

16. Armageddon

Haryo Nihei. Lived in Tokyo's downtown Kameido area. She was only eight when Tokyo was firebombed. She fled with her family and watched as many others were burned alive. As the flames swept over her, she was sheltered both by her father, who survived, and by many others who had piled on top of them, all of whom suffocated or burned to death. She and her father stayed with relatives and moved briefly to the countryside before eventually returning to their old neighbourhood. She was silent about her experiences during the firebombing for many decades.

Kazuo Watanabe. A translator and academic who worked at several Japanese universities and specialised in French and English.

Fūtarō Yamada. The pseudonym of Seiya Yamada, a Japanese author. He was born in Yabu Hyogo. In 1947, he wrote a mystery short story *The Incident on Dharma Pass*, and then became a novelist. Many of his works have been adapted for film, TV, manga and anime. He died in 2001.

17. The Radiance of a Thousand Suns

Shigenori Kubota. A senior medical officer attached to the Tokyo defence units during the war.

18. Enduring the Unendurable

Hisako Yoshizawa. Wrote a diary during the war, as a twenty-seven-year-old. She later became a lifestyle writer, and died in 2019 at the age of 101.

Musei Tokugawa. A prominent Japanese actor, raconteur and essayist, on radio and television. He specialised in foreign films. He was also a prolific writer, publishing nearly fifty books in his life.

Hisatsune Sakomizu. A government official and politician before, during and after the Asia-Pacific War. He served as chief secretary to Prime Minister Kantarō Suzuki's cabinet from April to August 1945, when he reported that Japan's resources were rapidly decreasing, and that it would be unable to continue fighting the war for more than a few months. After the war, he became a member of the Diet. He died in 1977.

Yasuo Kuwahara. In cooperation with American author Gordon Allred, Kuwahara's book *Kamikaze* was published in 1957. It has sold over 500,000 copies, and changed foreign attitudes towards kamikaze pilots.

JAPAN'S DISSIDENTS

Despite only modest coverage of their activities, both before and during the Asia-Pacific War, Japan had many people who, from various political perspectives, were opposed to national policies and actions from the late nineteenth century onwards. Sadly, their stories illustrate how the oppression of dissent began early along Japan's journey to modernity, and was usually unbendingly brutal.

Hideki Fukuda. She has been described as the 'Joan of Arc' of the Freedom and People's Rights Movement in Japan in the 1880s. She was also an editor of *Sekai Fujin* (*Women of the World*), a socialist women's paper. In 1885, Fukuda was arrested for her involvement in the 'Osaka Incident', a failed plan intended to overthrow the Meiji government through open revolt in various parts of Japan. Part of the plan also included assisting Korean independence activists in a coup against conservatives in the Korean monarchy. Before the plan was able to be implemented, the police arrested the conspirators and confiscated the weapons before they could leave Japan for Korea.

Shūsui Kōtoku. He was a socialist and anarchist, influenced by Russian anarchist Peter Kropotkin, and a vociferous critic of imperialism. In 1911, twelve people, including Kōtoku, were executed for their involvement in the 'High Treason Incident', a failed plot to assassinate Emperor Meiji. Also executed for involvement was **Suga Kanno**, an anarcho-feminist journalist and former common-law wife of Kōtoku. Kanno was clear about her reasons for participating in the plot.

'Basically, even among anarchists I was among the more radical thinkers. When I was imprisoned in June 1908 in connection with the Red Flag incident I was outraged at the brutal behaviour of the police. I concluded that a peaceful propagation of our principles could not be conducted under

these circumstances. It was necessary to arouse the people's awareness by staging riots or a revolution or by undertaking assassinations [...] I hoped to destroy not only the emperor but other elements too [...] Emperor Mutsuhito [Emperor Meiji], compared with other emperors in history, seems to be popular with the people and is a good individual. Although I feel sorry for him personally, he is, as emperor, the chief person responsible for the exploitation of the people economically. Politically he is at the root of all the crimes being committed, and intellectually he is the fundamental cause of superstitious beliefs. A person in such a position, I concluded, must be killed.'

Heimin Shimbun (*Commoners' Newspaper*). This was a socialist newspaper which served as the leading anti-war vehicle during the Russo-Japanese War. It was a weekly mouthpiece of the socialist **Heimin-sha** ('Society of Commoners'). The chief writers were **Shūsui Kōtoku** and **Toshihiko Sakai**. When the *Heimin* criticised the higher taxes levied to pay for the war, Sakai was sentenced to two months in jail. When the paper published the Communist Manifesto, Kōtoku was given five months in prison, and the paper was closed down. Multiple issues of the newspaper had been banned by the Meiji government because they were deemed politically offensive, and editors were arrested, fined and jailed. The paper ceased publication in 1905. The last issue, published in red, was printed on 18 January 1905.

Fumiko Kaneko. A Japanese anarchist and nihilist who lived in Japanese-occupied Korea. Along with Korean anarchist **Park Yeol**, she was accused of attempting to procure bombs from a Korean independence group in Shanghai, as well as plotting to assassinate members of the Japanese imperial family.

Kaneko and Park were convicted of high treason for attempting to kill the Emperor Taisho. They confessed to the crime and were legally married a few days prior to their sentencing. They were initially given a death sentence, but an imperial pardon commuted the sentence to life imprisonment. Instead of accepting the pardon, Kaneko tore it up and refused to thank the emperor. While Park survived his time in prison and was released years later, Kaneko was reported to have committed suicide in her cell in 1926. However, there were suspicious circumstances around her death.

Gudō Uchiyama was a Sōtō Zen Buddhist priest. Although Japanese Buddhism was generally subservient to the Japanese authoritarian system, there were some rare individuals who resisted. Gudō was an anarcho-socialist who spoke out against Japanese imperialism. He was a supporter of redistributive land reform, encouraged conscripts to desert in their masses, and championed democratic rights for all. He criticised Zen leaders who believed that low social status was justified by 'karma', and spoke out against those who sold abbotships to the highest bidder.

In January 1904, he wrote: *'As a propagator of Buddhism, I teach that "all sentient beings have the 'Buddha Nature'," and that "within the Dharma there is equality, with neither superior nor inferior". Furthermore, I teach that "all sentient beings are my children". Having taken these golden words as the basis of my faith, I discovered that they are in complete agreement with the principles of socialism. It was thus that I became a believer in socialism.'*

After government persecution forced movements opposed to the Russo-Japanese War into hiding, Gudō bought printing equipment to set up a secret press in his temple. He produced popular socialist texts and pamphlets, some of which were his own works. He was executed for his involvement in the attempt to assassinate Emperor Meiji in the 'High Treason Incident'.

Daisuke Nanba. A Japanese student communist who, in 1924, attempted to assassinate the Prince Regent Hirohito. He was horrified by the Kantō Massacre – the mass murder of Koreans and dissidents in the aftermath of the 1923 Great Kantō Earthquake. The victims included his partner, anarchist **Ōsugi Sakai**, feminist **Noe Itō** and Ōsugi's six-year-old nephew. They were beaten, strangled, and their bodies thrown down a well by Masahiko Amakasu, a Kempeitai officer, who would later become a propagandist for Japan's Kwantung Army. Amakasu was tried for the murders but received a very lenient sentence and was released early. Nanba made his assassination attempt, known as the 'Toranomon Incident', on 27 December 1923 at the intersection between the Imperial Akasaka Palace and the Diet of Japan, in Tokyo. Crown Prince and Regent Hirohito was on his way to the opening of the 48th Session of the Imperial Diet when Nanba fired a small pistol at his carriage. The bullet shattered a window of the carriage, injuring a chamberlain, but Hirohito was unharmed.

Although Nanba took responsibility for his actions, he was proclaimed to be insane by the authorities. He was found guilty of high treason in November 1924. When Chief Justice Yokota of the Supreme Court pronounced the death sentence, Nanba yelled back, 'Long live the Communist Party of Japan!' He was executed by hanging two days later at Ichigaya Prison.

Saionji Kinmochi. He was the last of the *genrō* (Japanese elder statesmen who acted as advisers to the emperor), and served three times as prime minister between 1906 and 1912. There were several critics of Japan's growing militarism among more mainstream political circles, such as classical liberals and moderate conservatives. He held progressive views, and was known to be among the aristocrats who supported parliamentary government. He was often at odds with the military throughout his lengthy career, which led him to become an assassination target. His influence on Japanese politics long gone, he died in 1940 at the age of ninety.

Freedom and People's Rights Movement. The American West Coast, which had a large Japanese population, was a haven for Japanese political dissidents in the early twentieth century, especially refugees from this movement. In 1907, an open letter was addressed to 'Mutsuhito, Emperor of Japan from Anarchists-Terrorists' (it was regarded as an insult to address the emperor by his personal name) and posted at the Consulate General of Japan in San Francisco. The letter began with the words, '*We demand the implementation of the principle of assassination.*' The letter also claimed that the emperor was not a god, and ended with the even more provocative words, '*Hey you, miserable Mutsuhito. Bombs are all around you, about to explode. Farewell to you.*' It is not known whether the emperor ever read the letter – but, needless to say, it was not well received in the consulate.

Ikuo Oyama. A member of the left-wing Labour-Farmer Party, which promoted universal suffrage, minimum wages and women's rights. His colleague **Senji Yamamoto** was elected to the House of Representatives in the February 1928 general election, along with fellow party member **Chozaburo Mizutani**. The party was banned less than a month after the election, but both men retained their parliamentary status. During his term Yamamoto criticised the torture and illegal detention of prisoners by the police and unsuccessfully spoke against the death penalty amendment to the Peace Preservation Law of 1925. The amendment was passed by a vote of 249 to 170. On that night, he was killed by a right-wing assassin at an inn in the Kanda district of Tokyo. Oyama fled Japan in 1933 to the United States and got a job at Northwestern University, in its library and political science department. During his exile, he worked closely with the US Government against the Empire of Japan.

Modan gāru ('modern girls'). These were Japanese women who followed Western fashions and lifestyles in the 1920s. They were the equivalent of America's flappers. Although not overtly political, they were young working-class women with access to consumer goods and the money to buy them. They lived in cities, were financially and emotionally independent, chose their own men. However, in the 1930s, extreme Japanese nationalism and the Great Depression brought a return to the nineteenth-century ideal of 'Good Wife, Wise Mother', a concept in which women were taught to fulfil that role for the sake of the nation and the empire.

Salon de thé François. A Western-style café established in Kyoto in 1934 by **Shoichi Tateno**, a supporter of labour movements, and also anti-war movements. The café was a secret source of funds for the then-banned Japanese Communist Party. The anti-fascist newspaper *Doyōbi* (*Saturday*) was produced and distributed from the café. It was distributed twice a month and had a circulation of about 8,000.

In July 1937, a week after the outbreak of the Second Sino-Japanese War, Tateno was arrested because of his anti-war activities. One of the staff members, **Rushiko Sato**, ran the salon. It continued in business even after the outbreak of the Asia-Pacific War in December 1941, although the name was temporarily changed to *Miyako Sabō* ('Kyoto Tea Room') because of the prohibition of the use of enemy languages. The salon remains in business to this day. In 2002, it was certified as a

'Registered Tangible Cultural Property'. Tateno's family now run the café.

Yukitoki Takigawa. A writer and academic at Kyoto Imperial University. In March 1933, the Japanese parliament attempted to control various education groups. The Interior Ministry banned two textbooks on criminal laws written by Takigawa. The following month, **Shigenao Konishi**, president of the university, was asked to dismiss Takigawa but refused. However, following intense pressure from military and nationalist groups, Takigawa was fired from the university. That led to the resignation of all thirty-nine members of the university's law faculty. The Ministry of Education was able to suppress the movement by firing Konishi. In addition to this attempt by the Japanese government to control educational institutions, during the term of the education minister, Ichirō Hatoyama, a number of elementary school teachers were also dismissed for having what were said to be 'dangerous thoughts'.

Wataru Kaji. A working-class writer who lived in Shanghai, China with his wife, **Yuki Ikeda**, who had been tortured in Japan. She fled the country and, to earn a living, worked as a ballroom dancer in Shanghai. They were friends with Chinese left-wing poet and author **Guo Moruo**. Kaji and Yuki were able to escape from Shanghai when the Japanese entered the city. They were both involved in the re-education of captured Japanese soldiers during the war. Kaji later worked with the secret American Office of Strategic Services (OSS) towards the end of the war.

Sanzō Nosaka. A founder of the Japanese Communist Party, he worked with the Chinese Communists during the war. He was in charge of the re-education of captured Japanese troops. Japanese Intelligence was desperate to eliminate him, but always failed in its attempts. His work with the Japanese POWs won him significant praise – and won many new recruits for the Chinese Communists.

Taro Yashima. An artist who joined a group of other progressive artists, sympathetic to the struggles of ordinary workers, and opposed to the rise of militarism in the early 1930s. Following the invasion of

Manchuria, the suppression of domestic dissent became widespread, including the use of arrests and torture by the Tokkō (a high-level branch of the Kempeitai, also called the 'Thought Police'). Yashima was imprisoned without trial, along with his pregnant wife, **Tomoe Sasako**, for protesting against militarism. The prison conditions were grim, and they were beaten. They eventually left for America where Yashima helped the OSS.

Eitaro Ishigaki. A painter who emigrated to America. At the outbreak of war, he painted anti-war and anti-fascist images, many of which became iconic propaganda pieces. With his wife, **Ayako**, he then worked for the United States Office of War Information.

Richard Sorge. Working under the identity of a Japanese correspondent for the German newspaper *Frankfurter Zeitung*, he acted as a Soviet military intelligence officer and conducted surveillance in both Germany and Japan. He arrived in Yokohama in 1933 and recruited two journalists: *Asahi Shimbun* journalist **Hotsumi Ozaki**, who wanted communist revolutions in both China and Japan, and **Yotoku Miyagi**, who translated Japanese newspaper articles and reports into English and created a wide network of informants. In 1941, Sorge passed intelligence to the Soviet Union that Prime Minister Fumimaro Konoe had decided against an immediate attack on the Soviets, choosing instead to keep forces in French Indochina. The information allowed the Soviet Union to move materiel to the western front without fear of Japanese attacks. Later that year, both Sorge and Ozaki were found guilty of treason and were hanged three years later, in 1944. Miyagi had died in prison in 1943, at the age of fifty.

George Ohsawa. A pacifist and the founder of the macrobiotic diet. He was imprisoned for his anti-war activities in January 1945. Pacifism was one of the many ideologies targeted by the Tokkō. Harshly treated while in prison, when he was finally released – one month after the bombing of Hiroshima – he was gaunt, crippled and 80 per cent blind.

Toyohiko Kagawa. A Christian pacifist. He wrote, spoke and worked tirelessly on ways to apply Christian principles to civilised society through cooperatives. His desire to help the poor led him to live among them. He promoted women's suffrage and a peaceful foreign policy. He was arrested in 1940 for apologising to the Republic of China for Japan's occupation of China. When he was released, he went to the United States to try to prevent war. After Japan's surrender, he became an adviser to the transitional government. During his life, Kagawa wrote over 150 books, and was twice nominated for the Nobel Prize in Literature (in 1947 and 1948), and for the Nobel Peace Prize (in 1954 and 1955).

Hiroshi Masaki. A lawyer who produced an independent bulletin called *Chikaki Yori* (*Nearby*). His method to fool the censors was to hide his criticism of the government behind thinly veiled sarcasm which, apparently, worked; he was able to continue publishing attacks on the government until the end of the war. After the war, Masaki became a defence lawyer, successfully fighting police malpractice, which put him in great danger

Toshirō Ubukata. Novelist, humorist and publisher of *Kojin Konjin*, a monthly critique of the army. Although two issues were banned, he used satire without any direct calls to political action, and managed to avoid prosecution until the end of the war. He ceased publication in 1968.

Fumio Kamei. A highly regarded documentary filmmaker who was arrested under the 1925 Peace Preservation Law after releasing two state-funded documentaries that, while claiming to be celebrations of Japan and its army, in fact showed civilian victims of Japanese war crimes and ridiculed the 'sacred war' message and 'beautiful Japan' propaganda. After making a film about the poet Issa Kobayashi, Kamei became the first filmmaker to lose his licence to direct, under the 1939 Film Law. He was released from custody after the war and continued to make anti-establishment films. Under the Allied Occupation, Kamei directed a documentary called *The Japanese Tragedy*. The film, produced from pre-war and wartime newsreels and still photographs, condemned the Japanese empire, which he argued was the result of capitalism. The film also reported on war criminals at Sugamo Prison and said that there were still more criminals at large, including Hirohito himself.

Karl Yoneda. A second-generation Japanese immigrant born in California. In the 1930s, he went to Japan to protest against the Japanese invasion of China. He later joined US military intelligence.

Tsunesaburō Makiguchi. A well-known educator who based his work on the teachings of the thirteenth-century religious revolutionary Nichiren Daishonin and attributed the various troubles Japan was experiencing to the acceptance of Nembutsu Buddhism and other false religious doctrines which slander human life. His religious beliefs compelled him to take a stand against the government, earning him a reputation as a political dissident. His faith in Nichiren Buddhism motivated him towards active engagement to promote social good, even if it led to defiance of state authority. Consequently, Makiguchi soon attracted the attention of the Thought Police. In 1943, Makiguchi was instrumental in persuading his priesthood to refuse a government-sponsored mandate based in the Religious Organisations Law, which had been established in 1939. As the war progressed, the Japanese government ordered that a talisman from the Shinto religion should be placed in every home and temple. Defending the purity of his teachings, Makiguchi refused. During his prison interrogation by the Thought Police, Makiguchi shared that his group had destroyed at least 500 of the talismans, a seditious act in those days.

In 1942, a monthly magazine published by Makiguchi, called *Kachi Sōzō*, was shut down by the militaristic government, after only nine issues. Makiguchi, his disciple **Josei Toda**, and nineteen other leaders of the *Soka Kyoiku Gakkai* ('Value Creating Education Society') were arrested on 6 July 1943, on charges of breaking the Peace Preservation Law. They were charged with denying the emperor's divinity and slandering the Grand Shrine of Ise. During interrogation, Makiguchi insisted that, '*The emperor is an ordinary man [. . .] the emperor makes mistakes like anyone else.*' The treatment in prison was harsh and, on 18 November 1944, Makiguchi died of malnutrition. He was aged seventy-three.

JAPAN'S WAR CRIMES

Much has been written in recent decades about Japan's war crimes. However, it should be noted that thousands of Japanese soldiers and civilians suffered death, injury and humiliation at the hands of the Allies.

Operation August Storm, launched by the Soviet Union's Red Army in 1945 – its Manchurian Campaign – was a brutal end to the war on Mainland Asia. Although the figures are suspect, the Soviets claimed that Japanese suffered 84,000 killed and 594,000 captured. Their own losses were given as 12,103 killed and 24,550 wounded. But the figures exclude Manchurian and Mongolian auxiliaries, as well as thousands of Japanese reservists and civilians killed during the campaign. Of the 2,726,000 Japanese nationals, two-thirds of whom were civilians, captured during the Manchurian Campaign, 254,000 died in Soviet captivity and a further 93,000 were listed as missing. One Japanese estimate indicates that as many as 376,000 died or went missing in the first winter in captivity. Another source states that of 220,000 Japanese civilian settlers, 80,000 died, either having starved to death, committed suicide, or been killed in massacres. Only 140,000 survivors returned to Japan. As happened when the Red Army overran Germany, tens of thousands of Japanese and Chinese women were raped, many repeatedly, as the Soviets completed their conquest of Manchuria.

Today, many in Japan and elsewhere question the morality of the Allied bombing raids on Japan. The mass incendiary attacks on Japan's cities created firestorms, were designed to undermine Japan's willingness to resist, killed hundreds of thousands, and destroyed vast areas. The casualty figures vary but may have been as high as 900,000, including the 300,000 casualties from the atomic bombs dropped on Hiroshima and Nagasaki.

We should also be mindful of the many acts of cruelty and oppression committed by the nations of Europe during the building and rule of their empires, and by the United States in its treatment of its indigenous populations (many of which were committed in modern times).

Nanking Massacre

In 1937, at the beginning of the Sino-Japanese War, the Japanese invaded Nanking, the capital city of Nationalist China. The atrocities began in late 1937 and ended in early 1938. It is estimated that as many as 300,000 Chinese soldiers and civilians were killed, and as many as 80,000 Chinese women were raped, many of whom were then killed.

Comfort Women

Over the course of the Sino-Japanese conflict and the Second World War, the Japanese army forced as many as 200,000 women into prostitution. Called 'comfort women', they worked in brothels for the Japanese military. The brothels operated long hours and the women were rarely granted time off. They endured repeated mistreatment every day for years.

Death on the Railway

During their occupation of Southeast Asian territories, the Japanese decided to build a railroad connecting Thailand and Burma. The railroad would run through incredibly dense jungle and was to be built largely by hand. The Japanese gathered 60,000 POWs and 200,000 enslaved local labourers and forced them to work day and night. Labourers were given nothing but rice to eat, and those who were injured were left to die. Dangers included dengue fever, cholera, tropical ulcers, and an extreme vitamin B deficiency that led to paralysis.

Unit 731

Among several other top-secret groups, Unit 731 was a Japanese military unit responsible for chemical and biological weapons research. The unit tested 'plague bombs' by dropping disease-infected weapons over cities to see whether they would cause infections, which led to many thousands of deaths. At its base in Pingfang, in China, doctors put people in pressure chambers to see how much pressure the human body could withstand before exploding. They also infected civilians with diseases and then dissected them to examine the effects of the disease. Other atrocities included leaving POWs outside to freeze until they died, in order to investigate potential cures for frostbite, and amputating subjects' limbs to learn about blood loss.

Beheading Competition

As part of the horrors of the Nanking Massacre, two Japanese army officers competed to determine who could behead 100 people. The contest was covered by Japanese newspapers. One of the reports read: *'Noda, "Hey, I got 105. What about you?" Mukai, "I got 106!" [. . .] Both men laughed. Because they didn't know who had reached 100 kills first, in the end someone said, "Well then, since it's a drawn game, what if we start again, this time going for 150 kills?"'*

Bataan Death March

The atrocities in Bataan, in the Philippines, began in 1942, when the region was surrendered to Japan. The Japanese, unprepared for the huge number of POWs, ordered all 75,000 of them to march through the jungle, a march that became known as the 'Bataan Death March'.

Japanese soldiers, who believed surrender to be a sign of weakness, beat the captives ceaselessly. Those who fell behind were beheaded or simply left to die. Around 2,500 Filipinos and 500 Americans died on the march, while a further 26,000 succumbed to disease or starvation in the prison camp.

Bangka Island Massacre

As Allied forces deserted Singapore after the Japanese invaded, imperial planes bombed the sea in an effort to sink as many fleeing transport ships as possible. One such ship was filled with sixty-five Australian nurses, fifty-three of whom managed to swim to the small,

Japanese-controlled island of Bangka after their transport sank. The Japanese army rounded up as many people as they could find, including injured servicemen, Allied soldiers and some of the nurses. The Japanese then set up a machine gun on the beach, ordered everyone to walk into the shallows, and mowed them down. Only two survived the incident.

Sandakan Death Marches

Considered the worst wartime atrocity in Australia's history, the incident occurred as the Japanese were retreating from Borneo. They abandoned the Sandakan POW camp in Sabah, forcing the soldiers interned there to march through the jungle with them until they died of starvation or disease. Any soldiers who actually made the entire trek were duly executed. Of the 2,700 internees at the camp, only six survived the march.

Cannibalism

There is substantial evidence, particularly from several eyewitness, that points to Japanese soldiers committing acts of cannibalism on Allied soldiers and captured civilians throughout Southeast Asia. Some accounts suggest the Japanese even executed some Allied soldiers for the sole purpose of harvesting them for food.

One of the most documented examples was the 'Chichijima Incident' which took place in September 1944. Nine American pilots escaped from their planes after being shot down during a bombing attack on Chichijima, a small island among the Ogasawara Islands, 700 miles south of Tokyo. Eight of the airmen were captured and eventually executed. The ninth, a twenty-year-old pilot, and the only one to avoid capture, was future US President George H. W. Bush. After the war, investigations found that the captured airmen had been beaten and tortured before being executed by beheading on the orders of Lt Gen. Yoshio Tachibana. Japanese officers then ate parts of four of the men, especially the liver (because of the traditional belief that a person's resolve came from the liver, and consuming it would grant strength and energy).

Tachibana and eleven others were tried in August 1946. Because international law did not specifically deal with cannibalism, they were tried for murder and the 'prevention of honourable burial'.

This case was investigated again in 1947 in a war crimes trial. Of the thirty Japanese soldiers prosecuted, four officers – including Tachibana, Major Matoba and Captain Yoshii – were found guilty and hanged. All enlisted men plus Probationary Medical Officer Tadashi Teraki were released within eight years. Vice Admiral Kunizo Mori, who commanded Chichijima air base at the time of the incident, was initially sentenced to life imprisonment. However, after his subordinates were convicted of other crimes in the Dutch East Indies, he was sentenced to death and subsequently hanged in a separate trial organised by the Dutch. They were buried in unmarked graves on Guam.

Parit Sulong Massacre

During the Battle of Muar, on 20 January 1942, the last major battle of the Malaya Campaign, Australian and Indian soldiers began a fighting withdrawal from Bukit Bakri, a town halfway between Kuala Lumpur and Singapore. The force withdrew in fifty vehicles carrying wounded men, ammunition and a limited supply of food. Despite repeated attacks, by the morning of 21 January, it had reached the outskirts of the village of Parit Sulong, which was held by Japan's Imperial Guard Division. The Allied force captured the village, but the only route out of the village was over a bridge that was still under Japanese control. Later that day, two ambulances loaded with dying Allied men approached the bridge and requested passage to friendly lines. However, the request was refused. All able-bodied Allied men were then dispersed into the jungle, to attempt to return to Allied lines. At least 150 Australian and Indian soldiers, too seriously injured to move, under the command of Captain Rewi Snelling, were left to surrender. Snelling approached the Japanese and offered his surrender, an offer that was met by beatings and the killing of those unable to move. The remaining soldiers were herded into a nearby building where they were stripped naked, kept in overcrowded rooms, and denied medical attention and water. The Imperial Guard soldiers began beheading the Indian soldiers and shot at others. The remaining soldiers were forced out of their building and were kicked and beaten with rifle butts. Some were tied with wire in the middle of the road and machine-gunned. Petrol was poured over them – some of whom were still alive – and they were set alight. Accounts by local people also reported that Allied prisoners were tied together and forced to stand on the bridge, before a Japanese soldier shot one of them, causing the rest to fall into the Simpang Kiri river and drown.

The Jesselton Revolt

Also known as the 'Jesselton Uprising' or the 'Double Tenth Revolt'/'Incident of 1943', it was led by Albert Kwok. This was a revolt by the Kinabalu Guerrillas, a combined ethnic force of locals around Jesselton, North Borneo, against the Japanese occupation forces. The guerrillas succeeded in killing several dozen Japanese police and soldiers, and temporarily took control of Jesselton and several neighbouring districts. However, with extremely limited arms supplies, the guerrillas were forced to retreat into their jungle base. The Kempeitai then launched vicious attacks against coastal settlements in western North Borneo to find the leaders, with many innocent civilians suffering various atrocities. Kwok finally decided to surrender, following Japanese threats to execute more civilians if the guerrillas did not turn themselves in, and was imprisoned in Batu Tiga. Along with 175 others, many of whom had nothing to do with the uprising, he was executed on 21 January 1944, in Petagas. Kwok, together with four other leaders – Charles Peter, Tsen Tsau Kong, Kong Tze Phui and Li Tet Phui – was beheaded, while others were machine-gunned or bayonetted.

Laha Airfield Massacre

Over the course of two weeks in February 1942, in reprisals for the destruction of a Japanese minesweeper that ran into a Dutch mine, the Japanese occupying force executed 300 Dutch and American POWs in the woods near the Laha Airfield on Ambon Island. Most of the soldiers were either beheaded or killed with a bayonet and were buried in mass graves.

Alexandra Hospital Massacre

In February 1942, the Japanese took Singapore. On the 14th, Japanese soldiers arrived at the British-run Alexandra Hospital, entered the building, and went from room to room indiscriminately beating patients, doctors, nurses, orderlies, and the military personnel who ran the hospital. They then took 100 men from the building, imprisoned them overnight in sweltering sheds behind the hospital, and began executing them the next day.

Palawan Massacre

On 14 December 1944, at the Palawan POW camp in the Philippines, the Japanese forced all 150 Americans in the camp into wooden buildings. They then set the buildings on fire. Between thirty and forty men managed to escape the burning buildings. Some tried to escape by swimming into a nearby bay and were shot, while others tried to hide among the rocks, but most were found and killed. Only eleven Americans survived.

Nauru Island Occupation

The Japanese occupied Nauru, a tiny equatorial island east of Papua New Guinea, from 1942 until the end of the war. During that time, they committed a series of atrocities, including the execution of several Australian officers. At the time, Nauru was home to a leper colony. The Japanese rounded up the lepers, put them on boats, sent them out to sea, and then blew up the boats, killing everyone aboard.

Operation Sook Ching

After seizing control of Singapore in February 1942, the Japanese decided to root out any Chinese in the city who might oppose Japanese rule, including military personnel, leftists, communists, and those with weapons. So began Operation Sook Ching, which is Chinese for 'purge through cleansing'. It resulted in multiple massacres, typically by machine gun, of groups of ethnic Chinese men. The official Japanese number for the operation was 5,000 casualties, although, according to a Japanese reporter in Singapore in 1942, the number was around 50,000.

Rape of Manila

In 1945, as the Japanese faced defeat, military leaders in Tokyo ordered the Japanese army to leave the Philippines, thus surrendering Manila to the Allies. Ignoring the order, the Japanese stationed in the city decided to destroy it, killing as many civilians as possible. As many as 100,000 Filipinos perished.

I-8 Submarine Massacres

The crew of the Japanese submarine *I-8* committed two atrocities during the war. First, they sank a Dutch freighter and took the crew hostage. They beat many of them with bayonets and swords until they died, then they lashed the survivors to the hull of the sub as it dived beneath the sea. Only six people survived. The crew of the *I-8* then sank an American cargo ship, taking more than 100 prisoners, who were then beaten. Only twenty-three Americans survived.

Pig Basket Massacre

When the Allies surrendered East Java to the Japanese in 1942, some soldiers – Dutch, American, British – escaped into the hills and formed resistance groups. The Kempeitai (military police) captured the escapees, forced them into three-foot-long bamboo boxes made for carting pigs, and transported them in exposed trucks to the coast, where they were loaded on to boats. They were then taken out to sea and dumped, still in the pig baskets, into shark-infested waters.

Port Blair Massacres

The Japanese committed several atrocities during their occupation of the Andamans, a pair of tropical islands off the Burmese coast in the Bay of Bengal. Among them were the Port Blair Executions. Japanese soldiers tortured high-ranking Indian officers for being 'in league' with Allied forces. They then buried them up to their chests and proceeded to bayonet, shoot and bludgeon their exposed heads and shoulders until they died.

Kempeitai

Often likened to Nazi Germany's Gestapo, the Kempeitai was the infamous Japanese secret military police (from 1881 to 1945). It was responsible for arresting and executing those who were suspected of being traitors or anti-Japanese. It became notorious for its multiple forms of torture and execution. Its officers were trained within Japan's War Ministry and had their own interrogation manual, which contained several ingenious but horrific forms of torture and execution.

Waterboarding. This involved water being poured over a cloth covering the face and breathing passages of an immobilised captive, causing the prisoner to experience the sensation of drowning. At Woosung prison camp in Shanghai in early 1942, there was a Japanese army interpreter, Isamu Ishihara, who worked for the Kempeitai, nicknamed the 'Beast of the East', and who developed his own version of waterboarding. He would put a ladder on a slope, tie the prisoner to it, feet higher than head, pound something into their nostrils to break the bones so they had to breathe through their mouth, then pour water into their mouth.

Rice torture. During the occupation of Borneo, under the command of Warrant Officer Murakami Seisaku, Kempeitai officers at Sandakan, Sabah would starve their prisoners for several days and then have a large amount of uncooked rice forced down their throats. They would then force a hose into the victim's mouth, so that the water made the rice expand. The pain would be excruciating as the stomach was stretched to its limit and would continue for days while the rice was digested, often resulting in internal and rectal bleeding.

Flogging. The 'Double Tenth Massacre' was so called because it took place on 10 October 1943 in Singapore. After an Allied raid on Singapore Harbour, fifty-seven civilians were arrested and tortured on suspicion of aiding the raid. One of them was the Anglican Bishop of Singapore, Dr Leonard Wilson. He was flogged until unconscious by seven different Kempeitai officers. He survived the flogging and the war, but fifteen other prisoners did not. Flogging was the most commonplace of the Kempeitai cruelties and was routinely carried out at POW camps and on 'hell ships' (prison ships). Floggings would be administered by a wide range of implements: wood, baseball bat, hose, riding crop or bamboo. On Sandakan, beatings were made more painful by the use of wet sand, which would be smeared over the victim's back and pressed into the skin, followed by beating with a wooden sandal.

Electric shock. Electrical cables were attached to nipples and/or genitals to induce pain. Metal chairs, tables and finger rings were connected to the mains. A torture was specifically designed for women, where an electrical prod was inserted into the vagina.

Sharp objects. Pieces of wood or metal were inserted into various parts of the body to produce pain, especially fingernails. Apart from removing the fingernails or toenails of victims using pliers, sometimes sharp objects were inserted beneath the fingernails until the whole nail came away.

Heat. Nail torture was just one of many forms of torture Sybil Kathigasu suffered when she was captured by the Kempeitai. Together with her husband, she was captured for aiding the resistance forces in Malaya. While they ran needles into her fingers through her nails, her hand was held firmly flat on the table, so that heated iron bars could be applied to her legs and back and between her fingers. She passed away in 1948 at the age of forty-eight as a result of a wound to her jaw inflicted by the Kempeitai. It had become infected and led to fatal septicaemia.

Burying. Burial was considered a non-lethal torture by the Kempeitai but served as a warning or was intended to scare the locals. On one occasion, in Kuala Terengganu, a magistrate was wrongfully accused of espionage and tortured to extract a false confession. After spending a night tied to a table leg, the next morning his captors dragged him outside and almost kicked him to death. He was then buried, leaving just his head above ground, and made to close his eyes as a sword was put to his neck for several minutes. He was then dug up and made to sit in the hot sun all day.

Shintarō Uno was assigned to the Kempeitai at an infantry regimental headquarters in China: *'A good clean sword could cause a head to drop with just an easy motion. But even I sometimes botched the job. They were physically weakened by torture. They were semiconscious. Their bodies tended to move. They swayed. Sometimes I'd hit the shoulder. Once a lung popped out, almost like a balloon. I was shocked. All I could do was hit the base of the neck with my full strength. Blood spurted out. Arteries were cut. The man fell immediately. You might ask how it would happen that we'd kill people like this. It was easy. Once, for instance, I got a call from divisional headquarters, "You've made grandiose claims, Uno, but the area you're responsible for isn't secure. How are you going to explain this?" I could only answer that I had no excuse. I then resolved to clean up things. I dispatched our reserve squad, took the village mayor and others captive, and tortured them. They claimed they didn't know anything. I was furious. I'll show them, I thought. I lined them up, nine of them, and cut their heads off. That night I went out drinking at a restaurant.'*

Human Vivisection

In recent times, stories have begun to emerge of Japanese medical experiments which used human vivisection, with and without anaesthesia, to find ways of testing human capacities, and in the training of doctors in battlefield surgical techniques. The victims were either captured military personnel or civilians.

Baltimore Sun writer Thomas Easton penned a shocking article, published on 4 June 1995, based on the admissions of Japanese army doctor Toshio Tono. Easton described what took place in the anatomy department of Kyushu University in May 1945, after nine US airmen were taken prisoner following a bombing raid on Tachiaral Air Base, in southwestern Japan.

'Teddy Ponczka was the first to be handed over to the doctors and their assistants [. . .] A doctor wanted to test surgery's effects on the respiratory system, so one lung was removed. The wound was then stitched closed [. . .] Tono remembers events [. . .] "The first experiment was followed by a second.

Ponczka was given intravenous injections of sea water, to determine if sea water could be used as a substitute for sterile saline solution, used to increase blood volume in the wounded or those in shock." Tono held the bottle of sea water. He says Ponczka bled to death.

'Then it was the turn of the others. The Japanese wanted to learn whether a patient could survive the partial loss of his liver. They wanted to learn if epilepsy could be controlled by removing part of the brain. According to US military records, physicians also operated on the prisoners' stomachs and necks. All the Americans died.'

Rumours of the experiments leaked out, and thirty people were eventually brought to trial by an Allied war crimes tribunal in Yokohama, Japan, on 11 March 1948. The charges included vivisection, wrongful removal of body parts and cannibalism (based on reports that doctors had eaten the livers of the Americans). Of the thirty defendants, twenty-three were found guilty of various charges. Five were sentenced to death, four to life imprisonment, with the other fourteen being handed shorter prison terms.

JAPAN'S WAR CRIMINALS

At the end of the war, using 2,200 tribunals – sitting both inside and outside Japan, in fifty-one locations – the Allied powers indicted twenty-five individuals as Class A war criminals, and 5,700 persons were indicted as Class B or Class C war criminals. Of those, 984 were initially condemned to death (920 were actually executed), 475 received life sentences, 2,944 received prison terms, 1,018 were acquitted, while 279 were not sentenced or not brought to trial. The indicted included 178 ethnic Taiwanese and 148 ethnic Koreans.

Class A criminals were accused of having been involved in the planning, preparation, initiation or waging of the war. They were all tried by the International Military Tribunal for the Far East (IMTFE), also known as the 'Tokyo Trials'. Other courts were held in numerous places across Asia and the Pacific. Below is a list of the most notorious or well-known war criminals.

Kōsō Abe (1892–1947), admiral in the Imperial Japanese Navy. In August 1942, a force of 200 US Marines landed by submarine and raided Makin Island. At the cost of thirty men, the US Marines killed an estimated 160 Japanese on the island, destroyed the radio station, fuel depot, supplies and installations. Nine US Marines were left behind during the raid. They were captured by Japanese forces, and moved to the Kwajalein Atoll, where they were held for about a month. Initially bound for Japan as POWs, they were executed by beheading on 16 October 1946, on the orders of Abe, reportedly overriding the protests of **Captain Yoshio Obara** (a local Japanese commander on Kwajalein) and **Commander Hiusakichi Naiki** (the chief of the Kempeitai on Kwajalein). After the war, Abe was arrested and charged with war crimes. He was extradited to Guam, where he was convicted, of 'violation of the law and custom of war and the moral standards of civilized society' and was executed by hanging in June 1947. Obara was sentenced to ten years in prison, and Naiki to five years, for their roles in the executions.

Kenji Doihara (1883–1948), general. A notorious intelligence officer, he used his military power to become a criminal gangster and to systematically undermine the fabric of Chinese society by using every kind of criminality available, including drug addiction, terrorism, assassinations, blackmail, bribery, opium trafficking and racketeering. After the surrender of Japan, he was arrested and tried as a Class A war criminal. He was found guilty and sentenced to death, while his close colleague, **Naoki Hoshino**, director of the Japanese State Opium Monopoly Bureau in Manchuria, was sentenced to life imprisonment. Doihara was hanged on 23 December 1948, at Sugamo Prison in Tokyo.

Koki Hirota (1878–1948), prime minister from 1936 to 1937. Convicted of crimes against humanity, he was hanged in Tokyo in 1948. The severity of his punishment remains controversial as he was the only civilian so punished. The prosecution case was that, as prime minister, he knew about the atrocities in China, but did nothing to stop them.

Masaharu Honma (1887–1946), general. He was in command during the Bataan Death March, and was convicted of violating the rules of war. He was shot by firing squad (granted a 'soldier's execution') in the Philippines in 1946. However, there remain doubts about his guilt. There is no direct evidence that he was complicit in the mistreatment of POWs – and indeed, he was regarded as a humane man and soldier – but nevertheless, he was found guilty.

Hitoshi Imamura (1886–1968), general. He became the commander of Japan's 16th Army in November 1941, and led it in the invasion of the Dutch East Indies (present-day Indonesia). As his fleet approached Java to take up his command, his transport – the *Shinshu (Ryujo) Maru* – was sunk by torpedoes, probably by friendly fire, and he had to swim to shore. Imamura adopted an unusually lenient policy towards the local population and was often in conflict with the senior staff of the

Southern Army and Imperial Headquarters. However, his policies won much support from the population, particularly in Java, where he was based. In late 1942, he assumed overall command of the New Guinea Campaign and was promoted to general.

The Pig Basket Massacre of 1942 took place under his command. His story is unusual in that not only did he accept responsibility for the actions of his subordinates, but he argued that his punishment was not sufficiently severe. In April 1946, he wrote to the Australian commander at Rabaul, requesting that his trial for war crimes be accelerated in order to speed up the prosecution of war criminals under his command. He was tried by an Australian military court at Rabaul in May 1947, was convicted and sentenced to imprisonment for ten years. Imamura served his imprisonment in Sugamo Prison in Tokyo, until he was released in 1954. He thought that his imprisonment was too lenient, so he had a replica of the prison built in his garden and stayed there until his death in 1968, aged eighty-two.

Shirō Ishii (1892–1959), surgeon general, and a trained microbiologist. He was the director of the infamous Unit 731 and has been called the 'Mengele of the East'. He was the son of Katsuya Ishii, a wealthy landowner and maker of sake. His family held feudal status over the local area. At school, he was a 'teacher's favourite' and was said to have a photographic memory, able to recite complex texts from cover to cover in one reading. Some of his classmates regarded him as rude and arrogant. In 1916, he enrolled at the Faculty of Medicine, at Kyoto Imperial University, from which he graduated in 1920. He married the daughter of Akari Torasaburō, the university's president, in the same year. A brilliant student, in 1921 Ishii was commissioned into the Imperial Japanese Army with the rank of Army Surgeon, First Class (surgeon lieutenant). During his studies, Ishii would often grow bacteria 'pets' in multiple petri dishes. One of his mentors, Professor Ren Kimura, recalled that Ishii had an odd habit of doing his laboratory work in the middle of the night, using laboratory equipment that had been carefully cleaned by his classmates earlier. His classmates would *really be mad when they came in and found the laboratory equipment dirty the next morning*. By 1927, Ishii was campaigning for the creation of a Japanese biological weapons programme, and in 1928 he began a two-year tour of the West, where he did extensive research on the effects of chemical and biological warfare in the Great War. In January 1931, Ishii was promoted to Senior Army Surgeon, Third Class (surgeon major).

According to Ishii's followers, he was extremely loyal to the emperor, a vehement nationalist and had peculiar habits like working late at night in the lab after being out late with friends. He was a heavy-drinking womaniser and embezzler. In 1935, he was promoted to Senior Army Surgeon, Second Class (surgeon lieutenant-colonel) and in August 1936 was given formal oversight of Unit 731 and its research facilities. A former member of Unit 731 wrote that when he first met Ishii in Tokyo, he was surprised at his commander's appearance: '*Ishii was slovenly dressed. His uniform was covered with food stains and ashes from numerous cigarettes. His officer's sword was poorly fastened and dragged on the floor.*' However, in Manchuria in charge of 731, '*he was dressed immaculately. His uniform was spotless, and his sword was tied correctly.*'

As the head of 731, Ishii conducted a variety of experiments, including vivisections, testing biological weapons on Chinese villages, poisoning by toxins and gases, and forcing prison inmates to inflict syphilis on one another. It is also reported that he showed Hideki Tōjō, who later became prime minister, films of the experiments. Tōjō thought them unpleasant, and eventually stopped watching them. By 1939, Ishii had become fully integrated into Japan's military elite.

'*Throughout this time Ishii, the orator, administrator and propagandist, was undoubtedly championing his cause in the upper hierarchies of Japan's military machine. A measure of his ability to hold an audience spellbound is to be found in the report of a lecture he gave in the War Ministry's Grand Conference Hall in 1939. The Military Surgeon Group Magazine recorded that Ishii "packed this vast hall with practically the entire officer staff of the War Ministry and Headquarters Staff for a full two-and-a-half-hour address on the subject of the 'real situation with frontline health and sanitation during the latest Sino-Japanese incident'. His Imperial Highness, Prince Chichibu, broke away from his busy military responsibilities and honoured the meeting with his royal presence and listened most intently to the proceedings."*'

He was promoted several times during the war, until he became Surgeon General (surgeon lieutenant general) in March 1945 and was awarded a special service medal by Hirohito. Towards the end of the war, scheduled for 22 September 1945, Ishii developed a plan to spread plague fleas along the west coast of the United States, known as 'Operation Cherry Blossoms at Night'. The plan involved Japanese seaplanes launched from submarines that would deliver weapons carrying bubonic plague. The operation was abandoned shortly after its planning was finalized in March 1945 because of the strong opposition of General Yoshijirō Umezu, Chief of the Army General Staff. Attempts by Ishii and the Japanese government to cover up their crimes failed, and he was arrested during the occupation of Japan.

In a remarkable example of US political pragmatism and moral deceit, Ishii and his team were given immunity from prosecution for war crimes in exchange for full disclosure of all their experiments and actions. The Soviet Union wanted them to be prosecuted but the US objected after reports by a team of military microbiologists, headed by Lieutenant Colonel Murray Sanders, said that the information was *'absolutely invaluable'* and *'could never have been obtained in the United States because of scruples attached to experiments on humans'* and that *'the information would be obtained fairly cheaply'*. Ishii's immunity deal was concluded in 1948. He was never prosecuted for any war crimes or crimes against humanity, and was hired by the US government to lecture American officers at Fort Detrick (the headquarters of the US Biological Warfare Program) on the uses of bioweapons and the findings of Unit 731. Although disputed by some historians, it is widely reported that Ishii helped the US army with the use of biological warfare weapons during the Korean War, especially in the use of contaminated insects dropped from the air.

After returning to Japan, Ishii opened a clinic, performing examinations and treatments for free. He kept a diary but failed to make any reference to his wartime activities with Unit 731. Ishii died on 9 October 1959, from laryngeal cancer, at the age of sixty-seven. According to his daughter, shortly before his death, Ishii's medical condition worsened: *'One day, he took some sample tissue from himself to the University of Tokyo's Faculty of Medicine and, without saying to whom it belonged, asked one of his former subordinates to examine it. When he was told that the tissue was riddled by cancer, he proudly shouted that he had thought so too. No doctor had dared tell him he was suffering from cancer of the throat. He eventually underwent surgery and lost his voice. He was an earnest student of medicine to his last day, taking notes on his physical condition. Writing the message because he could no longer speak, he told his old professor Ren Kimura who came to visit him "it's all over now".'*

Seishirō Itagaki (1885–1948), war minister from 1938 to 1939. After the war, Itagaki was taken into custody and charged with war crimes specifically in connection with the Japanese seizure of Manchuria, his escalation of the war against the Allies during his term as war minister, and for allowing inhumane treatment of prisoners of war during his term as commander of Japanese forces in Southeast Asia. He was found guilty, condemned to death and hanged on 23 December 1948, at Sugamo Prison in Tokyo.

Heitarō Kimura (1888–1948), a career soldier. He was involved in strategic planning for the war in China and the 1941 onslaught on the Western Allies. In late 1944, Kimura was assigned to the field as commander-in-chief in Burma. It was something of a poisoned chalice, as Japanese forces were under severe pressure and the Allies had total control of the skies. Unable to defend all of Burma, Kimura fell back, and was only able to use delaying tactics. Mercifully, he decided to spare his men rather than defend the capital, Rangoon, to the last man. After the war, Kimura was arrested and tried for war crimes and paid the price for being part of Japan's policy of overt aggression towards what it perceived were its enemies. His role in planning the strategy for the war in China and Southeast Asia was the central charge, and he was condemned for not preventing atrocities against POWs in Burma. Although the Death Railway was built from 1942 to 1943, and Kimura did not arrive in Burma until late 1944, he was also charged with the abuse and deaths of POWs and civilian labourers used to construct the railroad. He was condemned as a war criminal and hanged in 1948.

Kuniaki Koiso (1880–1950), politician and military leader. He was Prime Minister of Japan from 1944 to 1945 and Governor General of

Korea from 1942 to 1944. He was arrested and tried for war crimes, convicted and given life imprisonment for his role in starting the wars against China and the Allies. Although he was not directly responsible for the war crimes committed by the Japanese Army, he was found guilty of failing to prevent them – or to punish the perpetrators – when, as prime minister, it was within his power to have done so. Koiso died of cancer in Sugamo Prison in 1950.

Iwane Matsui (1878–1948), general. He was the commander of the expeditionary force sent to China in 1937. He was tried, sentenced to death and hanged for his involvement in the Nanking Massacre. It is not clear to what extent Matsui was aware of the atrocities perpetrated in the city. His former chief of staff later testified that Matsui had been informed that there had been a few cases of plunder and outrage. Matsui's field diary also mentioned rape and looting, which he suggested were unavoidable. When a representative from Japan's foreign ministry came to investigate, Matsui admitted that some crimes had occurred, and he blamed his subordinate commanders for allowing too many soldiers into the city, in violation of his orders.

Toshiaki Mukai (1912–1948), junior officer. He was sentenced to death for participating in the 'hundred man killing contest', part of the Nanking Massacre. He and his fellow defendant, **Tsuyoshi Noda**, were found guilty of war crimes and executed by firing squad in Yuhuatai Execution Ground in Nanking, China, in January 1948.

Akira Mutō (1883–1948), army commander and member of the General High Staff. He was chief of military intelligence in the Kwantung Army at the time of the 'Marco Polo Bridge Incident' – which began the war in China – and is thought to have been one of the planners behind it. He was accused of having conducted a campaign of slaughter, torture and other atrocities against the Filipino civilian population, prisoners of war and civilian internees, and was arrested and charged with war crimes. He was convicted for atrocities against civilians and POWS in both China and the Philippines and was hanged on 23 December 1948.

Hiromi Nakayama (died 1946), junior officer. Led by Lieutenant Nakayama, the Japanese Army launched Operation RY on 26 August

1942, with a company (100 men) of the 43rd Guard Force (Palau). They captured Nauru Island and, in March 1943, Nakayama proceeded to execute Colonel F. R. Chalmers and four other prisoners of war. He was tried, found guilty and hanged in Rabaul, Papua New Guinea, in August 1946.

Takuma Nishimura (1889–1951), general. He was commander of the 9th Infantry Regiment from 1936 to 1938. He then commanded the 1st Heavy Field Artillery Brigade from 1938 to 1939. He became Chief of Staff of the Eastern Defence Army from 1939 to 1940 and was promoted to the rank of major general in 1940. Nishimura was commander of the invasion of French Indochina in 1940 and was promoted to lieutenant general in 1941. He then commanded the Imperial Guard Division during the conquest of Malaya, during which 155 Australian and Indian POWs were killed in the Parit Sulong Massacre. Nishimura then commanded the eastern half of Singapore Island when the Sook Ching Massacre took place. However, he was accused of insubordination by his commander, General Tomoyuki Yamashita, and he was recalled to Japan and forced to retire in April 1942.

He was recalled to the army in June 1943 and became military governor of Sumatra in February 1944 until the end of the war. Nishimura was tried by a British military tribunal in Singapore for the Sook Ching Massacre, found guilty of war crimes, sentenced to imprisonment for life, served four years in Singapore, and was then sent to Tokyo to complete his sentence. On his way to Japan, Nishimura was arrested in Hong Kong harbour by Australian military police, brought before a military tribunal on Manus Island, in Papua New Guinea, and investigated for his role in the Parit Sulong Massacre. Despite much confusion about survivors of the massacre identifying the perpetrators, Nishimura was found guilty and hanged in June 1951. Controversy continues to this day, especially over a statement from **Lieutenant Fujita Seizaburo**, who confessed that he was directly responsible for the Parit Sulong Massacre. He later fled and was not charged, leaving his fate unknown.

Tasuku Okada (1890–1949), general. Okada was put on trial during the Yokohama War Crimes Trials for ordering the executions of thirty-eight captured American aircrew in 1945. He considered them to be war criminals because of the firebombings of Tokyo. He was found guilty, sentenced to death, and hanged in 1949 in Tokyo.

Hiroshi Ōshima (1886–1975), general and Japanese ambassador to Germany. After the war, he was convicted of war crimes and sentenced to life imprisonment but was paroled in 1955 and granted clemency three years later. He died in 1975, at the age of eighty-nine. Virtually all of Ōshima's dispatches as ambassador were intercepted: approximately seventy-five during the last eleven months of 1941, some 100 in 1942, 400 in 1943, 600 in 1944, and about 300 during the just over four months of 1945. He went to his grave not knowing that he had been a major source of intelligence for the Allies. The interceptions revealed many occasions when Ōshima was complicit in Germany's and Japan's aggressive intentions.

For example, following the Nazi invasion of the Soviet Union on 22 June 1941, pressure was put on the Japanese government to join the invasion. On 9 July 1942, Joachim von Ribbentrop, German foreign minister, tried to convince Ōshima to urge his government to join the invasion from the east: '*Never again would Japan have such an opportunity as existed at present to eliminate once and for all the Russian colossus in eastern Asia.*'

On 6 March 1943, Ōshima delivered to Ribbentrop the official statement from the Japanese government: '*The Japanese Government absolutely recognise the danger which threatens from Russia and completely understand the desire of their German ally that Japan on her part will also enter the war against Russia. However, it is not possible for the Japanese Government, considering the present war situation, to enter into the war. They are rather of the conviction that it would be in the common interest not to start the war against Russia now. On the other hand, the Japanese Government would never disregard the Russian question.*'

Shigematsu Sakaibara (1898–1947), admiral in the Imperial Japanese Navy. After the Battle of Wake Island, on 23 December 1941, Sakaibara was appointed the garrison commander of the Japanese occupation force. Fearing an imminent attempt by American forces to retake the island, Sakaibara put ninety-eight American civilians he had captured to work building a series of bunkers and fortifications in preparation for a suspected invasion.

On 5 October 1943, aircraft from USS *Yorktown* bombed Wake Island. Two days later, Sakaibara ordered the beheading of an American civilian worker who was caught stealing. Sakaibara then ordered the rest of them to be killed. They were taken to the northern end of the island, blindfolded and machine-gunned. One prisoner, whose name has never been discovered, escaped, carved a message into a rock about the incident, but was then recaptured and personally beheaded by Sakaibara.

After the war, Sakaibara, his subordinates **Lieutenant Commander Shoichi Tachibana** and **Toraji Ito**, were arrested. Initially, they claimed that the victims were killed in a US bombing raid, but later confessed to the massacre. Sakaibara, Tachibana and Ito were extradited to Kwajalein Island, where they were tried for war crimes. Ito killed himself in custody. Sakaibara and Tachibana were both found guilty and sentenced to death in December 1945. Tachibana's sentence was commuted to life in prison, and he was sent to Tokyo's Sugamo Prison to serve out his sentence. Sakaibara was extradited to Guam for execution. Just before he was sentenced, Sakaibara read out a final statement to the commission. He admitted that what he had done was wrong, and said he wished that he had never heard of Wake Island. However, Sakaibara also claimed that, after using nuclear weapons on Japan, the United States had no moral authority to try him or others. Sakaibara was hanged in Guam on 19 June 1947. Until the end, he maintained that his trial had been unfair and his sentence too harsh.

Mamoru Shigemitsu (1887–1957), general and foreign minister. Shigemitsu co-signed the Japanese surrender on board the battleship USS *Missouri* on 2 September 1945. Despite his well-known opposition to the war, the Soviet Union insisted that he be charged as a war criminal. However, the tribunal was lenient on the grounds that Shigemitsu had regularly opposed Japanese militarism and protested at the inhumane treatment of POWs. He was sentenced to seven years in prison, the lightest punishment that was handed down to anyone convicted at the war crimes trials. He was paroled in 1950 and died in 1957, at the age of sixty-nine.

Toshio Shiratori (1887–1949), Japanese ambassador to Italy. He was found guilty of 'crimes against peace' and sentenced to life imprisonment. He died of laryngeal cancer in Sugamo Prison, Tokyo in 1949, at the age of sixty-one. Shiratori was appointed ambassador to Italy and served from 1938 to 1940, when he became adviser to foreign minister Yōsuke Matsuoka in 1940. He was an advocate of military expansionism and promoted an alliance between Germany, Italy and Japan. He was a fervent believer in the emperor's divinity and Japan's path to world domination.

Teiichi Suzuki (1888–1989), a lieutenant general and politician who planned Japan's economy. After the surrender of Japan, Suzuki was arrested and charged with Class A war crimes in December 1945 for having advocated war at the October 1941 *Gozen Kaigi* ('Imperial Conference'). He was found guilty and sentenced to life imprisonment in 1948 but released in September 1955 and pardoned by the Japanese government in 1958. He was requested to serve as an adviser by several industrialists and asked to run for the post-war Diet (parliament) of Japan but refused all offers to return to public life. Suzuki died at home of heart failure on 15 July 1989, at 100 years of age. He was the last surviving defendant of the main Tokyo/Nuremberg trials, outliving Rudolf Hess, who had committed suicide two years earlier.

Yoshio Tachibana (1890–1947), general. He was commander of the Japanese garrison on Chichijima, part of the Ogasawara (Bonin) Islands, to the south of Tokyo. He was later tried and executed for war crimes involving torture, extra-judicial execution, and cannibalism of prisoners of war. In May 1944, Tachibana was tasked with the defence of the Ogasawara Islands against invasion by American forces during the preparations for Operation Downfall (the invasion of mainland Japan).

By mid-1945, because of the Allied naval blockade, the 25,000 Japanese troops on Chichijima were struggling with few supplies. In what later came to be called the 'Chichijima Incident', in February/

March 1945, Tachibana's senior staff turned to cannibalism. Nine American airmen escaped from their planes after being shot down during bombing raids on Chichijima, eight of whom were captured. Over a period of several months, the prisoners were executed, their bodies were butchered by the division's medical orderlies, and their livers and other organs were consumed by the senior staff, including Tachibana. At the end of the war, Tachibana and his staff were arrested and deported to Guam, where they stood trial for war crimes. Tachibana was sentenced to death by hanging, along with four other defendants.

Hideki Tōjō (1884–1948), general and prime minister. Tōjō was born to a relatively low-ranking former samurai family in Tokyo. He began his career in the army in 1902 and rose through the ranks to become a general by 1934. In March 1937, he was promoted to chief of staff of the Kwantung Army and led military operations against the Chinese in Inner Mongolia. By July 1940, he was appointed minister of the army in the Japanese government led by Prime Minister Fumimaro Konoe.

Tōjō was an ardent supporter of a pre-emptive attack on the United States and its European allies, and after being appointed prime minister on 17 October 1941, he oversaw the launch of Japan's Holy War and its subsequent conquests. During the course of the war, Tōjō's leadership was responsible for numerous war crimes. These included the widespread massacre and starvation of civilians and prisoners of war, in what has been called the 'Asian Holocaust' – a term much criticised in Japan. Nevertheless, it is estimated that between 10 and 30 million people died.

After the war turned against Japan, Tōjō resigned as prime minister on 18 July 1944. When Japan surrendered in 1945, he was arrested and accused of war crimes. As American soldiers surrounded his house, Tōjō shot himself in the chest with a pistol but missed his heart. As he bled, Tōjō began to talk. Two Japanese reporters recorded his words: *'I am very sorry it is taking me so long to die. The Greater East Asia War was justified and righteous. I am very sorry for the nation and all the races of the Greater Asiatic powers. I wait for the righteous judgment of history. I wished to commit suicide but sometimes that fails.'*

Tōjō was tried and found guilty of waging wars of aggression, in violation of international law, against various nations, and ordering, authorising and permitting inhumane treatment of prisoners of war. Tōjō accepted full responsibility for his actions during the war: '*It is natural that I should bear entire responsibility for the war in general, and, needless to say, I am prepared to do so. Consequently, now that the war has been lost, it is presumably necessary that I be judged so that the circumstances of the time can be clarified and the future peace of the world be assured. Therefore, with respect to my trial, it is my intention to speak frankly, according to my recollection, even though when the vanquished stands before the victor, who has over him the power of life and death, he may be apt to toady and flatter. I mean to pay considerable attention to this in my actions and say to the end that what is true is true and what is false is false. To shade one's words in flattery to the point of untruthfulness would falsify the trial and do incalculable harm to the nation, and great care must be taken to avoid this.*'

Tōjō was sentenced to death and hanged on 23 December 1948, a week before his sixty-fourth birthday. Before his execution, he gave his military ribbons to one of his guards; they are now on display at the National Naval Aviation Museum in Florida. In his final statement, he apologised for the atrocities committed by the Japanese military and urged the American military to show compassion towards the Japanese people, who had suffered devastating aerial attacks and the dropping of two atomic bombs. After his execution, Tōjō was cremated and his ashes scattered over the Pacific Ocean, thirty miles east of Yokohama, along with the ashes of six other Class A war criminals.

Yoshijirō Umezu (1882–1949), general. A career soldier, in May 1938 Umezu became commander-in-chief of Japan's 1st Army. From September 1939 he was commander-in-chief of the Kwantung Army. In July 1944, Umezu was appointed as the final Chief of the Imperial Japanese Army General Staff. Following the resignation of Hideki Tōjō, he became a member of the Supreme War Council. Umezu opposed the surrender in August 1945, believing that the military should fight on to inflict heavy losses in an invasion, allowing Japan to negotiate for peace under favourable terms. He was aware of the planned coup by junior officers opposed to the surrender, but did nothing to either aid or hinder it. He was personally ordered by Hirohito to sign the instrument of surrender on the USS *Missouri*, officially ending the war. He was then arrested and tried as a war criminal. He was found guilty of waging a war of aggression, and was sentenced to life imprisonment in 1948.

Umezu died from rectal cancer in 1949. He converted to Catholicism the day before his death and the last rites were performed at his bedside by a Catholic priest. Although Umezu had followed the country's Shinto religion, his family favoured Catholicism and his daughter became a Catholic nun.

Tomoyuki Yamashita (1885–1946), general. Yamashita led Japanese forces during the Malaya Campaign. His victory in just seventy days earned him the nickname the 'Tiger of Malaya'. Later in the war, he was appointed to defend the Philippines from the advancing Allies and despite dwindling supplies, he was able to hold on to part of Luzon until after the formal Surrender of Japan in August 1945. Under Yamashita's command, between 350,000 and 450,000 were killed, and he was in command during Sook Ching, the Rape of Manila and other atrocities.

Yamashita's culpability for war crimes remains a matter of controversy. Many have argued that his guilt derives from the fact that he failed to prevent them. On the other hand, other historians maintain that, according to post-war testimony, the order to execute 50,000 Chinese came from senior officers within Yamashita's staff. After the war, Yamashita apologised to the few survivors of the 650 bayoneted or shot at the Alexandra Hospital Massacre, and it is alleged that some soldiers caught looting in the aftermath of the slaughter were executed. Historian Akashi Yoji claims that this would have been in line with Yamashita's personality and beliefs. According to him, the first orders given by Yamashita to the soldiers were '*no looting; no rape; no arson*', with the warning that any soldier committing such acts would be severely punished and his superior held accountable.

Nevertheless, Yamashita's warnings to his troops were generally not heeded, and wanton acts of violence were reported. Akashi argues that the main issue was that, despite being an excellent tactician and leader, Yamashita's personal ideals constantly placed him at odds with the General Staff and War Ministry. His humane treatment of prisoners of war as well as British leaders was something the other officers had difficulty coming to terms with. Despite the blame for the Sook Ching Massacre being placed at Yamashita's door, it is now argued that he had no direct part in it, and his subordinates were the ones behind the incident.

After the war, regardless of the controversy, Yamashita was tried for war crimes. The court eventually found Yamashita guilty, and he was executed in February 1946. For his part, Yamashita denied he had any knowledge of the crimes committed by his men and claimed that he would have harshly punished them if he had known. Further, he argued that with an army as large as his, there was no way for him to control all the actions undertaken by all his subordinates.

'My command was as big as MacArthur's. How could I tell if some of my soldiers misbehaved themselves? It was impossible for any man in my position to control every action of his subordinate commanders, let alone the deeds of individual soldiers. The charges are completely new to me. If they had happened, and I had known about them, I would have punished the wrongdoers severely. But in war someone has to lose. What I am really being charged with is losing the war. It could have happened to General MacArthur, you know.'

Following the Supreme Court decision, an appeal for clemency was made to US President Harry S. Truman, who declined to intervene and, in due course, General MacArthur confirmed the sentence of the commission. On 23 February 1946, Yamashita was hanged at Los Banos Prison Camp, thirty miles south of Manila. After climbing the thirteen steps leading to the gallows, he was asked if he had a final statement. His reply was:

'As I said in the Manila Supreme Court that I have done with my all capacity, so I don't ashamed [sic] in front of the gods for what I have done when I have died. But if you say to me "you do not have any ability to command the Japanese Army" I should say nothing for it, because it is my own nature. Now, our war criminal trial going under your kindness and right. I know that all your American and American military affairs always

have tolerant and rightful judgment. When I have been investigated in Manila court I have had a good treatment, kindful [sic] attitude from your good-natured officers who protected me all the time. I never forget for what they have done for me even if I had died. I don't blame my executioner. I'll pray the gods bless them. Please send my thankful word to Col. Clarke and Lt. Col. Feldhaus, Lt. Col. Hendrix, Maj. Guy, Capt. Sandburg, Capt. Reel, at Manila court, and Col. Arnard. I thank you.'

Yamashita was hanged and he was buried first at the Japanese cemetery near the Los Baños Prison Camp, then his remains were moved to the Tama Cemetery, Fuchū, Tokyo. The ruling against Yamashita – holding the commander responsible for subordinates' war crimes where the commander did not attempt to discover and stop them from occurring – came to be known as the 'Yamashita Standard'.

Yasukuni Shrine

A place of great controversy, the Yasukuni Shrine is a Shinto shrine located in Chiyoda, Tokyo. It was founded by Emperor Meiji in June 1869 and commemorates those who died fighting for Japan. The shrine lists the name, origin, birthdate and place of death of 2,466,532 people. Among those are 1,066 convicted war criminals, including the names of some of the Class A criminals indicted at the Tokyo Trials. This is how they are listed:

Hideki Tōjō
Kenji Doihara
Iwane Matsui
Heitarō Kimura
Seishiro Itagaki
Akira Muto
Yosuke Matsuoka
Osami Nagano
Toshio Shiratori
Kichiro Hiranuma
Kuniaki Koiso
Shigenori Tōjō
Yoshijirō Umezu

CHRONOLOGY

1941

December	7	(December 8 in Japan) Japanese forces attack the Malay Peninsula and Pearl Harbor. They also attack the Philippines, Wake Island, Guam, Malaya, Thailand, Shanghai and Midway, and Japanese diplomatic staff in America submit ultimatum to American Secretary of State, commencing the Pacific War.
	8	US and Britain declare war on Japan. Japanese land near Singapore and enter Thailand.
	9	China declares war on Japan.
	11	Japanese invade Burma.
	15	First Japanese merchant ship sunk by a US submarine.
	16	Japanese invade British Borneo.
	18	Japanese invade Hong Kong.
	22	Japanese invade Luzon in the Philippines.
	23	US troops begin a withdrawal from Manila to Bataan; Japanese take Wake Island.
	25	British surrender at Hong Kong.
	27	Japanese bomb Manila.

1942

January	2	Manila and US naval base at Cavite captured by the Japanese.
	7	Japanese attack Bataan in the Philippines.

	11	Japanese invade Dutch East Indies and Dutch Borneo.
	16	Japanese begin an advance into Burma.
	18	German-Japanese-Italian military agreement signed in Berlin.
	19	Japanese take North Borneo.
	23	Japanese take Rabaul on New Britain in the Solomon Islands and also invade Bougainville, the largest island.
	30/31	The British withdraw into Singapore. The siege of Singapore then begins.
February	1	First US aircraft carrier offensive of the war as *Yorktown* and *Enterprise* conduct air raids on Japanese bases in the Gilbert and Marshall Islands.
	2	Japanese invade Java in the Dutch East Indies.
	8/9	Japanese invade Singapore.
	14	Japanese invade Sumatra in the Dutch East Indies.
	15	British surrender at Singapore.
	19	Largest Japanese air raid since Pearl Harbor occurs against Darwin, Australia; Japanese invade Bali.
	22	President Franklin D. Roosevelt orders American troops out of the Philippines.
	23	First Japanese attack on the US mainland as a submarine shells an oil refinery near Santa Barbara, California.
	24	USS *Enterprise* attacks Japanese on Wake Island.
	26	First US carrier, USS *Langley*, is sunk by Japanese bombers.
	27	Japanese naval victory in the Battle of the Java Sea as the largest US warship in the Far East, USS *Houston*, is sunk.
March	7	British evacuate Rangoon in Burma; Japanese invade Salamaua and Lae on New Guinea.
	8	The Dutch on Java surrender to the Japanese.

	23	Japanese invade the Andaman Islands in the Bay of Bengal.
April	3	Japanese attack US and Filipino troops at Bataan.
	6	First US troops arrive in Australia.
	9	US forces on Bataan surrender unconditionally to the Japanese.
	18	Surprise US 'Doolittle' B-25 air raid from USS *Hornet* against Tokyo boosts Allied morale.
	29	Japanese take central Burma.
May	1	Japanese occupy Mandalay in Burma.
	3	Japanese take Tulagi in the Solomon Islands.
	5	Japanese prepare to invade Midway and the Aleutian Islands.
	6	Unconditional surrender of all US and Filipino forces in the Philippines.
	7–8	Japan suffers its first defeat of the war during the Battle of the Coral Sea off New Guinea.
	20	Japanese complete the capture of Burma and reach India.
June	4–5	A turning point in the war occurs with a decisive victory for the US against Japan in the Battle of Midway.
	7	Japanese invade the Aleutian Islands.
	9	Japanese postpone further plans to take Midway.
	21	Japanese land troops near Gona on New Guinea.
August	7	The first US amphibious landing of the Pacific War occurs as US Marines invade Tulagi and Guadalcanal in the Solomon Islands.
	8	US Marines take the unfinished airfield on Guadalcanal and name it Henderson Field.
	8/9	A major US naval defeat off Savo Island, north of Guadalcanal, as eight Japanese warships wage a night attack.

September	12–14	Battle of Bloody Ridge on Guadalcanal.
	15	A Japanese submarine torpedo attack near the Solomon Islands.
	27	British offensive in Burma.
October	11/12	US cruisers and destroyers defeat a Japanese task force in the Battle of Cape Esperance off Guadalcanal.
	26	Battle of Santa Cruz off Guadalcanal between US and Japanese warships results in the loss of the Carrier *Hornet*.
November	14/15	US and Japanese warships clash again off Guadalcanal resulting in the sinking of the US cruiser *Juneau*.
	23/24	Japanese air raid on Darwin, Australia.
December	20–24	Japanese air raids on Calcutta, India.
	31	Emperor Hirohito gives permission to his troops to withdraw from Guadalcanal after five months of bloody fighting against US forces.

1943

January	2	Allies take Buna in New Guinea.
	22	Allies defeat Japanese at Sanananda on New Guinea.
February	1	Japanese begin evacuation of Guadalcanal.
	9	Japanese resistance on Guadalcanal ends.
March	2–4	US victory over Japan in the Battle of Bismarck Sea.
May	10	US troops invade Attu in the Aleutian Islands.
	31	The US completes the capture of Attu.
June	1	US begins submarine warfare against Japanese shipping.

	21	Allies advance to New Georgia, Solomon Islands.
July	8	B-24 Liberators flying from Midway bomb Japanese on Wake Island.
August	6/7	Battle of Vella Gulf in the Solomon Islands.
	25	Allies complete the occupation of New Georgia.
September	4	Allies recapture Lae-Salamaua, New Guinea.
October	26	Emperor Hirohito states his country's situation is now 'truly grave'.
November	1	US Marines invade Bougainville in the Solomon Islands.
	20	US troops invade Makin and Tarawa in the Gilbert Islands.
	23	Japan ends resistance on Makin and Tarawa.
December	26	Full Allied assault on New Britain at Cape Gloucester.

1944

January	9	British and Indian troops recapture Maungdaw in Burma.
	31	US troops invade Kwajalein in the Marshall Islands.
March	15	Japanese begin offensive towards Imphal and Kohima.
April	17	Japanese begin their last offensive in China, attacking US air bases in eastern China.
June	5	The first mission by B-29 Superfortress bombers occurs as 77 planes bomb Japanese railway facilities at Bangkok, Thailand.
	15	US Marines invade Saipan in the Mariana Islands.
	19	The 'Marianas Turkey Shoot' occurs as US carrier-

		based fighters shoot down 220 Japanese planes, while only 20 American planes are lost.
July	8	Japanese withdraw from Imphal.
	19	US Marines invade Guam in the Marianas.
	24	US Marines invade Tinian.
August	3	US and Chinese troops take Myitkyina after a two-month siege.
	8	American troops complete the capture of the Mariana Islands.
October	11	US air raids against Okinawa.
	18	Fourteen B-29s based on the Marianas attack the Japanese base at Truk.
	20	US Sixth Army invades Leyte in the Philippines.
	23–26	Battle of Leyte Gulf results in a decisive US naval victory.
November	11	Iwo Jima bombarded by the US Navy.
	24	Twenty-four B-29s bomb the Nakajima aircraft factory near Tokyo.
December	15	US troops invade Mindoro in the Philippines.

1945

January	4	British occupy Akyab in Burma.
	9	US Sixth Army invades Lingayen Gulf on Luzon in the Philippines.
	11	Air raid against Japanese bases in Indochina by US carrier-based planes.
February	3	US Sixth Army attacks Japanese in Manila.
	16	US troops recapture Bataan in the Philippines.
	19	US Marines invade Iwo Jima.
March	2	US airborne troops recapture Corregidor in the Philippines.

         3   US and Filipino troops take Manila.

  9/10   Fifteen square miles of Tokyo erupts in flames after it is firebombed by 279 B-29s.

    10   US Eighth Army invades Zamboanga Peninsula on Mindanao in the Philippines.

    20   British troops liberate Mandalay, Burma.

April   **1**   The final amphibious landing of the war occurs as the US Tenth Army invades Okinawa.

    7   B-29s fly their first fighter-escorted mission against Japan with P-51 Mustangs based on Iwo Jima, and US carrier-based fighters sink the super battleship Yamato and several escort vessels which planned to attack US forces on Okinawa.

    12   President Roosevelt dies, succeeded by Harry S. Truman.

May   **8**   VE-Day in Europe.

    20   Japan begins its withdrawal from China.

    25   US Joint Chiefs of Staff approve Operation Olympic, the invasion of Japan, scheduled for November 1.

June   **9**   Japanese Premier Suzuki announces Japan will fight to the very end rather than accept unconditional surrender.

    18   Japanese resistance ends on Mindanao in the Philippines.

    22   Japanese resistance ends on Okinawa as the US completes its capture.

July   **5**   The liberation of the Philippines is declared.

    10   1,000 bomber raids against Japan begin.

    14   The first US naval bombardment of Japanese home islands.

    16   An atomic bomb is successfully tested in the US.

    26   The components of the atomic bomb 'Little Boy'

		are unloaded on the Tinian Island in the South Pacific.
August	6	The first atomic bomb is dropped on Hiroshima from a B-29.
	8	The USSR declares war on Japan, then invades Manchuria.
	9	The second atomic bomb is dropped on Nagasaki from a B-29. Emperor Hirohito and Japanese Prime Minister Suzuki then decide to seek an immediate peace with the Allies.
	14	The Japanese accept unconditional surrender.
	29	US troops land near Tokyo to begin the occupation of Japan.
September	2	Japan ends its occupation of the Aleutian Islands. The formal Japanese surrender ceremony on the USS *Missouri* in Tokyo Bay. President Truman declares VJ-Day.

ENDNOTES

For all sources, full citation appears in the first instance, with a recognisable shortened form thereafter.

Epigraphs

page

vii **Japan will rise and fight** – W. G. Beasley, *Japanese Imperialism 1894–1945* (Oxford: The Clarendon Press, 1991), p. 28.

vii **For twenty-six centuries** – Hiroko Nakamoto, *My Japan 1930–1951* (Scranton, PA: University of Scranton Press, 2000), p. 52.

Preface: The 'Enigma' that is Japan

page

xxi **'One nation, one civilisation, one language'** – quoted in the *Japan Times*, October 2005, from a speech given at a ceremony at the new Kyushu National Museum in Dazaifu, Fukuoka Prefecture.

xxiii **When a serious observer** – Ruth Benedict, *The Chrysanthemum and the Sword* (Rutland, VT and Tokyo: Charles Tuttle and Company, 1954), p. 1.

xxiv **Did the idea ever occur to you . . . You seem to us** – Yoshisaburō Okakura, *The Life and Thought of Japan* (London: J. M. Dent & Sons, 1913), pp. 115–16.

xxv **The coats of varnish that are laid** – Komakichi Nohara, *Das wahre Gesicht Japans. Er über Japan* (Dresden: Zwingerverlag o.J., 1935); published in English as *The True Face of Japan, A Japanese on Japan* (London: Jarrolds Ltd, 1936), p. 29.

xxv **It is to this day . . . It is my strong belief . . . unless the wantonness** – Okakura, *The Life and Thought of Japan*, pp. 17–18.

1: The Way of the Warrior

page

6 Heaven is above and earth is below – David J. Lu, *Sources of Japanese History Vol. 1* (New York, NY: McGraw-Hill, 1974), p. 236.

6 is one who does not cultivate – Ryusaku Tsunoda et al, *Sources of Japanese Tradition*, revised edition (New York, NY: Columbia University Press, 1964), pp. 398–9.

9 Whether there is order or chaos in the nation – ibid., p. 401.

10 '*By the end of the Tenpō era*' – quoted in Romulus Hillsborough, *Samurai Revolution* (Rutland, VT and Tokyo: Tuttle, 2014), p. 26.

11 '*We must take the initiative*' – ibid., p. 452.

12 The Sacred Throne of Japan – Lu, *Sources of Japanese History Vol. 1*, p. 66.

13 When Japan began to modernise – Saburō Ienaga, *The Pacific War 1931–1945* (New York, NY: Knopf Doubleday, 1978), p. 4.

14 The Sino-Japanese War changed – ibid.

2. A Nation Galvanised

page

18 The phrase, 'for the sake of war' – David J. Lu, *Sources of Japanese History Vol. 2* (New York, NY: McGraw-Hill, 1974), p. 95.

20 An unconscious and irresistible power – Inazō Nitobe, *Bushidō, The Soul of Japan*, first published 1899 (New York, NY: Cosimo Classics, 2007), p. 27.

21 '*Since the absence of bodily comfort*' . . . '*Once I came into the room*' – Etsu Inagaki Sugimoto, *A daughter of the Samurai* (New York, NY: Warbler Press, 2021), p. 28.

22 The outcome of future wars – Conrad Totman, *A History of Japan* (Oxford: Blackwell, 2000), p. 377.

23 GROUP 1. The Japanese Government – Lu, *Sources of Japanese History Vol. 2*, p. 102.

3: Hirohito

page

26 '*I have visited the battlefields*' – the quotes from Emperor Hirohito, Yoshinaga Nakagawa, Daisuke Nanba and Nobuaki Makino on this and subsequent pages are from Herbert p. Bix, *Hirohito and the Making of Modern Japan* (London: Duckworth, 2000), pp. 141–2.

29 To protect and welcome the emperor – ibid., p. 197.

30 clean against unclean – ibid.

30 *'The enthronement showed'* – ibid., p. 198.

30 **Anyone who has formed** – Richard H. Mitchell, 1973. 'Japan's Peace Preservation Law of 1925: Its Origins and Significance'. *Monumenta Nipponica* 28 (3), 317.

31 **In 1928, the Tanaka government** – Daizaburo Yui & Nobuko Kosuge, *Rengō koku boryo gyakutai to sengo sekinin: Iwanami Bukkuretto no. 321*, (Tokyo: Iwanami Shoten, 1993), p. 19.

33 *'After destroying England'* – Conrad Totman, *A History of Japan* (Oxford: Blackwell, 2000), p. 378.

33 *'We must sweep clean'* – ibid., p. 379.

33 *'How can we farmers survive?'* – David Batty, *Japan's War in Colour*, NHK/Channel 4/TWI co-production, 2003 (from the author's personal archives), script for programme 1, p. 5 @ 04:56.

34 *'If you say anything bad'* – ibid., p. 6 @ 06:03.

4. China

page

37 **Today, the Great Powers openly** – Tomoko Masuda, *Saitō Makoto kyokoku itchi naikakuron* (Tokyo: Iwanami Shoten, 1993), p. 247.

38 *'Today's Japan'* – David Batty, *Japan's War in Colour*, NHK/Channel 4/ TWI co-production, 2003 (from the author's personal archives), script for programme 1, p. 4 @ 03:16.

38 *'Japanese–Chinese amity'* and *'As long as the Manchurian issue'* – Saburō Ienaga, *The Pacific War 1931–1945* (New York, NY: Knopf Doubleday, 1978), p. 64.

39 *'There were Japanese who rode'* – ibid., p. 162.

40 **'The Governments of Japan, Germany and Italy'** – The Avalon Law Project, archived from the original, August 2011. Available at https:// avalon.law.yale.edu/wwii/triparti.asp (accessed November 2024).

41 *'Let the government'* – Batty, *Japan's War in Colour*, programme 1, p. 11 @ 12:50.

41 *'At first the war brought only excitement'* – Hiroko Nakamoto, *My Japan 1930–1951* (Scranton, PA: University of Scranton Press, 2000), p. 20.

42 *'We Japanese soldiers simply formed a line'* – Haruko Taya Cook & Theodore F. Cook, *Japan at War: An Oral History* (London: Phoenix Press, 2000), p. 31.

42 *'When we arrived'* – Batty, *Japan's War in Colour*, programme 1, p. 12 @ 14:15.

43 *'In the middle of the night'* – Jean Lartéguy, *The Sun Goes Down: Last Letters from Japanese Suicide Pilots and Soldiers* (London: William Kimber & Co. Ltd, 1956), p. 31.

43 *'Rice became rationed'* – Nakamoto, *My Japan*, p. 22.

43 *'Seven thousand prisoners'* – Shirō Azuma's diary, *My Nanking Platoon* (translated into English in 1987), quoted in Batty, *Japan's War in Colour*, programme 1, p. 13 @ 15:47.

44 *'When I tried to cut off'* – diary entry by Shirō Azuma, reported by CNN, 16 August 1998.

44 *'While out foraging'* – Ienaga, *The Pacific War*, p. 50.

44 *'beat a Chinese with rocks'* – ibid.

45 *'I am proud'* – Batty, *Japan's War in Colour*, programme 1, p. 14 @ 17:05.

45 *'The area was filled'* . . . *'There are about 20,000'* – Ienaga, *The Pacific War*, p. 186.

46 *'5,000 prisoners were taken'* – Batty, *Japan's War in Colour*, programme 1, p. 15 @ 17:15.

46 *'One by one the prisoners fell'* – James Yin & Shi Young, *The Rape of Nanking* (Chicago, IL: Innovative Publishing, 1997), p. 81.

46 *'On Hsiakwan Wharves'* – Iris Chang, *The Rape of Nanking* (London: Penguin Books, 1997), p. 86.

46 *'Those in the first row'* – Yukio Omata, *Reports and Recollections of Japanese Military Correspondents* (Tokyo: Tokuma Shoten, 1985), p. 31.

47 *'The women suffered the most'* – Hu Hua-ling, 1991, 'Chinese Women Under the Rape of Nanking', *Journal of Studies of Japanese Aggression Against China* (November, vol. 103), 68.

47 *'Whatever you say'* – Katsuichi Honda, *The Nanking Massacre: A Japanese journalist confronts Japan's national shame* (London: Routledge, 1999), pp. 131–2.

47 *'One of the essential means'* – Cook & Cook, *Japan at War*, p. 155.

48 **By the august virtue of His Majesty** – Fumimaro Konoe, Statement of the Government, 3 November 1938. *Papers Relating to the Foreign Relations of the United States: Japan 1931–1941, Volume 1* (Washington, WA: Department of State, 1943), 793.94/14380.

49 *'The day after I arrived'* . . . *'the only thought I had'* – Cook & Cook, *Japan at War*, p. 42.

49 *'A new conscript'* – ibid., p. 44.

50 *'I heard a talk given'* – Kike Wadatsumi no Koe, *Listen to the Voices from the Sea: Writings of the Fallen Japanese Students*, compiled by the Japan Memorial Society for the Students Killed in the War (Wadatsumi Society), translated by Midori Yamanouchi and Joseph L. Quinn (Scranton, PA: University of Scranton Press, 2000), p. 176.

5. The Mighty Escalation

page

52 *Hinode* 'How will . . . The Emperor himself – 'Far East, Teeth Behind Smiles', *Time Magazine*, 25 November 1944.

53 *Two years from now* – quoted in Conrad Totman, *A History of Japan* (Oxford: Blackwell, 2000), p. 447.

54 **Emperor: 'In the event we must finally open hostilities'** – Sōkichi Takagi historical documents: *Seikai shojōhō-Shōwa jūninen kar* (Tokyo: National Diet Library), p. 389.

55 **The Imperial Army and Navy enjoyed** – Saburō Ienaga, *The Pacific War 1931–1945* (New York, NY: Knopf Doubleday, 1978), p. 33.

55 **A commander who allows** – James Bradley, *A True Story of Courage* (New York, NY: Little Brown, 2003), p. 38.

56 *'Get rid of'* . . . *'Assassinate Premier Konoe'* . . . *'Citizens of Tokyo!'* – Shigeru Nambara, *War and Conscience in Japan* (San Francisco, CA: Presidio Press, 2012), p. 216.

56 *'Draftings into the Service'* – Kike Wadatsumi no Koe, *Listen to the Voices from the Sea: Writings of the Fallen Japanese Students*, compiled by the Japan Memorial Society for the Students Killed in the War (Wadatsumi Society), translated by Midori Yamanouchi and Joseph L. Quinn (Scranton, PA: University of Scranton Press, 2000), p. 40.

58 *'To die for Emperor and Nation'* – Edwin Hoyt, *Yamamoto, The Man Who Planned Pearl Harbor* (New York, NY: McGraw-Hill, 2001), p. 101.

59 *'4am: Japan issued a final ultimatum'* – Herbert p. Bix, *Hirohito and the Making of Modern Japan* (London: Duckworth, 2000), p. 4.

60 **Motor vehicles get through** – R. H. p. Mason & J. G. Caiger, *A History of Japan* (Rutland, VT and Tokyo: Tuttle, 1997), p. 352.

6. Pacific Expansion

page

63 **This is Penang calling** – Penang City Archives. From the author's personal archives.

65 **When you encounter the enemy** – Jim Keys, 'The Fall of Singapore', *The History Herald*, 11 November 2020. Available at https://thehistoryherald.com/articles/military-history/world-war-ii/the-fall-of-singapore/2/ (accessed November 2024).

67 *'Not only the soldiers'* – Shigenori Tōgō, *The Cause of Japan* (New York, NY: Simon and Schuster, 1956), p. 229.

68 *'Against common sense'* – Shigeru Nambara, *War and Conscience in Japan* (Lanham, MD: Rowman & Littlefield, 2010), p. 117.

68 *'The executions were carried out'* – Saburō Ienaga, *Japan's Last War* (Oxford: Blackwell, 1979), p. 73.

69 In order to force Britain – Herbert p. Bix, *Hirohito and the Making of Modern Japan* (London: Duckworth, 2000), p. 446.

69 '*Was in a more pleasant mood*' – ibid., p. 452.

70 '*Should hostilities break out*' – stated in a letter to Ryoichi Sasakawa prior to the attack on Pearl Harbor. Quoted in Gordon W. Prange, *At Dawn We Slept* (London: Penguin Books, 1981), p. 11.

70 '*In the first six to twelve months*' – statement to Japanese cabinet minister Shigeharu Matsumoto and Japanese prime minister Fumimaro Matsumoto. Quoted in Ronald Spector, *Eagle Against the Sun: The American War With Japan* (New York, NY: Simon and Schuster, 1985), p. 78.

71 '*This must not be happening!*' – *Asahi Shimbun*, 19 April 1942.

71 '*Enemy bombers appeared*' – Clayton Chun, *The Doolittle Raid* (Oxford: Osprey, 2006), p. 83.

72 '*Can't you find*' – Bix, *Hirohito*, p. 449.

7. The Turning Point

page

76 '*I had presumed*' – Herbert p. Bix, *Hirohito and the Making of Modern Japan* (London: Duckworth, 2000), p. 450.

77 '*Petty officers would not hesitate*' – Saburō Sakai, *Samurai!* (New York, NY: E. p. Dutton & Company, Inc., 1957), p. 8.

78 '*Had I been ordered*' – ibid., p. 32.

78 '*We are deeply pleased*' – Bix, *Hirohito*, p. 458.

79 '*What I want to tell you*' – ibid.

79 '*We are dismayed*' – ibid., p. 459.

79 '*What I want to know*' – ibid.

80 '*No food is available*' . . . '*He who can rise*' – David Alan Johnson, January 2011, *Warfare History Network* 10 (2). Available at https://warfarehistorynetwork.com/issue/wwii-history-january-2011-issue/ (accessed November 2024).

80 '*It is unacceptable*' – Bix, *Hirohito*, p. 461.

80 '*No matter how good*' – ibid., p. 464.

81 '*Yesterday there was a report*' – Kiyoshi Kiyosawa, *A Diary of Darkness* (New Jersey, NJ: Princeton University Press, 1999), p. 32.

81 '*Our forces on Attu*' – Donald Keene, *So Lovely a Country Will Never Die: Wartime Diaries of Japanese* Writers (New York, NY: Columbia University Press, 2010), p. 32.

81 '*We Japanese are often*' – Jean Lartéguy, *The Sun Goes Down: Last Letters from Japanese Suicide Pilots and Soldiers* (London: William Kimber & Co. Ltd, 1956), p. 6.

82 '*I'm not going to tolerate*' – Bix, *Hirohito*, p. 466.

82 *'No matter how far we walk'* … *'eating roots'* … *'no cloth'* – Saburō Ienaga, *The Pacific War 1931–1945* (New York, NY: Knopf Doubleday, 1978), p. 144.

82 *'In late 1942'* – Haruko Taya Cook & Theodore F. Cook, *Japan at War: An Oral History* (London: Phoenix Press, 2000), p. 147.

8. A 'Truly Grave' Situation

page

84 *'Everywhere the war'* – Hiroko Nakamoto, *My Japan 1930–1951* (Scranton, PA: University of Scranton Press, 2000), p. 42.

84 *'Meantime there was'* – ibid., p. 49.

85 *'Our losses for this'* – Dan Van der Vat, *The Pacific Campaign: The US Naval War 1941–1945* (New York, NY: Simon and Schuster, 1991), p. 291.

86 *'I wonder if they will come'* – Toshihiro Ōura's diary entries on this and subsequent pages are taken from Jack H. McCall, '"I will fight to the last": WWII Japanese Soldier Diary, June 1943', *HistoryNet*, 21 February 2010. Available at https://www.historynet.com/i-will-fight-to-the-last-wwii-japanese-soldier-diary-june-1943/ (accessed November 2024).

88 *'We have an army'* – David Dexter, *The New Guinea Offensives: Australia in the war of 1939–1945*, Volume VI (Canberra: Australian War Memorial, 1961), p. 543.

88 *'As soon as we arrived'* – Kike Wadatsumi no Koe, *Listen to the Voices from the Sea: Writings of the Fallen Japanese Students*, compiled by the Japan Memorial Society for the Students Killed in the War (Wadatsumi Society), translated by Midori Yamanouchi and Joseph L. Quinn (Scranton, PA: University of Scranton Press, 2000), p. 86.

89 *'The words flashed into my mind'* – R. H. p. Mason & J. G. Caiger, *A History of Japan* (Rutland, VT and Tokyo: Tuttle, 1997), p. 352.

89 *'In air superiority'* – Harry A. Gailey, *Bougainville, 1943–1945: The Forgotten Campaign* (Lexington, KY: Kentucky University Press, 2003), p. 59.

9. Burma: A Portent of Things to Come

page

91 *'We took small boats'* … *'The forced march'* – Kazuo Tamayama and John Nunneley, *Tales by Japanese Soldiers* (London: Cassell, 2000), p. 30.

92 *'Every day we walked'* – ibid., p. 42.

92 *'We marched a long way'* – ibid., p. 60.

93 *'After a very relaxing'* – ibid., p. 61.

94 '*It was too much*' – Yoshimi Yoshiaki, *Grassroots Fascism: The War Experiences of the Japanese People* (New York, NY: Columbia University Press, 1987), p. 176.

94 '*I started off the Marco Polo Bridge Incident*' – Francis Pike, *Hirohito's War: The Pacific War 1941–1945* (London: Bloomsbury, 2015), p. 692.

95 '*We were told Operation U-go*' – Tamayama & Nunneley, *Tales*, p. 157.

95 '*The rule of the battlefield is*' – ibid., p. 160.

95 '*Although we kept fighting*' – ibid., p. 170.

98 '*Conditions were hard*' – ibid., p. 174.

98 '*The enemy's heavy artillery*' – ibid, pp. 175–6.

98 '*At the beginning of the Imphal Operation*' – ibid., p. 177.

99 '*Older soldiers, and my own generation*' – Kike Wadatsumi no Koe, *Listen to the Voices from the Sea: Writings of the Fallen Japanese Students*, compiled by the Japan Memorial Society for the Students Killed in the War (Wadatsumi Society), translated by Midori Yamanouchi and Joseph L. Quinn (Scranton, PA: University of Scranton Press, 2000), p. 131.

99 '*We disembarked at a station*' – Tamayama & Nunneley, *Tales*, p. 227.

100 '*In increasing numbers*' – ibid., p. 196.

100 '*Along the way, many soldiers*' – Yoshiaki, *Grassroots Fascism*, p. 176.

10. A Ferocious Defence

page

103 '*November 12th. We know*' – diary entries quoted in this chapter are from Jennifer N. Johnson, 2013, 'We're Still Alive Today: A Captured Japanese Diary from the Pacific Theater', *Genealogy Notes*, 45 (2), 54–61.

105 '*Our men on Tarawa*' – Donald Keene, *So Lovely a Country will Never Die: Wartime Diaries of Japanese Writers* (New York, NY: Columbia University Press, 2010), p. 47.

106 '*it would take one million men*' – see https://www.nationalww2museum.org/war/articles/photo-finish-battle-tarawa (accessed November 2024).

106 '*People like myself*' – Keene, *So Lovely a Country*, p. 4.

107 '*Defending isn't enough*' – Herbert p. Bix, *Hirohito and the Making of Modern Japan* (London: Duckworth, 2000), p. 471.

11. Gyokusai

page

110 '*Whether we attack*' – John Toland, *The Rising Sun: The Decline and Fall of the Japanese Empire 1936–1945* (New York, NY: Random House, 1970), p. 516.

111 '*Last night the heat was oppressive*' – Samuel Hideo Yamashita, *Leaves*

from an Autumn of Emergencies: Daily Life in Wartime Japan 1940–1945 (Honolulu: University of Hawai'i Press, 2005), p. 174.

111 *'19 July 1944. The fact that'* – Kiyoshi Kiyosawa, *A Diary of Darkness* (New Jersey, NJ: Princeton University Press, 1999), p. 227.

111 *'20 July 1944. The Tōjō Cabinet'* . . . *'Young boys died'* – ibid., p. 228.

112 *'They [the Japanese pilots] never had a chance'* – Barrett Tillman, *Clash of the Carriers: The True Story of the Marianas Turkey Shoot of World War II* (New York, NY: New American Library, 2006), p. 185.

112 *'I am firmly convinced'* – Mitsuo Fuchida & Masatake Okumiya, *Midway: The Battle that Doomed Japan; the Japanese Navy's Story*, original publication 1955 (Annapolis, MD: Bluejacket Books, 2000), p. 121.

113 *'It is with much embarrassment'* . . . *'We Japanese soldiers'* – Meilan Solly, 'The Japanese WWII Soldier Who Refused to Surrender for 27 Years', *Smithsonian Magazine*, 21 January 2022.

113 *'Your Majesty, I have returned home'* – Nicholas D. Kristof, 'Shōichi Yokoi, 82, Is Dead; Japan Soldier Hid 27 Years', *New York Times*, 26 September 1997.

113 *'The enemy circling overhead'* – W. D. Dickson, *The Battle of the Philippine Sea, June 1944* (Shepperton: Ian Allan, 1975), p. 146.

114 *'Tuesday, 7th August. This evening'* – Jean Lartéguy, *The Sun Goes Down: Last Letters from Japanese Suicide Pilots and Soldiers* (London: William Kimber & Co. Ltd, 1956) p. 79.

115 *'to remain in the divine land'* – Herbert p. Bix, *Hirohito and the Making of Modern Japan* (London: Duckworth, 2000), p. 480.

115 *'Any question of justice'* – David Batty, *Japan's War in Colour*, NHK/Channel 4/TWI co-production, 2003 (from the author's personal archives), script for programme 2, p. 4 @ 02:53.

116 *'The war was lost'* – Philip Crowl, *Campaign in the Marianas* (Washington, DC: Center of Military History, United States Army, 1960. Reissued by St John's Press, 2016), p. 445.

116 *'Rise to the challenge'* – Bix, *Hirohito*, p. 476.

12. Kamikaze

page

118 *'Now standing at the crossroads'* . . . *'I am truly sorry'* . . . *'My students, fall'* – Albert Axell & Kase Hideaki, *Kamikaze – Japan's Suicide Gods* (Harlow: Longman, 2002), p. 36.

119 *'Dear Parents, please congratulate'* – Chris Abell, *The Samurai Contract* (Ashland, OR: Blackstone Publishing, 2023), p. 42.

119 Upon sighting the target . . . You have lived – ibid.

120 *'We've made some'* . . . *'But we are not defeated'* – Samuel Hideo

Yamashita, *Leaves from an Autumn of Emergencies: Daily Life in Wartime Japan 1940–1945* (Honolulu, University of Hawai'i Press, 2005), p. 65.

120 *'I am full of the spirit'* – ibid., p. 67.

120 *'It was finally announced'* – ibid., p.72.

120 *'The Yamato people'* . . . *'The engines of our planes'* . . . *'Yasuo is happy'* – ibid., p. 75.

121 *'Captain Kuniyasu and'* . . . *'I have changed a lot'* – Jean Lartéguy, *The Sun Goes Down: Last Letters from Japanese Suicide Pilots and Soldiers* (London: William Kimber & Co. Ltd, 1956), p. 109.

122 *'We the Kamikaze are nothing but robots'* – Abell, *The Samurai Contract*, p. 72.

122 *'Dear Wife, the happy dream is over'* – ibid., p. 75.

122 The special attack pilots – Saburō Ienaga, *Japan's Last War* (Oxford: Blackwell, 1979), p. 183.

123 The Japanese Army was imbued – writing for *Seki Magazine*, in March 1946, quoted in Inoguchi Rikihei, Nakajima Tadashi & Pineau Roger, *The Divine Wind* (Annapolis, MD: United States Naval Institute, 1958), p. 169.

123 *'As one of the officers'* – Edwin Hoyt, *The Last Samurai: The Story of Admiral Matome Ugaki* (Westport, CT: Praeger Publishers, 1993), p. 207.

124 Despite brave fighting – ibid., p. 209.

125 *'I have already been inside'* – Lartéguy, *The Sun Goes Down*, p. 112.

126 'sunk or damaged beyond repair' – H. p. Willmott, Robin Cross & Charles Messenger, *World War II* (London: Dorling Kindersley, 2004), p. 99.

126 United States Strategic Bombing Survey – available at https://www. airuniversity.af.edu/Portals/10/AUPress/Books/B_0020_SPANGRUD_ STRATEGIC_BOMBING_SURVEYS.pdf (accessed November 2024).

13. The Pearl of the Orient

page

127 *'Today our imperial state'* – Herbert p. Bix, *Hirohito and the Making of Modern Japan* (London: Duckworth, 2000), p. 481.

127 *'Contrary to views of the Army'* – ibid., p. 486.

127 *'He suddenly stood up'* – ibid., p. 490.

130 When Filipinos are to be killed – James M. Scott, 'Battlefield as Crime Scene: The Japanese Massacre in Manila', *HistoryNet*, 1 December 2019. Available at https://www.historynet.com/worldwar2-japanese-massacre-in-manila/ (accessed November 2024).

131 The Americans who have penetrated – Bix, *Hirohito*, p. 490.

14. Iwo Jima

page
136 'The disadvantages' ... 'the ultimate priority' ...'a moment favourable'
     ...'If we hold out' – Shun Katsuno, Shōwa tennō no sensō (Tokyo:
     Tosho Shuppansha, 1990), pp. 205–6.

136 'This is a very quiet' – Isoko & Ichirō Hatano, Mother and Son, A
     Japanese Correspondence (Boston, MA: Houghton Mifflin, 1962), p. 67.

137 'At about midday' – ibid., p. 69.

137 'It's clear and cold' – Samuel Hideo Yamashita, Leaves From an Autumn
     of Emergencies: Daily Life in Wartime Japan 1940–1945 (Honolulu,
     University of Hawai'i Press, 2005), p. 105.

138 'So now Suwa has been bombed' – Hatano, Mother and Son, p. 75.

139 'He once organised a strike' – Derrick Wright, The Battle for Iwo Jima,
     1945 (Stroud: Sutton Publishing, 1999), p. 41.

139 'There is no spring water' – Tadamichi Kuribayashi, Picture Letters from
     the Commander in Chief (San Francisco, CA: Viz Media, 2007), p. 236.

139 'There are so many flies' – Kumiko Kakehashi, So Sad to Fall in Battle
     (New York, NY: Random House, 2005), p. 21.

140 'It must be destiny' – Kuribayashi, Picture Letters, p. 236.

140 1. We shall defend ... Preparations for battle – Kakehashi, So Sad to
     Fall in Battle, p. 39.

142 'Just as I expected' – ibid., p. 46.

143 'The guns that were trained' – ibid., p. 101.

143 'As we waited' – ibid., p. 165.

144 In the light of the above situation – quoted in Japanese Monograph
     No. 48 (a series of 187 operational histories, prepared under the
     direction of General Headquarters of the US Far East Command,
     beginning in 1945), p. 62.

145 'We were forced to' – Kuribayashi, Picture Letters, p. 228.

145 'I am fully satisfied' – Damon Shūhei, Tatakau Tennō (Tokyo: Kodansha,
     1989), p. 192.

145 The battle is entering its final chapter – Kakehashi, So Sad to Fall in
     Battle, pp. XVIII–XIX.

146 I have just 400 men – Wright, The Battle for Iwo Jima, p. 207.

146 'General Kuribayashi commanded' – ibid., p. 206.

147 'On the evening of March 17' – ibid., p. 207.

147 All officers and men – ibid., p. 208.

147 'I tried to communicate' – ibid.

147 'My father had believed' – ibid., p. 45.

15. Typhoon of Steel

page
153 '*He looked at me pensively*' – Hiromichi Yahara, *The Battle for Okinawa* (New York, NY: John Wiley & Sons, 1995), p. 41.

154 '*In mid-May came*' – ibid., p. 47.

154 '*The beautiful, peaceful countryside*' – ibid., p. 62.

154 '*The battle was at fever pitch*' – ibid.

155 '*We climbed down the ladder*' – ibid., p. 102.

155 '*We sat there on rugs*' – ibid., p. 103.

156 '*I had the American book*' – 'Commander's grandson fights to preserve Okinawa's wartime history', *NHK World-Japan*, 10 September 2020. Available at https://www3.nhk.or.jp/nhkworld/en/news/backstories/1277/ (accessed November 2024).

156 '*Wounded soldiers were being carried in*' – ibid.

156 '*May our fortunes in war*' – Yahara, *The Battle for Okinawa*, p. 125.

157 **My Beloved Soldiers** – ibid., p. 134.

157 **Nurse Miyagi and the other girls** – the history and experiences of the Himeyuri Corps are preserved and recorded at the Himeyuri Peace Museum, Okinawa. See the website at https://www.himeyuri.or.jp/en/ (accessed November 2024).

158 '*There was a rain of bullets*' – 'Commander's grandson fights', *NHK World-Japan*, 10 September 2020.

158 '*The fields had still glistened*' – Yahara, *The Battle for Okinawa*, p. 135.

158 **To General Ushijima** – Yahara, *The Battle for Okinawa*, p. 136.

159 '*Are there any civilians*' – 'Commander's grandson fights', *NHK World-Japan*, 10 September 2020.

16. Armageddon

page
162 '*Wartime conditions have come to prevail*' ... '*Enemy American aircraft*' – Samuel Hideo Yamashita, *Leaves from an Autumn of Emergencies: Daily Life in Wartime Japan 1940–1945* (Honolulu: University of Hawai'i Press, 2005), p. 108.

163 '*I've been holed up*' – ibid., p. 115.

164 '*the often-repeated expression*' – Thomas R. H. Havens, *Valley of Darkness: the Japanese People and World War Two* (Lanham, MD: University Press of America, 1986), p. 161.

165 '*We could hardly breathe*' – ibid., p. 179.

165 '*Countless bodies were floating*' – ibid.

165 '*But the swimming pool*' – John Toland, *The Rising Sun: The Decline and Fall of the Japanese Empire* (New York, NY: Random House, 1970), p. 674.

166 *'I had spent the day'* … *'He came dashing in'* … *'There was a strong wind'* – interview with Julian Ryall in *Deutsche Welle* magazine, 3 June 2015.

166 *'There were small raids'* – ibid.

166 *'I was shocked'* – Yamashita, *Leaves*, pp. 121–2.

167 *'The bombardment destroyed'* … *'I curse those'* … *'Our country must die'* – quoted in Donald Keene, *So Lovely a Country Will Never Die: Wartime Diaries of Japanese* Writers (New York, NY: Columbia University Press, 2010), pp. 73–7.

168 *'It was the morning after'* – Shigenori Tōgō, *The Cause of Japan* (New York, NY: Simon and Schuster, 1956), p. 265.

169 *'The city of Osaka'* – Yamashita, *Leaves*, p. 124.

169 *'Digging through the rubble'* – Herbert p. Bix, *Hirohito and the Making of Modern Japan* (London: Duckworth, 2000), p. 491.

170 *'Probably they do not recognise'* – Keene, *So Lovely a Country*, p. 65.

170 *'In the end Germany has lost'* – Isoko & Ichirō Hatano, *Mother and Son, A Japanese Correspondence* (Boston, MA: Houghton Mifflin, 1962), p. 79.

171 *'Those soldiers are glad to go'* ibid., p. 84.

171 *'Children in grade schools'* – David J. Lu, *Sources of Japanese History Vol. 2* (New York, NY: McGraw-Hill, 1974), p. 168.

17. The Radiance of a Thousand Suns

page

175 *'You must be ready'* – Thomas R. H. Havens, *Valley of Darkness: the Japanese People and World War Two* (Lanham, MD: University Press of America, 1986), p. 190.

175 *'Everything considered, I wish'* – ibid.

175 *'glorious to die for the holy emperor'* – Williamson Murray & Alan R. Millet, *A War to be Won* (Cambridge, MA: Harvard University Press, 2000), p. 34.

175 **Bombs dropped from 20,000 feet** – Saburō Ienaga, *Japan's Last War* (Oxford: Blackwell, 1979), p. 200.

178 *'Time went on and we knew'* – Hiroko Nakamoto, *My Japan 1930–1951* (Scranton, PA: University of Scranton Press, 2000), p. 52.

179 *'I wonder what truth there is'* – Isoko & Ichirō Hatano, *Mother and Son, A Japanese Correspondence* (Boston, MA: Houghton Mifflin, 1962), p. 100.

180 *'The hour was early'* … *'Where was my wife?'* – Michihiko Hachiya, *Hiroshima Diary* (Chapel Hill, NC: University of North Carolina Press, 1955), p. 1.

181 *'Suddenly, from nowhere, came a blinding flash'* … *'I followed them'* – Nakamoto, *My Japan*, p. 56.

181 *'I could still hear the very faint sound'* … *'I couldn't really see'* – Haruko
     Taya Cook & Theodore F. Cook, *Japan at War: An Oral History* (London:
     Phoenix Press, 2000), p. 384.
182 *'They say that Hiroshima'* – Hatano, *Mother and Son*, p. 62.
183 *'There was a terrific rush of wind'* – David Batty, *Japan's War in Colour*,
     NHK/Channel 4/TWI co-production, 2003 (from the author's personal
     archives), script for programme 2, p. 2 @ 26.01.
183 *'Three days later, I managed'* – ibid. @ 26.43.
183 *'We were taken completely by surprise'* – quoted in Donald Keene, *So
     Lovely a Country Will Never Die: Wartime Diaries of Japanese Writers*
     (New York, NY: Columbia University Press, 2010), p. 97.
183 *'The effects of the bombs'* – Hatano, *Mother and Son*, p. 105.
184 *'Japan is standing at the last line of defence'* – Keene, *So Lovely a
     Country*, p. 93.

18. Enduring the Unendurable

page
185 *'A siren went off'* … *'The expression on people's faces'* – Samuel Hideo
     Yamashita, *Leaves from an Autumn of Emergencies: Daily Life in Wartime
     Japan 1940–1945* (Honolulu: University of Hawai'i Press, 2005), p. 217.
186 *'For the first time'* – Hiroko Nakamoto, *My Japan 1930–1951* (Scranton,
     PA: University of Scranton Press, 2000), p. 72.
186 *'Noon came'* – David J. Lu, *Sources of Japanese History Vol. 2* (New York,
     NY: McGraw-Hill, 1974), p. 168.
186 *'The sound of a gong'* – Donald Keene, *So Lovely a Country Will Never
     Die: Wartime Diaries of Japanese* Writers (New York, NY: Columbia
     University Press, 2010), p. 102.
186 *'I never dreamt the Emperor would'* – David Batty, *Japan's War in
     Colour*, NHK/Channel 4/TWI co-production, 2003 (from the author's
     personal archives), script for programme 2, p. 23 @ 30:38.
186 *'At the news of the surrender'* – ibid. @ 31:20.
187 *'quickly control the situation'* … *'the Soviet Union'* – Kōichi Kido, *The
     Diary of Marquis Kido 1931–1945* (Frederick, MD: University of
     America Publications, 1984), p. 1223.
187 *'The emperor then spoke'* – Shigenori Tōgō, *The Cause of Japan* (New
     York, NY: Simon and Schuster, 1956), p. 331.
187 **The Japanese Government is ready** – Zenshiro Hoshina, *Daitoa Senso
     Hishi [Secret History of the Greater East Asia War]*, Section 5 (Tokyo:
     Hara-Shobo, 1975), pp. 139–49.
188 *'We ourselves invited a situation'* – Akiko Takeyama, *Gyokuon bōsō*
     (Tokyo: Banseisha, 1989), p. 128.

189 '*A score of men sprang up*' – Yasuo Kuwahara and Gordon T. Allred, *Kamikaze* (New York, NY: Ballantine Books, 1957), p. 183.

191 '*People who appeared to be recovering*' – Batty, programme 2, p. 34 @ 44:11.

191 '*A fierce pain jolted my body*' – ibid. @ 45:10.

192 '*What will happen to the emperor?*' – Keene, *So Lovely a Country*, p. 82.

192 To the honourable General MacArthur – Batty, programme 2, p. 25 @ 49:54.

192 The emperor made the country – ibid. @ 50:07.

192 If it ever happens that – ibid. @ 50:22.

192 '*Why didn't General Tōjō*' – Keene, *So Lovely a Country*, p. 116.

193 '*There were rumours*' – Batty, programme 2, p. 25 @ 35:05.

193 '*The Supreme Commander paused*' – ibid.

193 '*The police are giving orders*' – ibid. @ 36:50.

194 '*Japan's leaders have tried*' – ibid. @ 37:50.

194 '*The word came*' – ibid. @ 41:39.

194 '*I was astonished to read*' – Keene, *So Lovely a Country*, p. 127.

195 '*It took three days*' – Batty, programme 2, p. 26 @ 42:58.

196 '*I finally got enough money*' – Haruko Taya Cook & Theodore F. Cook, *Japan at War: An Oral History* (London: Phoenix Press, 2000), p. 408.

196 '*We beat and kicked*' – Batty, programme 2, p. 25 @ 33:27.

196 '*I really didn't do anything wrong*' – ibid. @ 32:53.

197 '*The period of feudal darkness*' – ibid. @ 48:41.

197 '*A young Japanese woman*' – Keene, *So Lovely a Country*, pp. 170–71.

198 Sadly, we police – Seiichi Kaburagi, from his 1972 memoir, reported in the *Gainesville Sun*, 15 August 2015.

199 I rushed there – ibid.

Epilogue

page

201 '*At the appropriate time*' – Donald Keene, *So Lovely a Country Will Never Die: Wartime Diaries of Japanese Writers* (New York, NY: Columbia University Press, 2010), p. 174.

201 '*We cannot deny*' – David Batty, *Japan's War in Colour*, NHK/Channel 4/TWI co-production, 2003 (from the author's personal archives), script for programme 2, p. 40 @ 51:29.

Japan's Dissidents

page
229 *'Basically, even among anarchists'* – Hane Mikiso, *Reflections on the Way to the Gallows* (Berkeley, CA: University of California Press, 1988), p. 54.

231 *'As a propagator of Buddhism'* – Victoria Brian, *Zen at War* (Boulder, CO: Weatherhill, 1988), p. 41.

232 *'We demand the implementation'* . . . *'Hey you, miserable Mutsuhito'* – Ian Buruma, *Inventing Japan 1853–1964* (Albany, NY: Modern Library, 2003), p. 91.

237 *'The emperor is an ordinary man'* – Jacqueline Stone, 1994, 'Rebuking the Enemies of the Lotus: Nichirenist Exclusivism in Historical Perspective', *Japanese Journal of Religious Studies*, 21 (2–3), 231–59.

Japan's War Crimes

page
240 *'Noda, "Hey, I got 105 . . ."'* – *Tokyo Nichi-Nichi Shimbun*, 13 December 1937.

248 *'A good clean sword'* . . . – Haruko Taya Cook & Theodore F. Cook, *Japan at War: An Oral History* (London: Phoenix Press, 2000), pp. 156.

248 *'Teddy Ponczka was the first'* – Thomas Easton, 'Grisly WWII Fact: Japanese Dissected American POWs Alive', *Baltimore Sun*, 4 June 1995.

Japan's War Criminals

page
252 *'really be mad'* – Sheldon Harris, *Factories of Death: Japanese Biological Warfare, 1932–1945, and the American Cover-up* (New York, NY: Routledge, 2002), pp. 16–17.

253 *'Ishii was slovenly dressed'* . . . *'he was dressed immaculately'* – Ibid., p. 15.

253 *'Throughout this time Ishii, the orator'* – *Current Events Titbits (Jiji Henpen)*, Group News Column, *Military Surgeon Group Magazine*, no. 311, April 1939; quoted in David Williams & Peter Wallace, *Unit 731: The Japanese Army's Secret of Secrets* (London: Grafton Books, 1989), p. 131.

254 *'absolutely invaluable'* . . . *'could never have been obtained'* . . . *'the information would be'* – BBC, *Horizon: Plague in the Wind*, documentary broadcast 29 October 1984.

254 *'One day, he took some sample tissue'* – interview with Harumi Ishii, recorded in 1984 (New York, NY: Vimeo).

258 *'Never again would Japan have'* – US National Archives, *Trials of German Major War Criminals*, Volume 3 (Washington, DC: US Government Printing Office, 1951), p. 386.

258 *'The Japanese Government absolutely recognise'* – Ibid., p. 387.

261 *'I am very sorry'* – John Toland, *The Rising Sun: The Decline and Fall of the Japanese Empire 1936–1945* (New York, NY: Random House, 1970), pp. 871–2.

262 *'It is natural that I should bear'* – David Crowe, *War Crimes, Genocide and Justice: A Global History* (New York, NY: St Martin's Press, 2014), p. 217.

262 In his final statement – Toland, *The Rising Sun*, p. 873.

263 *'no looting; no rape; no arson'* – Brian Farrell & Sandy Hunter (eds), *Sixty Years On: The Fall of Singapore Revisited* (Singapore: Eastern Universities Press, 2003), p. 190.

264 *'My command was as big as MacArthur's'* – Alan Warren, *Singapore 1942: Britain's Greatest Defeat* (London: Hambledon Continuum, 2001), p. 291.

264 *'As I said in the Manila Supreme Court'* – 'Yamashita hanged for war crimes', *Arizona Republic*, 23 February 1946.

SELECT BIBLIOGRAPHY

Abell, Chris, *The Samurai Contract* (Ashland, OR: Blackstone Publishing, 2023)

Allen, Thomas B., *Remember Pearl Harbor: American and Japanese Survivors Tell Their Stories* (Washington, DC: National Geographic Society, 2001)

Axell, Albert & Hideaki, Kase, *Kamikaze – Japan's Suicide Gods* (Harlow: Longman, 2002)

Beasley, W.G., *Japanese Imperialism 1894–1945* (Oxford: The Clarendon Press, 1991)

Beasley, W. G., *The Japanese Experience: A Short History of Japan* (London: Weidenfeld and Nicholson, 1999)

Benedict, Ruth, *The Chrysanthemum and the Sword* (Rutland, VT and Tokyo: Charles Tuttle and Company, 1954)

Bergamini, David, *Japan's Imperial Conspiracy* (New York, NY: William Morrow & Co., 1971)

Bix, Herbert P., *Hirohito and the Making of Modern Japan* (London: Duckworth, 2000)

Brooks, Lester, *Behind Japan's Surrender* (Stamford, CT: Carpe Veritas Books, De Gustibus Ltd., 1968)

Butow, Robert J. C., *Tōjō and the Coming of War* (Stanford, CA: Stanford University Press, 1961)

Chang, Iris, *The Rape of Nanking* (London: Penguin, 1997)

Clements, Jonathan, *Admiral Togo, Nelson of the East* (London: Haus Publishing, 2010)

Clements, Jonathan, *Japan at War in the Pacific: The Rise and Fall of the Japanese Empire in Asia 1868–1945* (Rutland, VT and Tokyo: Tuttle, 2022)

Clements, Thomas Cleaver, *Tidal Wave: From Leyte Gulf to Tokyo Bay* (Oxford: Osprey, 2018)

Cook, Haruko Taya & Cook, Theodore F., *Japan at War: An Oral History* (London: Phoenix Press, 2000)

Cox, Jeffrey R., *Morning Star, Midnight Sun* (Oxford: Osprey, 2018)

Crowl, Philip, *Campaign in the Marianas* (Washington, DC: Center of Military History, United States Army, 1960. Reissued by St John's Press, 2016)

Dexter, David, *The New Guinea Offensives: Australia in the war of 1939–1945*, Volume VI (Canberra: Australian War Memorial, 1961)

Dickson, W. D., *The Battle of the Philippine Sea, June 1944* (Shepperton: Ian Allan, 1975)

Dower, John W., *Embracing Defeat: Japan in the Aftermath of World War II* (London: Penguin, 1999)

Felton, Mark, *Japan's Gestapo: Murder, Mayhem and Torture in Wartime Asia* (Barnsley, Pen & Sword Military, 2009)

Gailey, Harry A., *The War in the Pacific* (Novato, CA: Presidio Press, 1995)

Gailey, Harry A., *Bougainville, 1943–1945: The Forgotten Campaign*, (Lexington, KY: University Press of Kentucky, 2003)

Gordon, Andrew, *A Modern History of Japan: From Tokugawa Times to the Present*, 2nd edition (Oxford: OUP, 2008)

Hachiya, Michihiko, *Hiroshima Diary* (Chapel Hill, NC: The University of North Carolina Press, 1955)

Hagoromo Society of Kamikaze Divine Thunderbolt Corps Survivors, *Born to Die: The Cherry Blossom Squadrons* (Los Angeles, CA: O'Hara Publications, 1973)

Hanayama Shinsho, *The Way of Deliverance: Three Years with the Condemned Japanese War Criminals* (London: Victor Gollancz, 1955)

Havens, Thomas, R. H., *Valley of Darkness: The Japanese People and World War Two* (Lanham, MD: University Press of America, 1986)

Henshall, Kenneth, *A History of Japan: From Stone Age to Superpower* (Basingstoke: Palgrave Macmillan, 1999)

Hoyt, Edwin P., *The Last Kamikaze: The Story of Admiral Matome Ugaki* (Westport, CT: Greenwood Publishing Group, 1993)

Hoyt, Edwin, *Yamamoto, The Man Who Planned Pearl Harbor* (New York, NY: McGraw-Hill, 2001)

Ienaga, Saburō, *The Pacific War 1931–1945* (New York, NY: Knopf Doubleday, 1978)

Ienaga, Saburō, *Japan's Last War* (Oxford: Blackwell, 1979)

Inoguchi, Rikihei & Nakajima, Tadashi, *The Divine Wind: Japan's Kamikaze Force in World War II* (New York, NY: Ballantine Books, 1968)

Ishimaru, Lt-Comdr Tōta, *Japan Must Fight Britain* (London: Hurst & Blackett, 1936)

Japan Memorial Society for the Students Killed in the War, *Listen to the Voices from the Sea* (Scranton, PA: University of Scranton Press, 2000)

Kakehashi, Kumiko, *So Sad to Fall in Battle* (New York, NY: Random House, 2005)

Keene, Donald, *So Lovely a Country Will Never Die: Wartime Diaries of Japanese Writers* (New York, NY: Columbia University Press, 2010)

Kido, Kōichi, *The Diary of Marquis Kido 1931–1945* (Frederick, MD: University of America Publications, 1984)

Kiyosawa, Kiyoshi, *A Diary of Darkness: The Wartime Diary of Kiyosawa Kiyoshi* (New Jersey, NJ: Princeton University Press, 1999)

Kuribayashi, Tadamichi, *Picture Letters from the Commander in Chief* (San Francisco, CA: Viz Media, 2007)

Kuwahara, Yasuo & Allred, Gordon T., *Kamikaze* (New York, NY: Ballantine Books, 1957)

Lartéguy, Jean, *The Sun Goes Down: Last Letters From Japanese Suicide Pilots and Soldiers* (London: William Kimber & Co. Ltd, 1956)

Leckie, Robert, *Okinawa: The Last Battle of World War II* (New York, NY: Penguin, 1995)

Lu, David J., *Sources of Japanese History*, in two volumes (New York, NY: McGraw-Hill, 1974)

Lyman, Robert, *A War of Empires: Japan, India, Burma & Britain 1941–45* (Oxford: Osprey, 2021)

Mason, R. H. P., & Caiger, J. G., *A History of Japan* (Rutland, VT and Tokyo: Tuttle, 1997)

Mitter, Rana, *China's War with Japan 1937–1945: The Struggle for Survival* (London: Allen Lane, 2013)

Morris-Suzuki, Tessa, *Shōwa: An Inside History of Hirohito's Japan* (London: The Athlone Press, 1984)

Nagatsuka, Ryuji, *I Was Kamikaze* (New York, NY: Macmillan Publishing Co. Inc., 1972)

Naito, Hatsuho, *Thunder Gods: The Kamikaze Pilots Tell Their Story* (New York, NY: Kodansha International, 1982)

Nakamoto, Hiroko, *My Japan 1930–1951* (Scranton, PA: University of Scranton Press, 2000)

Nambara, Shigeru, *War and Conscience in Japan* (Lanham, MD: Rowan & Littlefield, 2011)

Nitobe, Inazō, *Bushidō, The Soul of Japan*, first published 1899, revised and updated 1905 (New York, NY: Cosimo Classics 2007)

Nohara, Komakichi, *Das wahre Gesicht Japans. Er über Japan* (Dresden: Zwingerverlag o.J., 1935); published in English as *The True Face of Japan, A Japanese on Japan* (London: Jarrolds Ltd, 1936)

Oates, Leslie Russell, *Populist Nationalism in Prewar Japan: A Biography of Nakano Seigo* (Sydney: George Allen & Unwin, 1985)

Ohnuko-Tierney, Emiko, *Kamikaze Diaries: Reflections of Japanese Student Soldiers* (Chicago, IL: The University of Chicago Press, 2006)

Pacific War Research Society, *Japan's Longest Day* (Tokyo: Kodansha International, 1968)

Pagnamenta, Peter & Williams, Momoko, *Falling Blossom: A British Officer's Love for a Japanese Woman* (London: Century, 2006)

Pike, Francis, *Hirohito's War: The Pacific War 1941–1945* (London: Bloomsbury, 2015)

Reischauer, Edwin, O., *The Japanese* (Rutland, VT and Tokyo: Tuttle, 1977)

Sakai, Saburō, *Samurai!* (New York, NY: E.P. Dutton & Company, Inc., 1957)

Sakaida, Henry et al., *1-400: Japan's Secret Aircraft-Carrying Strike Submarine* (Manchester: Hikoki Publications, 2006)

Sakaida, Henry & Takaki, Koji, *Genda's Blade: Japan's Squadron of Aces, 343 Kokutai* (Hersham: Chevron Publishing Ltd, 2003)

Sakurai, Tadayoshi, *Human Bullets: A Soldier's Story of the Russo-Japanese War* (London: Kegan Paul, 2005)

Sawamura, Sadako, *My Asakusa: Coming of Age in Pre-War Tokyo* (Rutland, VT and Tokyo: Tuttle, 2000)

Sheftall, Mordecai G., *Blossoms in the Wind: Human Legacies of the Kamikaze* (London: Penguin Books, 2005)

Storry, Richard, *A History of Modern Japan* (London: Penguin, 1960)

Sugimoto, Etsu Inagaki, *A Daughter of the Samurai* (New York, NY: Warbler Press, 2021)

Takeyama, Michio, *The Scars of War: Tokyo During World War II* (Lanham, MD: Rowan & Littlefield, 2007)

Tamayama, Kazuo & Nunneley, John, *Tales by Japanese Soldiers* (London: Cassell, 2000)

Tillman, Barrett, *Clash of the Carriers: The True Story of the Marianas Turkey Shoot of World War II* (New York, NY: New American Library, 2006)

Tōgō, Shigenori, *The Cause of Japan* (New York, NY: Simon and Schuster, 1956)

Toland, John, *The Rising Sun: The Decline and Fall of the Japanese Empire 1936–1945* (New York, NY: Random House, 1970)

Totman, Conrad, *A History of Japan* (Oxford: Blackwell, 2000)

Van der Vat, Dan, *The Pacific Campaign: The US Naval War 1941–1945* (New York, NY: Simon and Schuster, 1991)

Volpicelli, Vladimir, *The China-Japan War Compiled from Japanese, Chinese, and Foreign Sources Vol. 1*, first published in New York by Charles Scribner, 1896 (London: Forgotten Books, 2018)

Williams, David, *Defending Japan's Pacific War: The Kyoto School Philosophers and Post-White Power* (London: Routledge, 2012)

Wilson, Dick, *When Tigers Fight, The Story of the Sino-Japanese War 1937–1945* (London: Penguin, 1982)

Wright, Derrick, *The Battle for Iwo Jima, 1945* (Stroud: Sutton Publishing, 1999)

Yahara, Hiromichi, *The Battle for Okinawa* (New York, NY: John Wiley & Sons, 1995)

Yamashita, Samuel Hideo, *Leaves From an Autumn of Emergencies: Daily Life in Wartime Japan 1940–1945* (Honolulu: University of Hawai'i Press, 2005)
Yin, James & Young, Shi, *Rape of Nanking* (Chicago, IL: Triumph Books, 1997)
Yoshiaki, Yoshimi, *Grassroots Fascism: The War Experiences of the Japanese People* (New York, NY: Columbia University Press, 1987)

Osprey Publishing: Essential Histories

Jukes, Geoffrey, *The Russo-Japanese War, 1904–1905* (Oxford: Osprey, 2002)

Osprey Publishing: Elite

Jowett, Philip, *The Japanese Home Front 1937–45* (Oxford: Osprey, 2021)
Osprey Publishing: Air Campaign
Lardas, Mark, *The Kamikaze Campaign 1944–45: Imperial Japan's Last Throw of the Dice* (Oxford: Osprey, 2022)

Osprey Publishing: Men at Arms

Bodin, Lynn E., *The Boxer Rebellion* (Oxford: Osprey, 2021)
Jowett, Philip, *The Japanese Army 1931–45 (Vols 1 & 2)* (Oxford: Osprey 2002)

Osprey Publishing: Campaign

Chun, Clayton K. S., *Japan 1945: From Operation Downfall to Hiroshima and Nagasaki* (Oxford: Osprey, 2008)
Harrington, Peter, *Peking 1900: The Boxer Rebellion* (Oxford: Osprey, 2001)
Lardas, Mark, *Tsushima 1905: Death of a Russian Fleet* (Oxford: Osprey, 2018)
Stile, Mark, *The Coral Sea: The First Carrier Battle* (Oxford: Osprey, 2009)
Stile, Mark, *Leyte Gulf 1944 (Vol. 1) The Battles of the Sibuyan Sea and Samar* (Oxford: Osprey, 2021)
Stile, Mark, *Leyte Gulf 1944 (Vol. 2) Surigao Strait and Cape Engaño* (Oxford: Osprey, 2022)

RAISING READERS
Books Build Bright Futures

Dear Reader,

We'd love your attention for one more page to tell you about the crisis in children's reading, and what we can all do.

Studies have shown that reading for fun is the **single biggest predictor of a child's future success** – more than family circumstance, parents' educational background or income. It improves academic results, mental health, wealth, communication skills and ambition.

The number of children reading for fun is in rapid decline. Young people have a lot of competition for their time, and a worryingly high number do not have a single book at home.

Our business works extensively with schools, libraries and literacy charities, but here are some ways we can all raise more readers:

- Reading to children for just 10 minutes a day makes a difference
- Don't give up if your children aren't regular readers – there will be books for them!
- Visit bookshops and libraries to get recommendations
- Encourage them to listen to audiobooks
- Support school libraries
- Give books as gifts

Thank you for reading.
www.JoinRaisingReaders.com